THE
GOLDEN
RULE

THE
GOLDEN
RULE

JEFFREY WATTLES

New York   Oxford
Oxford University Press
1996

Oxford University Press

Oxford   New York
Athens   Auckland   Bangkok   Bogota   Bombay
Buenos Aires   Calcutta   Cape Town   Dar es Salaam
Delhi   Florence   Hong Kong   Istanbul   Karachi
Kuala Lumpur   Madras   Madrid   Melbourne
Mexico City   Nairobi   Paris   Singapore
Taipei   Tokyo   Toronto

and associated companies in
Berlin   Ibadan

Published by Oxford University Press, Inc.
198 Madison Avenue, New York, New York 10016

Oxford is a registered trademark of Oxford University Press

Library of Congress Cataloging-in-Publication Data
Wattles, Jeffrey Hamilton
The Golden Rule / Jeffrey Wattles.
p. cm.
Includes bibliographical references and index.
ISBN 0-19-510187-1; ISBN 0-19-511036-6 (pbk.)
1. Golden rule—Comparative studies.   1. Title.
BL85.W3   1996
170'.44—dc20   95-49824

9 8 7 6 5 4 3 2 1
Printed in the United States of America
on acid-free paper

Preface

How is one to move beyond shock and cynicism as one confronts the evidence of moral decline in society? What reaction comes more easily than to blame *them*? We may be driven to act on the tendency to separate humankind into two camps—the ones who are the problem and those of us with higher standards—but such is not the ultimate solution. I believe that we can all learn to relate more humanely and reach out more effectively by discovering the golden rule in its full implications.

The need even for morally active people to discover the golden rule is greater that I realized over a decade ago when I began my research. I used to assume that nearly everyone was raised so that when they heard the phrase "the golden rule" they could supply a principle worded, approximately, "Do to others as you want others to do to you." I also assumed that nearly everyone who heard that principle spelled out had a roughly accurate initial grasp of its meaning. And I assumed that those who thought highly of the principle would occasionally spend time thinking about how to apply it. I have not made a scientific survey and would not hazard an estimate in percentage terms, but my experiences talking about the rule with individuals and groups during the past several years incline me to doubt these assumptions.

A volunteer soliciting contributions for an environmental group guessed that the golden rule was "An eye for an eye and a tooth for a tooth." A reporter misquoted the rule: "Do to others as will be done to you." Given a correct formulation, two students debated at length with their professor that the rule meant the same as the motto "Get even." A pastor's wife doubted that the rule was biblical. Philosophers often distort the rule and dismiss it, while others who prefer a charitable interpretation find no reply.

This book is intended both for beginners and scholars in the fields of philosophy and religion, but students of psychology and cultural history will profit from it as well. Presupposing a course or two in philosophy or religion, in these chapters I present the heritage of many cultures and academic disciplines in order to develop a many-sided yet, I trust, coherent concept of the golden rule. This approach takes a middle way between highlighting difference at the expense of universal concerns and reading a single concept of the rule into every tradition. The present is enriched through a review of the past, while the past is studied with an eye to present problems. The major section of the book, "Histories of the Golden Rule," treats of Confucianism, ancient Greek culture, classical Jewish thought, the New Testament, medieval and Reformation theology, early modern philosophy, late nineteenth- and early twentieth-century American history, and contemporary psychology, philosophy, and religious thought. It concludes with a proposal for a new ethics centered on the golden rule.

My experience of working on this book was initially an exercise of piety. Next it turned into an effort to construct the appearance and reality of an academic specialty. Then it became an affair of self-redefinition. The book culminates as a gift, an invitation to come and see what I have found.

The rule began to be brightly real to me a few years ago, not during a time for study, nor as a result of any deliberate experiment to put the rule into practice, but through the experience of taking over all the kitchen tasks for the family during a two-week period when my wife, Hagiko, needed to concentrate on her literary studies. One day, as our then eight-year-old son handed me his dishes, for a moment I seemed to sense a slight, unspoken, unconsciously derogatory attitude: "Here. You are the one who takes care of this sort of thing." In that moment I realized that I had related to my wife in such a way.

In my intellectual and personal adventure, I sought and I found, but I did not find by seeking, and now I know why it is said that you only understand the golden rule by living it.

Stow, Ohio   J. H. W.
March 1996

Acknowledgments

The idea for this book originated in a 1985 Stanford University seminar on the golden rule in which I was privileged to assist David S. Nivison. His work on the Confucian golden rule inspired me, and his friendship and scholarly experience have been most helpful. I could not name all the authors and friends who have contributed to this work, nor have I been able to profit sufficiently from the perspectives they have offered. Nevertheless, I want to mention additional help I received regarding the Confucian tradition from John Berthrong, Antonio Cua, Julia Ching, Herbert Fingarette, Craig Ihara, Kwang-Sae Lee, Barry Steben, Lee Rainey, Tang Yi-jie, James Ware, and Yang Xiao-jie. With respect to the chapter on ancient Greek philosophy, I am especially indebted to Mitchell H. Miller, Jr. In addition, I wish to acknowledge help received from Jonathan Barnes, Julia Barkowiak, James Dickoff, Albrecht Dihle, Daniel Dombrowski, Norman Fischer, Daniel Guerrière, Patricia James, and Diane Yeager. Torsti Äärelä commented on the chapter on Judaism; David A. Fraser and David Odell-Scott commented on the New Testament chapter. John V. Apczynski and George L. Murphy commented on the chapter on medieval and Reformation thought. Robert P. Swierenga commented on the chapter concerning American history; and Rob Davis and Philip A. Rolnick helped in the area of nineteenth- and twentieth-century theology. C. Daniel Batson's thorough remarks on the chapter devoted to psychology prompted a major revision; and Bret Lathwell helped me sharpen social science perspectives. Regarding the golden rule in contemporary ethics, my ongoing dialogue with Harry J. Gensler S.J., has led to a fine friendship and continued enlightenment. I am grateful for careful comments by Bruce Alton, Daniel O. Dahlstrom, Donald Evans, Louis Pojman, and William Lad Sessions, all of whom read parts of an earlier draft. In addition, I owe much to conversations with Ronald M. Green, R. M. Hare, George R. Lucas, Jr., John Morreall, Onora O'Neill, Manuel Velasquez, and Carol White. Joseph T. O'Connell and Julian Woods helped with Hinduism, Abrahim I. Khan with Islam, Robert L.

Haynes with African-American perspectives, and Sioux Harvey with American Indian traditions.

I acknowledge the fine opportunity I was granted to share my discoveries as a visiting scholar at three schools in the North Carolina Independent College Association. A second series of presentations were supported, in part, by the Ohio Humanities Council and the National Endowment for the Humanities. I am grateful to the students who attended my Kent State University seminar on the golden rule, as well as to fellow panelists Richard Berg and Antonio Gualtieri, who participated in the 1994 session on the golden rule and the law of love sponsored by the Canadian Council for the Study of Religion.

Portions of chapter 2 are reprinted, with changes, from "Plato's Brush with the Golden Rule," *Journal of Religious Ethics* 21, no. 1 (Spring 1993): 69–85, by permission of the publisher, © 1987 by Religious Ethics, Inc. Portions of chapter 10 originally appeared, in a slightly different form, in "Levels of Meaning in the Golden Rule," *Journal of Religious Ethics* 15, no. 1 (Spring 1987): 106–29, © by Religious Ethics, Inc.

The Scripture quotations contained herein are from the New Revised Standard Version Bible, copyright © 1989 by the Division of Christian Education of the National Council of the Churches of Christ in the U.S.A., and are used by permission. All rights reserved.

A contemporary scholar owes much to librarians and bibliographic services, and I want to acknowledge the help I received from Gladys Smiley Bell and Michael Cole of Kent State University Library and librarians at the University of Toronto and Santa Clara University.

It has been a genuine privilege to work with the people at Oxford University Press, including my executive editor, Cynthia Read, associate editor, Peter Ohlin, manuscript editor, Henry Krawitz, and production editor, Rob Dilworth. I am also grateful to the freelance copy editor, Maura High, and to an anonymous reviewer. Their patience and helpfulness have been extraordinary.

Lastly, I owe a great debt of gratitude to my parents, George Wattles and Louise Howard, who initiated me into the golden rule. Family life with Hagiko Ichihara Wattles and our son, Benjamin Ichihara Wattles, has been a sustaining delight.

Contents

THE
GOLDEN
RULE

one

Introduction

The Golden Rule—One or Many, Gold or Glitter?

Children are taught to respect parents and other authority figures. Adolescents are urged to control their impulses. Adults are told to conduct themselves in accord with certain moral
and ethical standards. Morality, then, may seem to be just an affair of imposition, a cultural voice that says "no" in various ways to our desires. To
be sure, there are times when the word "no" must be spoken and enforced. But, time and again, people have discovered something more to
morality, something rooted in life itself. The "no" is but one word in the
voice of life, a voice that has other words, including the golden rule: Do
to others as you want others to do to you. This book is about the life in
that principle.

THE UNITY OF THE RULE

What could be easier to grasp intuitively than the golden rule? It has such
an immediate intelligibility that it serves as a ladder that anyone can step
onto without a great stretch. I know how I like to be treated; and that is
how I am to treat others. The rule asks me to be considerate of others
rather than indulging in self-centeredness. The study of the rule, however,
leads beyond conventional interpretation, and the practice of the rule
leads beyond conventional morality.

The rule is widely regarded as obvious and self-evident. Nearly everyone is familiar with it in some formulation or other. An angry parent uses
it as a weapon: "Is that how you want others to treat you?" A defense
attorney invites the members of the jury to put themselves in the shoes
of his or her client. Noting that particular rules and interpretations do not
cover every situation, a manual of professional ethics exhorts members to
treat other professionals with the same consideration and respect that
they would wish for themselves. Formulated in one way or another, the
rule finds its way into countless speeches, sermons, documents, and
books on the assumption that that it has a single, clear sense that the

listener or reader grasps and approves of. In an age where differences so often occasion violence, here, it seems, is something that everyone can agree on.

Promoting the notion that the golden rule is "taught by all the world's religions," advocates have collected maxims from various traditions, producing lists with entries like the following: "Hinduism: 'Let no man do to another that which would be repugnant to himself.' "[1] "Islam: 'None of you [truly] believes until he wishes for his brother what he wishes for himself.' "[2] The point of these lists is self-evident. Despite the differences in phrasing, all religions acknowledge the same basic, universal moral teaching.[3] Moreover, this principle may be accepted as common ground by secular ethics as well.

Under the microscope of analysis, however, things are not so simple. Different formulations have different implications, and differences in context raise the question of whether the same concept is at work in passages where the wording is nearly identical. Is the meaning of the rule constant whenever one of these phrases is mentioned? There is a persistent debate, for example, about the relative merit of the positive formulation versus the negative one, "Do not do to others what you do not want others to do to you." Nor can the full meaning of a sentence be grasped in isolation. For example, to point to "the golden rule in Confucianism" by quoting a fifteen-word sentence from the *Analects* of Confucius does not convey the historical dynamism of the rule's evolving social, ethical, and spiritual connotations. What do the words mean in their original context? How prominent is the rule within that particular tradition? Finally, how does the rule function in a given interaction between the speaker or writer and the listener or reader? The rule may function as an authoritative reproach, a pious rehearsal of tradition, a specimen for analytic dissection, or a confession of personal commitment. Is the rule one or many? Can we even properly speak of *the* golden rule at all?[4] Some Hindus interpret the injunction to treat others as oneself as an invitation to identify with the divine spirit within each person. Some Muslims take the golden rule to apply primarily to the brotherhood of Islam. Some Christians regard the rule as a shorthand summary of the morality of Jesus' religion. And countless people think of the rule without any religious associations at all.

Raising the question about the meanings of the golden rule in different contexts is not intended to reduce similarities to dust and ashes merely by appealing to the imponderable weight of cultural differences. Context is not the last word on meaning; the sentence expressing the golden rule contributes meaning of its own to its context. Meaning does involve context, but the fact that contexts differ does not prove that there is no commonality of meaning. Language and culture, moreover, are not reliable clues for identifying conceptual similarity and difference, since conceptual harmony is experienced across these boundaries.[5]

The golden rule, happily, has more than a single sense. It is not a static, one-dimensional proposition with a single meaning to be accepted or rejected, defended or refuted. Nor is its multiplicity chaotic. There is enough continuity of meaning in its varied uses to justify speaking of the golden rule. My own thesis is that the rule's unity is best comprehended not in terms of a single meaning but as a symbol of a process of growth on emotional, intellectual, and spiritual levels.

THE QUALITY OF THE RULE

"Gold is where you find it" runs a proverb coined by miners who found what they were seeking in unexpected places. So what sort of ore or alloy or sculpture is the teaching that, since the seventeenth century, has been called "the golden rule"? Is it gold or glitter? Certain appreciative remarks on the golden rule seem to bear witness to a discovery. "Eureka!" they seem to say. "There is a supreme principle of living! It can be expressed in a single statement!"

By contrast, theologian Paul Tillich found the rule an inferior principle. For him, the biblical commandment to love and the assurance that God is love "infinitely transcend" the golden rule. The problem with the rule is that it "does not tell us what we should wish."[6]

Is the rule golden? In other words, is it worthy to be cherished as a rule of living or even as the rule of living? The values of the rule are as much in dispute as its meanings. Most people, it seems, intuitively regard the golden rule as a good principle, and some have spoken as though there is within the rule a special kind of agency with the power to transform humankind.

It is understandable that the golden rule has been regarded as the supreme moral principle. I do not want to be murdered; therefore I should not murder another. I do not want my spouse to commit adultery, my property to be stolen, and so forth; therefore I should treat others with comparable consideration. Others have comparable interests, and the rule calls me to treat the other as someone akin to myself. Moreover, I realize that I sometimes have desires to be treated in ways that do not represent my considered best judgment, and this reflection makes it obvious that reason is required for the proper application of the golden rule. Finally, in personal relationships, I want to be loved, and, in consequence, the rule directs me to be loving.[7] From the perspective of someone simply interested in living right rather than in the construction and critique of theories, the rule has much to recommend it.

Some writers have put the rule on a pedestal, giving the impression that the rule is sufficient for ethics in the sense that no one could ever go wrong by adhering to it or in the sense that all duties may be inferred from it. Others have claimed that the rule is a necessary criterion for right action; in other words, an action must be able to pass the test of the golden rule if it is to be validated as right, and any action that fails the test is wrong. Some philosophers have hoped for an ethical theory that would be self-sufficient (depending on no controversial axioms), perfectly good (invulnerable to counterexamples), and all-powerful (enabling the derivation of every correct moral judgment, given appropriate data about the situation). They have dreamed of sculpting ethics into an independent, rational, deductive system, on the model of geometry, with a single normative axiom. However much reason may hanker for such a system, once the golden rule is taken as a candidate for such an axiom, a minor flexing of the analytic bicep is enough to humiliate it. A single counterexample suffices to defeat a pretender to this throne.

Many scholars today regard the rule as an acceptable principle for popular use but as embarrassing if taken with philosophic seriousness. Most professional ethicists rely instead on other principles, since the rule seems vulnerable to counterexamples, such as the current favorite, "What if a sadomasochist goes forth to treat others as he wants to be treated?"

Technically, the golden rule can defend itself from objections, since it contains within itself the seed of its own self-correction. Any easily abused interpretation may be challenged: "Would you want to be treated according to a rule construed in this way?" The recursive use of the rule—applying it to the results of its own earlier application—is a lever that extricates it from many tangles. Close examination of the counterexample of the sadomasochist (offered in chapter 13) shows that to use the rule properly requires a certain degree of maturity. The counterexample does not refute the golden rule, properly understood; rather, it serves to clarify the interpretation of the rule—that the golden rule functions appropriately in a *growing* personality; indeed, the practice of the rule itself promotes the required growth. Since the rule is such a compressed statement of morality, it takes for granted at least a minimum sincerity that refuses to manipulate the rule sophistically to "justify" patently immoral conduct. Where that prerequisite cannot be assumed, problems multiply.

The objections that have been raised against the rule are useful to illustrate misinterpretations of the rule and to make clear assumptions that must be satisfied for the rule to function in moral theory.

It has been objected that the golden rule assumes that human beings are basically alike and thereby fails to do justice to the differences between people. In particular, the rule allegedly implies that what we want is what others want. As George Bernard Shaw quipped, "Don't do to others as you want them to do unto you. Their tastes may be different."[8] The golden rule may also seem to imply that what we want for ourselves is good for ourselves and that what is good for ourselves is good for others. The positive formulation, in particular, is accused of harboring the potential for presumption; thus, the rule is suited for immediate application only among those whose beliefs and needs are similar. In fact, however, the rule calls for due consideration for any relevant difference between persons—just as the agent would want such consideration from others.

Another criticism is that the golden rule sets too low a standard because it makes ordinary wants and desires the criterion of morality. On one interpretation, the rule asks individuals to do whatever they imagine they might wish to have done to them in a given situation; thus a judge would be obliged by the golden rule to sentence a convicted criminal with extreme leniency. As a mere principle of sympathy, therefore, it is argued, the rule is incapable of guiding judgment in cases where the necessary action is unwelcome to its immediate recipient.

A related problem is that the rule, taken merely as a policy of sympathy, amounts to the advice "Treat others as they want you to treat them," as in a puzzle from the opening chapter of Herman Melville's *Moby-Dick*, where Ishmael is invited by his new friend, Queequeg, to join in pagan worship. Ishmael pauses to think it over:

> But what is worship?—to do the will of God—*that* is worship. And what is the will of God?—to do to my fellow man what I would have my fellow man to do to me—*that* is the will of God. Now, Queequeg is my fellow man. And what do I wish that this Queequeg would do to me? Why, unite with me in my particular Presbyterian form of worship. Consequently, I must then unite with him in his; ergo, I must turn idolator.[9]

If the golden rule is taken to require the agent to identify with the other in a simplistic and uncritical way, the result is a loss of the higher perspective toward which the rule moves the thoughtful practitioner.

The next clusters of objections have a depth that a quick, initial reply would betray, so I defer my response until later. If the rule is not to be interpreted as setting up the agent's idiosyncratic desires—or those of the recipient—as a supreme standard of goodness, then problems arise because the rule does not specify what the agent ought to desire. The rule merely requires consistency of moral judgment: one must apply the same standards to one's treatment of others that one applies to others' treatment of oneself. The lack of specificity in the rule, its merely formal or merely procedural character, allegedly renders its guidance insubstantial.

The rule seems to exhibit the limitations of any general moral principle: it does not carry sufficiently rich substantive implications to be helpful in the thicket of life's problems. Even though most people live with some allegiance to integrating principles, action guides, mottoes, proverbs, or commandments that serve to unify the mind, the deficiency of any principle is that it is merely a principle, merely a beginning; only the full exposition of a system of ethics can validate the place of an asserted principle. An appeal to a general principle, moreover, can function as a retreat and a refusal to think through issues in their concreteness.

There is also criticism of a practice widely associated with the rule—imagining oneself in the other person's situation.[10] The charge is that this practice is an abstract, derivative, artificial, male, manipulative device, which can never compensate for the lack of human understanding and spontaneous goodness.

The rule has been criticized as a naively idealistic standard, unsuited to a world of rugged competition. The rule may seem to require that, if I am trustworthy and want to be trusted, I must treat everyone as being equally trustworthy. Furthermore, the broad humanitarianism of the golden rule allegedly makes unrealistic psychological demands; it is unfair to family and friends to embrace the universal concerns of the golden rule.

Last, some religious issues. The golden rule has been criticized for being a teaching that misleadingly lets people avoid confronting the higher teachings of religious ethics, for example, Jesus' commandment, "Love one another as I have loved you." Some find the rule of only intermediate usefulness, proposing that spiritual living moves beyond the standpoint of rules. Others have criticized the golden rule's traditional links to religion, arguing that moral intuition and moral reason can operate without reference to any religious foundation.

For responding to all these objections, there are three possible strategies: abandon the rule, reformulate it, or retain it as commonly worded, while taking advantage of objections to clarify its proper interpretation. I take the third way.

THE NATURE AND SCOPE OF THIS BOOK

To focus on the golden rule is not to begin at the beginning in a philosophy of living. Morality comes to its highest fruition in a life devoted to truth, beauty, and goodness on material, intellectual, and spiritual levels. Thus an adequate context for ethics would include reflections on scientific, philosophic, and spiritual truth, and on beauty in nature and the arts. Without a certain fullness in the realization of truth and beauty, the insightfulness and spontaneity that should grace moral action are lacking. This book does not presuppose specific commitments from this broader philosophic context; nevertheless, genuine moral inquiry does presuppose that one reject false freedom, the claim that one has a right to do whatever one chooses.

This book is designed to erode familiarity with the golden rule. These chapters provide an evolutionary path to discovery, a series of historical studies of the golden rule in various cultural traditions and in contemporary psychology, philosophy, and religion. The writing of each chapter is informed by issues at work in other chapters, so that each partially establishes the agenda for the others. Special attention is devoted to the following:

1. the practice of imaginative perspective-taking, putting oneself in the other person's situation
2. the question of spontaneity and self-forgetfulness
3. philosophical analyses, objections, and responses
4. virtues associated with the rule
5. the theme of human kinship

The rule is usually linked, in one way or another, with the conviction that human beings are somehow akin; and exploring that link is the secondary theme of the book. In the concluding chapters, I propose a revitalized ethics centered on the golden rule. Since the ultimate foundation of this ethics is religious, this book is finally an essay in religious ethics.

I have not aimed at encyclopedic coverage of everything published on the golden rule but at an integrated look at materials relevant to the rule as a principle in the philosophy of living. I have been selective, too, in my examination of traditions. Despite the fact that the golden rule has been expressed, in some form, in most or all of the world's religions, only in the Confucian and Judeo-Christian traditions did the rule become a prominent theme for sustained reflection. The emergence of the golden rule in some traditions is incomplete: a phrase is all that may be found, such as "If your neighbor's jackal escapes into your garden, you should return the animal to its owner; this is how you would want your neighbor to treat you"[11]; "Great Spirit, grant that I may not criticize my neighbor until I have walked a mile in his moccasins."[12] That the focus of the book is thus limited does not imply that the virtues symbolized by the golden rule are any less present in traditions such as Hinduism and Buddhism that are not discussed here.

There remain possibilities for alternative accounts of living the golden rule, in science-based, humanistic, and religious philosophies. These approaches compete partly on their ability to produce an account of what the others emphasize and to include somehow within their own systems of thinking the others' cherished facts, meanings, and values. Thus, science-based philosophies aim to explain altruism in terms of biological and social-psychological categories. Humanists acknowledge the scientific factors and the contribution of religion in sometimes motivating altruism, while insisting that human goodness is properly understood in strictly human terms. Religionists acknowledge the truths of science and the meanings and values that humanists emphasize, while proposing faith as the means of access to supreme values and to the source of human kinship.[13]

This book presents *scientific* perspectives in two senses. In part I, chapter 9 surveys research in psychology, while the chapters presenting philosophical and religious interpretations are scientific in the sense that they are histories: the discipline of history functions as the all-embracing science here. These histories aspire to historical objectivity in the following senses: I have tried to keep my redescriptions within bounds acceptable to those whose work is being described, to stay within what specialists in the area could regard as fair (however much they may disagree), and to give information in such a way that the reader who disagrees can use it to tell a better story. Likewise, the book presents *philosophic* perspectives in the very structure and texture of the book, by chronicling the ideas of philosophers, by including occasional comments in the histories (which are, from the standpoint of a professional historian, *philosophic* histories), and in the concluding exposition contained in part II. The same may be said about the *religious* perspectives discussed and active in the book. I have tried to present information for a general audience in such a way as to facilitate independent judgment. Though the perspective of Christianity is featured more than others, on every key point in the concluding chapter I give analogous illustrations from other religions as well.

If religious perspectives in ethics are to have a widely acknowledged place in the field of ethics generally, the currently predominant conception of ethics must open up. According to that conception, the purpose of ethics is to help individuals in conflict come to reasoned agreement about moral issues; and since convictions about religion are so intractable, the quest for universal agreement must operate independently of religion. But how can universal agreement be secured on a secularist premise with which a majority of the world's population disagree? All voices, religious and nonreligious, need to be part of public dialogue in ethics, since one never knows from what voices the next idea will come to benefit us all.

This book works with concepts of levels of living—emotional, intellectual, and spiritual—and this practice requires a caveat. Talk of levels is justified by the discontinuities in human experience, such that each breakthrough to a new and "higher" level yields new perspective on previously achieved levels. There is an asymmetry, such that from one level one can comprehend lower levels, but not vice versa. The interrelation of levels, however, is so thorough that one must take care to avoid overemphasizing the talk of levels and to retain a profound sense of the unity of the personality and of the equality of all men and women.

In gathering materials for this inquiry, I searched electronic databases and indexes for books and articles on the golden rule in English, German, and French in philosophy, religion, and the social sciences. In psychology I sought out literature on empathy, sympathy, and altruism. Even within the traditions on which I have focused, the reader will notice gaps that, in part, reflect the gaps in the literature on the golden rule that I have been able to locate and read.[14]

Concerning the practice of reforming language to make explicit the essential truth of the equality of women and men, though I have migrated from the complacent habits of an earlier generation, I do make occasional use of the phrase, "the brotherhood of man." A couple of times I use "the siblinghood of humankind," a phrase with the necessary familial connotations that may become standard in the next generation. I do not banish the older phrase, which elicits intuitive understanding and much favorable recognition around the world. When explaining the texts of other authors, I do not hesitate to reproduce their terminology, whatever its conscious or unconscious associations with sexism may have been, though I avoid "languageism"—taking an author's terminology as sufficient ground for accusation. English is in rapid flux, and it takes an extra measure of good will for communication to be successful in the environment of contemporary sensitivities.

OVERVIEW

This study gathers meanings of the golden rule by examining it in the context of issues from particular cultural traditions and academic disciplines. The histories in part I are organized roughly in chronological sequence. The evolution traced here is not a simple progression from inchoate barbarism to civilized magnificence. Origins are not so crude as may be imagined. Some of the steps along the way are ambiguous. And by the end of a story, much of the best is in the past. Nonetheless, a synoptic perspective may discern progress under way.

Chapter 2 examines the Confucian golden rule, which is embedded in an ethics of character, where the virtues are relational and centered in the family. On this foundation, beneficence extends, ultimately, to all humankind. The ideals are clear, and keen self-discipline is called for in pursuit of these ideals. The goal, however, is not conscientious conformity to norms but spontaneous living. The chapter focuses on the role of the golden rule in the movement to spontaneity.

Chapter 3 traces the gradual emergence of the golden rule in ancient Greece and Rome, where the first problem was to disentangle the rule from the popular sophistry of common practices and maxims of reciprocity and retaliation, helping friends and harming enemies. This chapter tells how, as the popular and sophistic use of the rule was set aside, the universal scope of the golden rule gained recognition.

Chapter 4 deals with occurrences of the golden rule in early Jewish literature. By the first century, Rabbi Hillel could propose the rule as a summary of the entire Torah. This chapter explores the evolution that made it possible for the rule to function in that way.

Chapter 5 explores the rule in the Gospels of Matthew and Luke. The writers of the New Testament faced the problem of distinguishing the rule from conventional notions of reciprocity and retaliation and the problem of connecting the rule with the elevated standards of Jesus' life and teachings. This chapter shows why the most reasonable understanding of the rule in these contexts distinguishes different levels of interpretation.

Chapters 6 and 7 discuss the European Middle Ages and early modern period, highlighting the theologians Augustine, Aquinas, and Luther; English religious writers of the seventeenth century; and philosophers Samuel Clarke, Immanuel Kant, and John Stuart Mill. At the beginning of the period, the golden rule was widely regarded as an important statement of "natural law," recognized by the human mind without having to rely on special revelation or divine grace. Two problems with the golden rule begin to stimulate writers during this period. First, what difference does the presence or absence of religious faith make to the practice of the rule? Second, how is one to respond to objections to the golden rule?

Chapter 8 recounts the heyday of the golden rule as a popular slogan in America during the late nineteenth and early twentieth centuries. For the religious leaders, politicians, and businessmen highlighted in this chapter, the challenge to the golden rule was not theoretical. Rather, in the rough competition of the age, when need for reforms was obvious and uncertainties about wealth and poverty were pressing, what sort of human response would prevail? Amid the spectrum of possible answers, ranging from ruthless self-aggrandizement to mystic renunciation, social Darwinism posed a vigorous challenge to Christianity. In what cases would the golden rule, cherished by many as the principle of the practice of the fatherhood of God and the brotherhood of man, validate itself as a superior principle of evolution, rather than a naive recipe for economic and political suicide?

Chapter 9 brings together psychological perspectives on the golden rule. Several theorists, including Piaget, Kohlberg, and Erikson, discuss the golden rule as part of a theory of a developmental sequence. In addition, the work of clinical and experimental psychologists has proved helpful in the application of the rule.

Chapters 10 and 11 examine the golden rule in twentieth-century philosophy, focusing on a number of related questions. What are the strengths and weaknesses of the rule taken strictly as a principle of consistency in moral judgment? What do philosophers have to say about empathy and the imaginative role reversal? What implications for interpreting the rule are there in the contemporary heightening of awareness of the otherness of the other person?

Chapter 12 relates contemporary interpretations of the rule in religious philosophy and theology. How is practicing the rule to lead to the positive transformation of one's desires? What levels of meaning are implicit in the rule? Does the spiritual practice of the rule aid in the solution of moral problems? How does it function—ideally—within the Christian community? The chapter closes with a contemporary Baha'i interpretation of the rule.

Part II sets forth a philosophical and religious context for the replete practice of the rule. The resulting ethics honors moral intuition, sharpens intuition through moral thinking, acknowledges the complex social context of interaction, and leads the practitioner beyond duty-conscious rule following to loving spontaneity.

I.

HISTORIES
OF THE
GOLDEN RULE

two

A Confucian Path from Conscientiousness to Spontaneity

Confucian tradition has honored the beauty in genuine goodness, where the shadow of self-conscious hesitation is gone and nobility of character expresses itself spontaneously. The ideal is appealing, but how shall this beautiful spontaneity dawn in human character? How can one live spontaneously without betraying duty? Is it possible to *cultivate* such a manner of living?

Confucius' autobiographical sketch indicates something of his steps along the way.

> At fifteen I set my heart upon learning. At thirty, I had planted my feet firmly upon the ground. At forty, I no longer suffered from perplexities. At fifty, I knew what were the biddings of Heaven. At sixty, I heard them with docile ear. At seventy, I could follow the dictates of my own heart; for I no longer overstepped the boundaries of right.[1]

A spontaneity that "follows the dictates of one's heart" while remaining "within the boundaries of right" can hardly be confused with impulsiveness.

In the program to achieve a noble and spontaneously expressive character, the golden rule plays an important and many-faceted role. First, the practice of the rule strengthens the virtues conducive to humane relationships in an orderly society. Second, the rule symbolizes the goal itself, the way of relating that is ideal. Third, the rule functions as a thread of continuity between levels of interpretation that range in focus from social-ethical norms to philosophical and spiritual realization.

The literary tradition of the Chinese golden rule appears to originate in the writings of Confucius (551–479 B.C.E). During a period of political corruption, warfare, disintegrating society, and declining personal standards, Confucius synthesized and added to traditional Chinese teachings in an effort to reestablish social and political order on a firm foundation. The cornerstone of his edifice was excellence of character, expressed especially in the basic relationships of society: father and son, husband and wife, older brother and younger brother, emperor and minister, and friend and friend. The primary emphasis was on the family; and every relationship but the last was asymmetrical, involving a superior and a subordinate. To be sure, insofar as the norms of any relationship involved unjustified notions of superiority and subordination, it would be harder for students of the golden rule to achieve gracious spontaneity in their practice.

The major philosophers who developed the Confucian golden rule further were Mencius (371–289 B.C.E.) and Chu Hsi (1130–1200 C.E.). While Confucius had occupied himself with character and society and had very little of the religious or the metaphysical in his discourses, and while Mencius took a only step or two into the realms of the invisible, things changed in that phase of the tradition called neo-Confucianism that developed under the stimulus of Buddhist intellectual speculation and meditation, in addition to the continuing challenge of Taoism. The first neo-Confucian thinker comparable to the major medieval thinkers of other traditions was Chu Hsi. Like Confucius, he served as an editor of tradition as well as a pioneer. He taught "the investigation of things" leading to the discovery of the cosmic principle; and he proposed a maxim of spiritual practice: "A half-day of study and a half-day of quiet sitting." He developed the concept of the Supreme Ultimate, whose tranquillity is at the root of the mind's initiatives of thought and whose activity conditions the processes of the universe. It is to be expected that these changes would substantially affect the interpretation of the golden rule.[2]

ANCHORING THE GOLDEN RULE IN RELATIONAL VIRTUES

The most ancient source for the golden rule is the *Analects* of Confucius, a collection of sayings attributed to Confucius and other disciples along with brief dialogues between Confucius and his students. Character achievement is the dominant concern in the *Analects*, and we find Confucius openly remarking on his own deficiencies, his progress, and the qualities that he possesses securely. The clearest initial sense of the golden rule emerges from the following dialogue:

> Tzu-kung asked, "Is there single word which can serve as the guiding principle for conduct throughout one's life?" Confucius said, "It is the word 'consideration' [shu]. Do not impose on others what you do not desire others to impose upon you."[3]

Confucius answers in terms of a relational virtue and then immediately defines that virtue in terms of a principle. His answer implies that there are maxims that one may outgrow. Particular maxims, such as "Obey the emperor," will have exceptions and will only be relevant at those times when someone is faced with an emperor's command, whereas the golden rule is continually pertinent.

Though Western philosophers have wrestled with counterexamples to the rule, the need to do so did not arise in early Chinese thought, which never isolated the rule from its character context as an abstract, independent criterion of right action. The ethical implications of the Chinese golden rule were so stoutly built in from the outset that such concerns did not arise.[4] The rule itself, expressing the virtue of consideration, was linked to with a companion virtue, loyalty (chung)[5] in the most influential Confucian golden rule text, Analects 4.15.

> Confucius said, "Ts'an, there is one thread that runs through my doctrines." Tseng Tzu said, "Yes." After Confucius had left, the disciples asked him, "What did he mean?" Tseng Tzu replied, "The Way of our Master is none other than conscientiousness [chung] and altruism [shu]."[6]

The metaphor of the one (thread)—actually a twofold weave of virtues—symbolizes the unity pervading the diversity of Confucian teachings.

Though it may seem implausible that Confucius would permit the one thread running through his teaching to be stated, in his absence, by a student, this interpretation by Tseng Tzu became standard Confucian doctrine.[7] In any case, the text acquired the status of scripture, and, by setting forth loyalty and consideration as the unifying theme of the Confucian Way, it assured the perennial status of the golden rule. The one thread would inspire continuous commentary, carrying implications for the embedded golden rule in its wake. For ensuing tradition, the topic of the golden rule became the topic of loyalty and consideration.

There is an etymological reason for pairing "loyalty" and "consideration." Each term comprises two characters, and both terms have the same lower character. In "loyalty," chung, the upper character means center; the lower character means mind or heart. Thus chung suggests that the mind or heart is centered. In consideration, shu, the upper character means like or as; the lower one, mind or heart. Etymologically, shu implies sympathy with the feelings and thoughts of another person, being of like mind and heart.[8]

There is an additional reason for pairing loyalty with consideration. As David S. Nivison has argued, in classical Chinese literature the two virtues are complementary in that the first tends to connote social relations to superiors, while the second tends to connote social relations to subordinates. Loyalty involves doing one's utmost in the fulfillment of a duty—especially to a superior. Indeed, loyalty sometimes connotes devotion to the emperor and the government; thus there might be a political motive for advocating this virtue. Consideration involves a generous attitude to subordinates, not being excessively rigorous in one's demands.[9] Both attitudes are also appropriate in relating to equals. Nivison notes that the

word "do" used in the phrase "do to others" has a connotation of bestow-
ing (or inflicting) something upon a subordinate: "Do not inflict on others
what you do not want others to inflict upon you."[10]

Confucius does not portray the golden rule as a moderate, merely
conventional, or easily attained standard. Tzu-kung said, "What I do not
want others to do to me, I do not want to do to them." Confucius said,
"Ah Tz'u! That is beyond you!"[11] Part of the challenge, presumably, is that
the rule pertains not only to actions but also to desires. The high ethical
implications of the golden rule are explicit in an influential third-century
text, *The Doctrine of the Mean*:

> Loyalty and consideration are not far from the Way (*tao*). If you would
> not be willing to have something done to yourself, then don't do it to
> others. The ways of the morally noble man are four, and I (Confucius)
> have not yet mastered even one of them: What you would require of
> your son, use in serving your father; . . . what you would require of
> your subordinate, use in serving your prince; . . . what you would re-
> quire of your younger brother, use in serving you elder brother; . . .
> what you would require of your friend, first apply in your treatment of
> him.[12]

If loyalty and consideration are virtues of the second rank—not far from
the Way—what virtue is higher?

Though there is no single, hierarchal map of the virtues that fits all
the Confucian classics, one quality is usually taken as the culminating and
integrating virtue in the *Analects* (though sometimes it is ranked just below
sagehood). The supreme virtue is *jen*, cohumanity (also translated "humanity," "benevolence," or "love").[13] One can fulfill major political responsibilities excellently and still fall short of cohumanity. A ruler needs the virtue
of cohumanity in order to attend properly to the needs of the people,
and members of society need the virtue of cohumanity to participate genuinely in rites, or traditional rituals such as prayer, sacrifices, and funerals.
At the core, cohumanity involves being truly humane in one-to-one relationships. Cohumanity, according to Antonio S. Cua, cannot be totally defined in terms of rules or criteria for moral conduct or a list of virtues
such as filial piety, loyalty, and so on. It can only be done situationally,
spontaneously, with moral creativity.[14]

How is the virtue of cohumanity expressed, and what is the best path
to it? The golden rule is a prominent answer to both questions. Expressing
such a high standard, it could be intimately connected with cohumanity,
as two passages in the *Analects* show. In the first, consideration is one of
the virtues included in cohumanity:

> Chung-kung asked about humanity. Confucius said, "When you go
> abroad, behave to everyone as if you were receiving a great guest. Employ
> the common people as if you were assisting at a great sacrifice. Do not
> do to others what you do not want them to do to you. Then there will

be no complaint against you in the state or in the family (the ruling clan)."
Chung-kung said, "Although I am not intelligent, may I put your saying
into practice."[15]

Here golden rule conduct is associated with hospitality, and hospitality is
extended beyond the confines of one's own community. Such an extension of generosity is a mark of cohumanity. The second passage describes
cohumanity in terms of the golden rule.

> A man of humanity, wishing to establish his own character, also estab-
> lishes the character of others, and wishing to be prominent himself, also
> helps others to be prominent. To be able to judge others by what is near
> to ourselves may be called the method of realizing humanity.[16]

Here the high level of cohumanity is described as satisfying the golden
rule. In addition, the practice of comparing self and others (estimating, by
our own case, "what is near to ourselves") is the way to attain cohumanity;
as Mencius said, "Be considerate, and you will find that this is the shortest
way to co-humanity."[17]

COMPARING SELF AND OTHER

The practice of the golden rule sometimes involves an explicit imaginative
role reversal, putting oneself in the other person's situation. In the second
of the passages just quoted, Confucius directs the agent to compare himself
with the recipient. But what is involved in comparing? Traditional Chinese
sources give no psychological description or philosophical analysis of it,
though it is possible to assemble pieces for a surprisingly rich mosaic,
blending classical and neo-Confucian authors (plus one, Mo Tzu, not
counted in the Confucian line).

   1. In comparing self and other, the agent imagines him- or herself in the situation
of the recipient.   One assumes that others also get hungry and thirsty, desire
to succeed, to establish a noble character, and so on. In general terms, the
agent discerns desires of the recipient, analogous to (legitimate) desires of
the agent. The assumption that writers of every period seem to share is
expressed by Chu Hsi: "By 'comparison' I mean to compare the mind of
another with my own, and so put myself in their place."[18]

   2. Though our empathic understanding of one another is not perfect, we do have an
intuitive grasp of others.   The modern Western philosophic question of how
we can justifiably claim to know other persons (at all) contrasts sharply
with Confucian trust in our intuitive grasp of human relationships. The
intuitive quality of empathy—especially in action—is evident in the following passage from one of the classics, The Great Learning:

> The "Announcement of K'ang" says, "Act as if you were watching over an
> infant." If a mother sincerely and earnestly looks for what the infant
> wants, she may not hit the mark but she will not be far from it. A young
> woman has never had to learn about nursing a baby before she marries.[19]

Since our intuitive grasp of others is both the root of our knowledge of others and also fallible, the goal of the process of comparing is to sharpen this intuition. Confucianism, however, failed to incorporate its scientific interest in "the investigation of things" into its expanding concept of comparing.[20]

3. *The agent sees the recipient in terms of a relational pattern, such as father and son.* In a simple case the agent may take himself as an example, in the sense that he recognizes himself as a person in a relational pattern, for instance, of father and son. A Taoist story amplifies the Confucian point about seeing oneself in a relational pattern. The power of discovering oneself in such a pattern is illustrated in one of the stories of Chuang Tzu (from ca. 395–295 B.C.E.). He was hunting a surrealistic bird, which had forgotten itself in pursuit of a praying mantis, which in turn had forgotten itself in pursuit of a cicada, which had simply forgotten itself. Pondering the cycle of predation, he abandoned the hunt, only to find that he, too, was a target—he was being pursued by the park keeper who took him for a poacher. He fled and pondered the matter for months.[21] It is through the norms implicit in relationships that comparing is guided by ethical concerns.

4. *Comparing is a matter of heart as well as mind.* The separation of heart and mind is un-Chinese, inasmuch as the term *hsin* comprehends both. The involvement of the heart in discovering the similarity of self and others is emphasized in the neo-Confucian treatment of loyalty and consideration developed by Ch'en Ch'un (1159–1223 C.E.), representing the school of Chu Hsi. He bases his explanation on etymology and comments, "When one extends one's own mind to others to the point that their desires are like one's own, that is empathy [shu]."[22]

5. *Comparing is a creative, artistic activity.* Understanding another person is as much an art as a science. Herbert Fingarette found that comparing (*p'i*) in the *Analects* is consistently used with bold, creative comparisons. "Thus when Confucius is interested in the enterprise of teaching, he remarks that it is *p'i* raising a hill out of buckets of earth."[23]

6. *In order to elicit the appropriate feeling for a challenging situation, the agent may need to construct an analogy between the immediate situation and one that spontaneously elicits the appropriate feeling.* Mencius writes of extending feelings. Once the appropriate attitude and action have been realized in one case, they can be extended to other cases. Encouraging a king who has shown compassion toward an ox but who lacks it for his people, Mencius advises, "[T]ake this very heart here and apply it to what is over there."[24] Mencius shows that such comparing may be more complex than a self–other comparison. In order adequately to identify with a stranger's situation, the agent may need to take a preliminary step, to bring to mind his or her sympathy for some person (or animal) closer to the agent. Mencius ties extending feelings with "extending actions":

To respect the elders in your family and then to extend this respect to others' elders, to love the young in your family and then extend this love to
others' youths . . . extending your kindness, you can protect all people
within the four seas . . . . The reason that the ancient sages were greater
than ordinary people is that they were good at extending their actions.[25]

The notion of extending implies a home base in one's own family.

7. *The agent identifies with concrete aspects of the recipient's situation.*   The complexity of the process of identifying with another person is suggested by
Mo Tzu (470–391 B.C.E.), a figure outside the Confucian line.[26] Mo Tzu
does not explicate the notion of loving others as oneself except in terms
of its practical consequences: that one will strive to do the same good to
others that one would want for oneself—feeding the hungry, clothing the
naked, and so on. Intuitively obvious human needs are Mo's examples.[27]
The kind of identification that one can have, for example, with another's
country is not the same as identification with another person; but the first
may be required for the second. The agent may need to be able to empathize with the patriotism of a recipient of an action who comes from another country in order to identify appropriately with the recipient. Mo
Tzu taught that universal love of all humankind will follow when people
regard other persons as themselves, and other families, states, and so on
as their own. He argues that it is foolish not to act from this perspective—
once one understands its consequences and loses the fear of its allegedly
self-sacrificial implications.[28]

8. *There is a scientific dimension to understanding others.*   The scientific component of understanding, so prominent in Chinese tradition, is missing in
the traditional texts on the golden rule. It is interesting to consider why
the notion of "the investigation of things," featured in discussions of self-
cultivation, was never used to develop the concept of interpersonal comparing. If comparing is all about gaining an understanding of the other,
and the investigation of things is the gateway to understanding (as proclaimed in *The Great Learning* and by Chu Hsi), then why is this scientific
approach neglected in the practice of the golden rule? The explanation
seems to lie in the intuitive character of comparing previously noted.
Nonetheless, a full contemporary practice of the golden rule must welcome the contributions of the sciences.

9. *We can see the recipient in terms of the Way without explicit comparing.*   Mencius reports that one can find the Way in oneself and in the other person:

A noble man steeps himself in the Way (tao) because he wishes to find it
in himself. When he finds it in himself, he will be at ease in it; when he
is at ease in it, he can draw deeply upon it; when he can draw deeply
upon it, he finds its source wherever he turns.[29]

Having found the (source of the) Way wherever one turns, the agent presumably finds that the Way as experienced within aligns with the Way as

realized through identifying with the other person. There is no felt need for explicit attention to the characteristics of the other or explicit comparing of self and other. Spiritual experience outshines any hierarchal aspect of the relationship.[30] On this level there is no explicit following of the golden rule.

10. *Comparing occurs within the context of the universal family.* Comparing is a matter of recognizing similarities between self and other, and, finally, of recognizing human kinship. This approach, however, was not associated with explicit comparing in the sense of imagining oneself in the other's situation. Rather, it may be called identifying with the universal family of Heaven and Earth.

For Confucius' sage, "[a]ll within the four seas are his brothers."[31] The *Doctrine of the Mean* advocates "treating the common people as one's own children."[32] If this sounds condescending, it is partly because the philosophers were fond of offering advice to rulers and would identify with the ruler's perspective; moreover, neo-Confucianism nurtured the ambition that the sage, through self-perfection, would bring blessings to all the people. Finally, the model of parental love was extrapolated to become a norm for the ruler and sage as well, who would act so as to bring blessings to everyone.

In neo-Confucianism the theme of the universal family becomes more prominent. For Chang Tsai (1020–1077 C.E.), "Heaven is my father and Earth is my mother. . . . All people are my brothers and sisters."[33] This quotation begins the famous Western Inscription that Chang Tsai placed on the western wall of his academy; the line was included among Chu Hsi's selections of prominent Confucian and neo-Confucian words of wisdom and thence gained prominence in subsequent neo-Confucian thought. For Wang Yang-ming (1472–1529), "[t]he sage . . . regards all the people of the world as his brothers and children."[34]

A popular neo-Confucian image of identifying with others was "forming one body with" others. Chu Hsi links this metaphysical unity with the practice of the golden rule:

> The man of humanity regards Heaven and Earth and all things as one body. To him there is nothing that is not himself. Since he has recognized all things as himself, how can there be any limit to his humanity? . . . It is most difficult to describe humanity. Hence Confucius merely said that the man of humanity "wishing to establish his own character, also establishes the character of others . . . ." The hope was that by looking at it this way we might get at the substance of humanity.[35]

Here the self appears to relate to others as a nucleus to its satellite members. Nevertheless, Chu's egalitarian commitments are strong. He emphasizes impartiality, in which there is no favoritism toward self or other, and uses the metaphor of "mutually reflecting" persons.[36] He also writes,

"Among living things men and women form the same species and are on the highest level. Therefore they are called brothers and sisters."[37]

SPONTANEITY AND THE GOLDEN RULE

Spontaneity is a mark of the sage: "He who is sincere is one who hits upon what is right without effort and apprehends without thinking. He is naturally and easily in harmony with the Way."[38] Anxiety about what to do and about one's ability simply do not arise.

The ideal manner of living, however, is remote because of the complexity and difficulty of ethical living. Even one who knows the right thing to do may have to contend with unregulated desires and hatreds[39] and laziness.[40] More subtle obstacles include compulsive concern with duty,[41] admixture of selfish motivation deriving from overkeen awareness of the benefits of virtue,[42] and intellectualism which concentrates upon general principles at the expense of noticing what is at hand.[43]

Because of these difficulties, according to the Confucian program, mature spontaneity would arise only gradually, thanks to a self-discipline that will gradually teach the heart to rechannel the energies of unacceptable impulses and to entertain only right motives. Habitual commitments are to be reinforced that should make spontaneity safe when it occurs. Efforts at one stage sustain the course of experience that culminates in transformation to the next stage.

If moral spontaneity is the goal, must not the naturalness of the sage be somehow reflected in the approach to the goal as well? Mencius explained how. He recognized that there is no way to create create cohumanity in a vacuum, simply by forceful intention. One must rely on the basic goodness within each person. In his classic exposition, Mencius sets forth a good-heartedness intrinsic to human nature: four pure human motives, the heart of compassion, the heart of shame, the heart of courtesy and modesty, the heart of right and wrong.[44] Though immanent within human nature, these four initiatives or sprouts or germs are not at the beck and call of the will. Character may be "cultivated" by facilitating the expression and growth of these initiatives. Mencius called for a mean between extremes and satirized misguided self-effort for personal growth with a story of a farmer who wanted to help rice grow by pulling on the sprouts:

> You must work at [rightness] and never let it out of your mind. At the same time, while you must never let it out of your mind, you must not forcibly help it grow either. You must not be like the man from Sung. There was a man from Sung who pulled at his rice plants because he was worried about their failure to grow. Having done so, he went on his way home, not realizing what he had done. "I am worn out today," said he to his family. "I have been helping the rice plants to grow." His son rushed

out to take a look and there the plants were, all shrivelled up. There are few in the world who can resist the urge to help their rice plants grow. There are some who leave the plants unattended, thinking that nothing they can do will be of any use. They are the people who do not even bother to weed. There are others who help the plants grow. They are the people who pull at them. Not only do they fail to help them but they do the plants positive harm.[45]

Thus Mencius presents proper moral development as a mean between the deficiency of neglect and the extreme of trying to hasten growth.

In the neo-Confucian period, spontaneity was interpreted metaphysically. A note of mysticism is present as Chu Hsi introduces a new symbol to interpret the traditional image of the one thread. In this comment on the one thread of Analects 4.15 (the classic link between golden rule consideration and loyalty) he begins with an unidentified quotation and adds a simile: " 'Empty and tranquil, and without any sign, and yet all things are luxuriantly present.' It is like a tree 100 feet tall. From the root to the branches and leaves, there is one thread running throughout."[46] The Mencian agricultural metaphor of self-cultivation gives way to the simply botanical metaphor of root and branches. In the Analects the one thread was said to run through all the teachings of Confucius. Here it unifies life. In this context, the roots symbolize attunement with the transcendent; the branch is loving service. The metaphor is based on Chu Hsi's metaphysics, giving new meanings to traditional terms. For Chu Hsi, loyalty (chung) is no longer simply a matter of being loyal to one's superiors or true to oneself; now it denotes being rooted or centered in the Supreme Ultimate. Consideration (shu) here denotes overflowing beneficence.[47]

Despite the theory of progressive conscientiousness, golden rule consideration was taken, in several texts, neither as a description of the goal, nor as a way to approach the goal, but precisely as that which lacks the desired quality. Chu Hsi once put it bluntly: "Jen [cohumanity] is spontaneous; altruism (shu) is cultivated."[48] Wang Yang-ming was even more explicit;

What men do to me, that I do not wish, I do not do to them. What I do wish, proceeds from the desire of my heart, naturally and spontaneously, without being forced. Not doing to others is possible after some effort. This indicates the difference between jen . . . and shu.[49]

How, then, is conscientious self-restraint, emphasized by the negative formulation of the rule, compatible with growth in spontaneity?

According to Robert Allinson, restraining inappropriate acts is intended to make room for the original goodness within human nature to manifest spontaneously.[50] Epistemological modesty and humility make one reluctant to claim to know what is good for somebody else; sometimes we can certainly know what not to do without being able to formulate a clear idea of what is to be done. The negative version of the rule is more consonant with these attitudes, while the presumptuous abuse of the positive golden rule has allegedly caused much harm. If we believe in the inherent goodness of human nature, then there is no need for positive moral rules. According to Allinson, "One would need only to ensure that one's nature be given an opportunity to express itself in its original character."[51] The negative rule, on this reading, prevents moral harm and facilitates moral growth. Allinson's reading is sensitive to major themes in Chinese tradition, and he finds in the golden rule a principle whereby the naturalness of the sage is best available to the student.

There must be more to the story, though. If the golden rule required only self-restraint of inappropriate impulses, it would make no sense for the Confucius of the *Analects* both to say that at age seventy he could follow the leadings of his heart (2.4) and also to recommend the golden rule as a rule for the whole of life (15.24). The elderly sage would have no more use for a rule of restraint. The examples used to illustrate the golden rule in *Analects* 6.28 and *The Doctrine of the Mean* make it clear that positive action is required to fulfill the rule. Ch'en Ch'un solves the problem with a harmonizing synthesis.

> When the Grand Master said, "Do not do to others what you do not want them to do to you," he was speaking about one side of the question. Actually one should not only refrain from doing to others what one does not want others to do to him; whatever one wants others to do to him he should do to others.[52]

Ch'en Ch'un goes on to distinguish three levels in the golden rule practice of loyalty and consideration: its approximation in the effort of the student, its heavenly essence and function, and its true practice by the sage:

> Generally, loyalty and consideration are basically matters of the student's effort only. Master Ch'eng (Cheng I) said, " 'The Mandate of Heaven, how beautiful and unceasing.' This is loyalty. 'The Way of (Heaven) is to change and transform so that everything will obtain its correct nature and destiny.' This is [consideration]." . . . In the case of the Sage, it is simply a completely merged great foundation in his mind operating and responding everywhere so that everything will come to rest where it should rest. . . . The [consideration] of the sage is co-humanity, which does not require an extension. . . . Extending oneself means exerting some effort."[53]

The balanced practice of the golden rule, then, evolves from conscientious striving, monitored by self-examination, to a level where the metaphysical-spiritual foundation so infuses the mind as to eclipse distracting selfish and material urges.

CONCLUSION

A few points of difference and similarity between the golden rule in Confucianism and in modern Western thought should be noted. First, the

Chinese sources for the concept of comparing self and other provide a strikingly comprehensive concept of the imaginative role reversal often associated with the practice of the golden rule. Imagining oneself in the other's position can involve an ethically informed intuition of heart and mind, seeing patterns of relationships, using scientific knowledge ("the investigation of things") and creative imagination, extending feelings into the present situation that have been previously realized in a similar relationship, attending to the Way that is immanent to the other person and interior to the agent, and identifying with the other as a member in the universal family. Although mentioning these many antecedents of moral conduct may seem to erect a burdensome ideal, an adequate understanding is often intuitively available to someone who approaches a situation with a loving, action-ready attitude.

Second, the Confucian golden rule could never become a principle abstracted from ideas about character growth, since it was initially set forth as an explication of a cardinal social virtue, consideration.

Third (as with many Western scholars), the rule came to be understood as a principle that would have different meanings at different stages of practice. Initially, it represents the careful comparing of self and other that marks the early stage of conscientious Confucian self-cultivation; ultimately, though, it symbolizes the spontaneous overflow of loving service in the person abiding in harmony with supreme reality.

Fourth, in contrast with Christian thought, it must be noted that at no point in Confucian philosophy did the affirmation arise that Heaven is our father and that all men and women are brothers and sisters—and that this realization is the foundation for the replete practice of the golden rule. The Confucian concept of humankind as one family was derived initially not from faith in a heavenly Parent but from golden rule comparing, extending to others the consideration that the agent had for his or her own family.

In sum, in Confucian philosophy, an ethics of the proper conduct of social relations and a metaphysics of the tranquillity and activity of the Supreme Ultimate have served as approaches to living the golden rule in spiritual beauty.

three

From Greek Reciprocity
to Cosmopolitan Idealism

"Sophistry" is a term of abuse. Used by the greatest thinkers of ancient Greece to characterize their opponents as purveyors of sham wisdom, "sophistry" connotes deceptive reasoning and rhetoric that sacrifices truth on the altar of social power. As characterized by Socrates (ca. 470–399), Plato (ca. 428–348 or 347), and Aristotle (384–322), the Sophists were the ones who entered the field of philosophy armed with talent, skill, and broad information, but refused to submit to the reconstruction of popular opinion required by honest logic and philosophical insight. Sophistic oratory, whether spoken or written—when it was not confrontational and abusive—was marked by *a pleasing and ambiguous mix of social propriety, vague idealism, and partisan self-interest.* Yet it was the Sophist Isocrates (436–335) who, more than anyone else, was responsible for the burst of golden rule thinking that entered fourth-century Greek culture.

Since the golden rule does not specify a particular moral standard, it can consort with social conventions whose mediocrity will be evident only to a later age or another culture. In this instance the popular code of repaying good for good and harm for harm—helping friends and harming enemies—was the convention in question. The drama of the evolution of the Greek golden rule is that, as it emerged, it became mingled with the "repayment ethic" as that code deconstructed itself; in other words, factionalism during the Peloponnesian War between Athens and Sparta (431–401) resulted in social and political disintegration, and the inwardly divided and mutually disunited Greek city-states were conquered by Philip of Macedon in 338.

The golden rule had a difficult birth in the West. It rarely received a general formulation. A general formulation would have tended to bring to light the rule's full human scope, undermining the ethic of factionalism, so that every person, friend or enemy, would be regarded as comparable to oneself. Neither was there a canonical version of the rule in Greek or Roman antiquity, such that those who wrote along its lines regarded themselves as producing variations on a formula that everyone honored and knew by heart. No author used a golden rule maxim as a hub around which to gather great themes. None proposed the rule as the leading principle of morality. Even at the close of this period (prior to the Christian invasion of the Mediterranean world) golden rule thinking functioned primarily through specific maxims, for example, about the treatment of slaves.

The rule developed in Greek literature, then, not by reflective commentaries on a recognized principle, but by the practice of a certain style of thinking. The golden rule thinking coming to birth in various expressions and maxims includes an idea, a recommendation, and a command: *Those affected by your actions are comparable to you. Imagine yourself in the other person's position as an aid to discovering how to apply to yourself the same high moral standard that you apply to others. Do not treat others as you do not want to be treated.*

The rule evolved unconsciously as a by-product of deliberate effort on two issues: How is the maxim of helping friends and harming enemies to be judged? And should we extend beneficence only to those who are dear to us or to all humankind? Once Socrates and Plato achieved a breakthrough on the first question, the implications for the second question would, within a few centuries, become clear to the Stoics.

It is noteworthy, especially in the light of later discussions of the doctrine (associated with "natural law" ethics) that there are cosmic truths that operate in every human mind, that a survey of Greco-Roman moral literature seems to show deliberate variations on a theme that is widely appreciated but usually not articulated in a general way. In the absence of such a canonical formulation of the golden rule, applications are nonetheless discernible as such, and the rule already functions with some degree of effectiveness before it is commonly quoted, agreed upon, and given institutional recognition. So it appears, at least in retrospect.

MORAL CLARITY IN EARLY GOLDEN RULE THINKING

The earliest Greek expression of golden rule thinking is in Homer's *Odyssey* (eighth century B.C.E.). Calypso is the goddess who has kept Odysseus as her love prisoner, and she has just received a message from Zeus that she must release her beloved and speed him homeward on pain of (un)godly retribution. Odysseus, who does not love Calypso, distrusts her offer to let him go. He demands that she promise not to harm him covertly, and Calypso reassures him:

> Now then: I swear by heaven above and by earth beneath and the pouring force of Styx—that is the most awful oath of the blessed gods: I will work no secret mischief against you. No, I mean what I say; I will be as careful for you as I should be for myself in the same need. I know what is fair and right, my heart is not made of iron, and I am really sorry for you.[1]

Calypso does not announce and apply the golden rule as a general formula for right conduct. Nevertheless, one may note behind the words "in the same need" a harbinger of the generalizing tendencies inherent in our intuitions of what is fair. One should be willing to accept the treatment that one gives to another, if the roles should be reversed. Calypso imagines herself in a situation similar to that of her recipient, Odysseus. She associates her promise with her assurance of moral dignity and sincerity. She is acting from a mind (*noos*) of justice and a heart (*thumos*) of compassion, and she showed herself trustworthy in carrying out her pledge.

Thales, according to Diogenes Laertius, is reputed to have said that men might live most virtuously and justly, "if we never do ourselves what we blame in others."[2] Another general formulation occurs in Herodotus (ca. 484–424) where he recounts the story of King Maeandrius of Samos in the days just prior to the Persian invasion of that island. Meandrius made a radical attempt to inaugurate a just political order in place of the former kingship. His proposal, soon to be frustrated by the suspicion and treachery of his associates, begins thus:

> You know, friends, that the sceptre of Polycrates, and all his power, has passed into my hands, and if I choose I may rule over you. But what I condemn in another I will, if I may, avoid myself. I never approved the ambition of Polycrates to lord it over men as good as himself, nor looked with favour on any of those who have done the like. Now therefore, since he has fulfilled his destiny, I lay down my office, and proclaim equal rights.[3]

The criterion in this speech—"what I condemn"—is unambiguously moral, not an appeal to desire—"what I do not want." The generality of this formulation is that it covers all the agent's deeds, not only the immediately present one. The association of the golden rule with equal rights was radical; Maeandrius' gesture of fairness made him vulnerable in an environment where the prevailing ethic was, as we are about to see, very different. The scope of the rule here extended to the entire relevant political unit, to a group he regarded as friends.

THE GOLDEN RULE MINGLED WITH PARTISAN SELF-INTEREST

Ancient Greece was awash with the practice of doing good to one's friends and harm to one's enemies—cardinal virtues of the age. Wars between Greek city-states were frequent, as were clashes between individuals within a given city-state. "A long-standing feud, year after year of provocation and retaliation, is a conspicuous phenomenon of . . . upper-class society. . . . It was not the Athenian custom to disguise hatred."[4] To be sure, returning a favor was often done without self-regarding calculation, and revenge sometimes deliberately sacrificed self-interest. The practice of repaying in kind involved not only mercilessly blind and suicidal feuding but also risk and sacrifice and self-protection in a violent world.

As the golden rule emerged within the tradition of repaying in kind, it was not always differentiated from it. The evolution of the ethic of helping friends and harming enemies is documented in the most massive and focused study of the golden rule, *Die goldene Regel* by Albrecht Dihle. He carried the connection he noticed to the extreme of interpreting every occurrence of golden rule thinking in the ancient cultures of the Mediterranean world as blended with, and dominated by, the popular ethic, which he called "repayment thinking" (*Vergeltungsdenken*).[5] Dihle saw the golden rule as a product of the Sophists, the traveling professional teachers of rhetoric and diverse knowledge of the fifth and fourth centuries B.C.E. Though the Sophists were like Plato in some ways, they denounced his quest for transcendent truth. Their formulations had a generality transcending earlier particular maxims such as "He who kills a person shall be killed." The new formulations cover not only action in response to what others have done, but also action in which the agent takes the initiative and anticipates others' response.[6] Dihle credited the Sophists with developing the capacity for abstraction and rational analysis; and he emphasized that the golden rule bears the mark of what the Sophists wanted to offer: a popular, commonsense technique for social success.[7] In the words of James Robinson, the Sophists transformed "commonsense ethical practice into rational abstract maxims and these maxims into prose gnomic sentences impressive on the memory and aesthetically satisfying in terms of the rhetoric of the day."[8]

On the whole, it is misleading to link the golden rule with repayment thinking. Edward Westermarck's encyclopedic study of planetary evolutionary ideas of morality associates primitive retaliation with nonmoral resentment, personal hatred, and revenge. Moral disapproval, by contrast, is distinguished by three factors: (1) nonselfishness; (2) the supposed independence of one's moral judgment from one's sympathy or hostility toward those whose acts are being judged; and (3) the presumption (false, in fact, for Westermarck) that a moral judgment "must be shared by everybody who possesses both a sufficient knowledge of the case and a 'sufficiently developed' moral consciousness."[9]

The initial plausibility of Dihle's interpretation may be gathered from the following train of thought. Consider that the golden rule may be adopted from desire and fear, as a policy designed to maintain a flow of benefits from allies and to forestall or minimize conflict. It is natural to respond in a friendly way to those who are friendly to us and to respond with antagonism to those antagonistic to us. To the extent that a society holds it as normative to repay persons in kind, it becomes prudent to act in accordance with a maxim of prudence: "Treat others in the light of the expectation that they will repay good for good and evil for evil." From this maxim one could develop a further rule, "Treat others as you want others to treat you," while remaining within the technology of self-interest.

The best illustrations of the blending of the golden rule with the pursuit of personal or factional advantage are found in the writings of the Sophist Isocrates, a vigorous advocate of the ethic of repaying in kind. His most impressive composition, *Panegyricus*, published around 380 B.C.E., appeals to the rule of helping friends and harming enemies in order to persuade the Greek cities to unite against the threat from Macedonia (which would conquer them in 338 B.C.E.). Isocrates had a school in Athens contemporary with and critical of Plato. He was a Sophist in the Platonic sense: brilliant, talented in (literary) oratory, and contemptuous of speculative philosophy. One of Isocrates' letters, composed in 374 B.C.E, during the period when Plato's *Phaedo* was probably written, is sprinkled with such observations.

In Isocrates' maxims (mostly positively formulated) revolving around an emerging golden rule, self and others are portrayed as comparable; and this insight becomes the hub for a variety of psychological observations and bits of moral and political advice.[10] At the close of a speech to the jury that will decide a lawsuit he has brought, Isocrates exhorts the jurors to "give a just verdict, and prove yourselves to be for me such judges as you would want to have for yourselves."[11] He advises, "Conduct yourself toward your parents as you would have your children conduct themselves toward you."[12] But this advice, which apparently expresses a high moral tone, is immediately preceded by the counsel to "do honour to the divine power at all times, but especially on occasions of public worship; for thus you will have the reputation both of sacrificing to the gods and of abiding by the laws." On the basis of the comparability of states, Isocrates does argue for a moderate, reasonable, and fair symmetry in power relations. "Deal with weaker states as you think it appropriate for stronger states to deal with you."[13] This advice, again apparently of high moral tone, is followed in the very next sentence by the following words: "Do not be contentious in all things, but only where it will profit you to have your own way." A similar ambiguity may be observed in a companion essay titled "Nicocles," where Isocrates writes by putting himself in the place of the ruler—it is as though Isocrates is ghostwriting a speech for Nicocles.[14] Here we find a quite general formulation of the emerging rule, but again set in an immediate context of repayment thinking: "Those things which provoke anger when you suffer them from others, do not do to others. Practice nothing in your deeds for which you condemn others in your words. Expect to fare well or ill according as you are disposed well or ill toward me."[15] In other words, the "ruler"-author is counseling his subjects to follow the golden rule in their relations toward the ruler . . . and if they do not, they can expect retaliation.

In order to get clear about the issues surrounding repayment thinking (both in Greek thought and in the New Testament), it is necessary to distinguish several principles that are logically independent, even though they may be combined or confused in a given text.

1. *The Repayment Principle:* We should repay good with good and harm

with harm. This is a formulation of repayment thinking, and it is a maxim about what one *ought* to do.

2. *The Principle of Social or Cosmic Justice:* Acts have consequences: if we do good, we can expect good in return; if we do evil, we can expect to suffer. This is an observation from experience about how reality is often seen to work. Dihle quotes the sophist Antiphon, "Whoever thinks he can do evil to his neighbor and not suffer evil is not wise."[16]

3. *The Principle of Moral Prudence:* We ought to do good rather than evil because it is in our own long-range self-interest to do so. Dihle cites exhortations to give a portion of our treasure to the god, because the god will reward us in turn; and he documents a belief that the high proportion of eunuchs among the Scythians can be explained as a punishment from the gods, since the Scythians had been lax in offering sacrifices to them.[17]

4. *The Golden Rule:* We ought not to do to others what we do not want others to do to us. None of the three previous principles implies an ethic of repaying in kind. Those who accept the principle of cosmic justice have reason to affirm the principle of prudence. But the repayment principle is inconsistent with the principles of cosmic justice and prudence, since doing harm to others provokes a spiral of never-ending vengeance. Golden rule thinking, exemplified by King Maeandrius in Herodotus' narrative, abandons the motive of prudence, stands for what is regarded as intrinsically right, does not presuppose any doctrine of cosmic retaliation, and does not engage in doing evil at all.

PLATO'S LIMITED USE FOR GOLDEN RULE THINKING: THE *CRITO*

Greek philosophy, born in the quest for the source or principles of all things, took a turn with Socrates, who focused on the cognitive foundations of virtuous character. Plato located the key to character growth in a conversion of the mind to inquiry into knowable patterns or structures ("forms"), leading toward insight into their ultimate source, an eternal, perfect, divine, unitary principle, "the good."[18] Socrates and Plato attacked the Sophists; whereas Plato's dialogues are consistent and militant in exposing and criticizing the ethic of helping friends and harming enemies.[19]

In the Crito, Plato portrays Socrates in prison, condemned to death by the Athenian assembly for allegedly teaching impiety and corrupting the youth. His friend Crito offers to bribe the prison guard to let Socrates escape, since Crito does not want to lose his friend, nor does he want his own reputation to suffer among those who might regard him as unwilling to spend the money to save his friend. Crito illustrates a tendency of character that Plato classifies as unduly influenced by social-emotional concern about what others think. In response to Crito, Socrates challenges the hegemony of popular opinion and then wins agreement on a major premise (repudiating the retaliation component of repayment thinking): never do harm, even in return for harm. The agreement on this principle is the philosophic fulcrum of the dialogue. In the subsequent and final section of the dialogue, Socrates begins by asking how that principle may be applied to the present situation. Does breaking jail amount to breaking a just agreement? At this point, Crito has trouble understanding him. Then Socrates replies,

> Look at it in this way. Suppose that while we were preparing to run away from here—or however one should describe it—the laws and constitution of Athens were to come and confront us and ask this question, Now Socrates, what are you proposing to do? Can you deny that by this act which you are contemplating you intend, so far as you have the power, to destroy us, the laws, and the whole city as well?[20]

Using golden rule thinking to clarify reasoning, Socrates imagines himself in the position of the one(s) who may be hurt by his action. He constructs what the laws, personified, might say if they were to catch him escaping from prison; indeed, his project is to gain an impartial perspective on what is just and what is harmful. This point remains true, regardless of the controversy about the degree of irony present here.

PLATO'S ARGUMENT IN THE *PHAEDO* FOR LOYALTY TO ONE'S DIVINE SPIRIT

In the *Phaedo* Plato describes Socrates in prison on the day when he will be put to death by drinking hemlock. The topic of the immortality of soul is the focus of his final conversation with friends. The question arises whether it is permissible to follow Socrates, not by imitating his sustained philosophic inquiry, but by committing suicide. Then, at *Phaedo* 62b–e, there is an argument that we should not commit suicide because we belong in the service of the god, the very best master, with whom a wise man would want to remain as long as possible. Socrates uses an argument that could be derived from the golden rule: Just as we would not want our property to destroy itself without our permission, so we should not frustrate the god by taking our lives prematurely.

Socrates begins by mentioning a questionable source of information: "The allegory which the mystics tell us—that we men are put in a sort of guard post, from which one must not release oneself or run away—seems to me to be a high doctrine with difficult implications."[21] The reference to an allegory of the mystics is a flag for irony, because a goal of Platonic philosophy is to transcend popular religion with its passions and opinions and fears and retaliatory notions of justice. However, Socrates' following sentence exemplifies the philosopher's effort to penetrate religious myth so as to distill its universal meaning: "All the same, Cebes, I believe that this much is true, that the gods are our keepers, and we men are one of their possessions. Don't you think so?" Cebes' simple agreement with Socrates establishes the shared foundation for this part of their dialogue: we belong to the gods.

The golden rule argument in this passage occurs in the next speech by Socrates, which he begins by calling Cebes to think of himself as an illustration: "Then take your own case. If one of your possessions were to destroy itself without intimation from you that you wanted it to die, wouldn't you be angry with it and punish it, if you had any means of doing so?"[22] This use of the imaginative role reversal shows the capacity of golden rule thinking to mingle what Plato regards as inferior psychological and religious notions with moral insight. The passage invokes the motive of retaliation, part of repayment thinking that Plato opposes, associated with an anthropomorphic conception of a vengeful god. Such a concept of God is displaced in the dialogues by the Socratic experience of the personally present divine spirit (daimon) and by a philosophic concept of eternal goodness. In this context the hierarchal relation of superior to subordinate is unquestionably legitimate, and the possibility of our own property being disloyal is fanciful (unless we think of Plato's Euthyphro, in which the fatal beating of a runaway slave led to the occasion for philosophic inquiry). Despite the fact that the reader should discern irony in the passage, the reader should also, I believe, discern a genuine Platonic affirmation here. Socrates' flight of imagination about runaway property is associated with ideas that Plato actually holds: that evil has consequences in human lives; that punishment has a place in a just order; that the harvest of earthly character-sowing cannot be presumed to terminate at death. The morally correct conclusion about suicide becomes clearer as a result of putting oneself in the position of the divine superior.

If we believe that Plato was at least partly serious about an afterlife, new questions arise. Can any moral theory maintain its integrity if it posits a cosmic order of rewards and punishments? Must self-interest invade the motivation of an agent who believes in such a scheme? If one who anticipates life beyond death wants to distinguish morality from self-interest, how can he manage to avoid cultivating virtue primarily as an ornament for his own immortal soul? It is easy to understand the suspicion, but difficult to prove that a given belief must cause the believer's motivation to be impure. Reply could be made with counterquestions: What if virtue really does coincide with our true self-interest in the long run? What if there really is an afterlife? What if our earthly loyalties really do matter to our immortal soul? Should we repress our beliefs about that? Or is our duty rather to put those beliefs in perspective by noting their epistemological limitations and their psychological functions and by emphasizing the realization in this life upon which the purported future of the soul depends? In Socrates we see Plato's exemplar of the proper emphasis of attention: he is not looking over his shoulder at the prospects for heavenly reward and punishment, but living with philosophic responsibility, examining arguments, and promoting virtue for its intrinsic value.

What philosophic possibilities of golden rule thinking might be gleaned from the *Phaedo* passage? There is no parity of interaction between gods and mortals such that we should treat the gods as we want the gods to treat us. When we say, "Do not treat others as you do not want others to treat you," there is the unspoken assumption "in (essentially) the same situation." This assumption can be extended to yield a new application of the golden rule: the agent should treat a superior as the agent would like to be treated by a subordinate. The domain of the golden rule is thus not restricted to interactions among social equals. The golden rule applies to those who are *comparable*. What is surprising is that God is included among the comparables. (Socrates does use the singular, *theos*, at 62b7.) The structure of this particular extension of golden rule thinking is this. We have an asymmetrical relationship to God analogous to asymmetrical relationships in which we are in the superior role. Our experience as recipients of an action (when others are obedient, or not, to our legitimate requirements) enables us to anticipate the attitude of God to the action we are considering. The implicit rule is that we should treat our divine superiors as we want our subordinates to treat us. In this sense, we should treat God as we would be treated. The principle that can be constructed on the basis of the golden rule arguments of the *Crito* and *Phaedo* is "When deliberating about how to treat a divine superior, imagine yourself (as best you can) in the superior perspective, and do not violate what you can thus recognize to be fair."[23] The force of such arguments is to remind us that actions relating to self and human others are also subsumed by our relationship with God.

THE REASONING IN PLATO'S *LAWS* ABOUT RESPECTING OTHERS' PROPERTY

In the *Laws* Plato considers in detail the legislation appropriate to a well-ordered state. Regarding business transactions, the Athenian, using a piece of reasoning clearly akin to the golden rule, proposes a "simple general rule": "I would have no one touch my property, if I can help it, or disturb it in the slightest way without some kind of consent on my part; if I am a man of reason, I must treat the property of others in the same way."[24] The previous adventures in golden rule thinking involved loyalty to superiors; here we have a symmetrical maxim for use between human beings. Again, ambiguity could be alleged. The Athenian's desire that others not touch his property seems extreme. The subsequent lines of his speech explain why business people should be motivated to respect others' property. According to the Athenian, what virtuous restraint costs him financially will be made up by the gain of his soul in goodness, a consideration that may seem "self-interested." There follows a discussion of punishments for thieves. As before, the maxim pertains to property considerations.

Nevertheless, there does seem to be more than reward-and-punishment thinking here. The rewards in question are treasures of the soul, incompatible with greed ("mere self-interest"). The Athenian, a mature citizen, sees that it is virtuous to abstain from taking others' property—not simply that retaliation is possible. The maxim is proposed as a practical guide, *not as a substitute for theoretic insight into reality*. It is not *offered as a free-floating criterion of what is right.*

A PLATONIC TRANSFORMATION OF GOLDEN RULE THINKING

On its face, the rule "Do not do to others what you do not want others to do to you" sets up what the agent *wants* as a criterion of morality. Plato, in sustained opposition to the Sophistic maxim of Protagoras, "Man is the measure," emphasized, above all, the pursuit of intellectual insight into eternal, perfect, unchanging, divine "forms" and their relations with the things we sense around us.[25] If Plato had ever explicitly discussed a generally formulated golden rule, his basic objection would have been expressed in a remark Socrates makes in the *Republic*: "Nothing imperfect is the measure of anything."[26] Unregulated wants are no measure at all. It is striking, however, that all occurrences of golden rule thinking in Plato's dialogues incorporate conditions that block this objection.[27] The person using golden rule thinking, Socrates or the Athenian, is virtuous, loyal to the highest conceivable standard of goodness. The conditions that block the objection are, first, that no free-floating golden rule is presented as a sufficient moral measure; and, second, that the wants of Socrates and the Athenian are hardly unregulated—they both strive for the divine measure. Such idealism would facilitate the insight necessary to apply the golden rule appropriately. Ennobled wants do not exceed what is fair.

In the interest of a more completely developed theory, one might ask what concepts of idealism, divine measure, and perfection are required for a non-Sophistic golden rule. The answer need not be spelled out in detail here. Any intuitively repulsive counterexample to the rule would suffice to indicate, by contrast, the requisite idealism. Any idealism worthy of the name will have the resources to condemn abuses that satisfy the letter but not the spirit of the golden rule—manipulative shows of benevolence, vengeful excesses, imperialistic impositions of one's own standards on another, including the caricatured adulterer or sadomasochist who goes forth to treat others, and so on. The bulwark against abuse of the rule and the key to its higher interpretation is its link to ideals of character.

AN ARISTOTELIAN NORM AMONG FRIENDS

Aristotle saw the golden rule operating legitimately among friends. According to Diogenes Laertius, when asked how to behave toward friends, Aristotle replied, "As we should wish our friends to behave to us."[28] We have concentric circles of friends. At the center is self-love, friendship with oneself. In persons of high character this is not a materialistic and antisocial trait, but the self-love possible in one who is not torn by inner conflict, has no anxiety about being alone with himself, is content with his life in retrospect, and choses, above all, noble deeds for himself. Such a person enjoys a truly happy life—full of excellent activities in which human capacities find satisfying exercise under the leadership of reason. Though Aristotle writes glowingly of philosophic contemplation of God, he does not regard the supreme experience of theoretical reason as particularly beneficial for ethics. Instead, he emphasizes cultivating virtuous habits through emotional discipline and careful deliberation based on a balanced understanding of the situation.

Then comes one's closest circle of friends and family. Though one might dream of being divinely self-sufficient (tasting contemplatively the self-reflective thinking that is God), having friends is one of the necessary goods in life. Companion friends like the same activities and share political convictions.[29] What goods shall one then wish for one's friend? The same goods that one wishes for oneself. "The decent person . . . is related to his friend as he is to himself, since the friend is another himself [allos autos]."[30] (Aristotle is not merely noting that each of them is a self; the implication rather is, for example, that you, my friend, are to me another Jeff.) The same idea applies within the family: "A parent loves his children as [he loves] himself."[31] Friendship includes goodwill—wishing goods for the other, for the other's sake; and a friend is also motivated to act to do good to his or her friend.[32]

The next circle of friends comprises one's fellow citizens. These, too, are people that one cares about, and a virtuous person is prepared to die for his or her city.[33] Though Aristotle's concept of justice differs from repayment thinking, in the Nicomachean Ethics he speaks tolerantly of this popular custom.[34] Though Plato evaluated reciprocity on the basis of its manipulative forms, Aristotle evaluates it more as a reasonable practice of social balance. Discussing justice, Aristotle does not advocate returning evil or harming the wrongdoer; rather he focuses on restoring proper proportion, for example, where property has been wrongly taken or a distribution improperly carried out. Moreover, punishment is not directed to "enemies" but to those who have violated due proportion by a particular action.

Life in the city is an affair of transactions; without exchange, there would be no relationships. Aristotle's overarching concern is to preserve proportion in interactions. Equality is the ideal, though it does not require exchanging the same kind of good in the same quantity. Friends make an appropriate return, reciprocating the spirit of the gift received.[35] In the case of benefactor and beneficiary, however, there may be an inequality. "Doing good is proper to the superior person, and receiving it to the inferior."[36] Where one cannot return a comparable good to a benefactor, the way to compensate is to accord the greater honor to the benefactor.

Aristotle finds what might be called a golden rule reasonableness in normal social life. This evident in a friendship among those whose goodwill springs from certain similarities.

> People are also friends if the same things are good and bad for them, or if they are friends to the same people and enemies to the same people. Necessarily these people wish the same things, and so, since one wishes the same things for the other as one wishes for oneself, one appears to be a friend to him.[37]

A golden rule consistency between feelings and actions becomes explicit in a passage concerning popular ways of thinking. "For what a man does himself, he is said not to resent when his neighbors do it, so that what he does not do, it follows that he resents."[38] The inference, though fallacious, is interesting. If I interpret it properly, the first part amounts to a social-psychological generalization that people usually accept it when others engage in the same kinds of behavior that they engage in themselves. The second part says that people generally do not do what they resent when others do it. An example of this kind of consistency is found in Aristotle's discussion of humor. There are certain jokes that are so abusive that a decent person would not tell them; neither does he welcome others' telling jokes of that sort.[39] In other words, Aristotle finds a general consistency between people's feelings about what others do and their own actions. Most people are not hypocrites. Thus far, they satisfy a golden rule that Aristotle never quite formulates as a norm; but his ethics is not in the business of giving rules for conduct. Normative description, with prescriptions latent, is his method.

The outermost circle of friendship includes every human being. Toward humanity one can be expected to acknowledge the capacity for community, to relax decently any legalistic insistence on having the exact measure that is due to one, and to have an attitude of goodwill. There is a basis for limited friendship with slaves *qua* human beings, since "every human being seems to have some relations of justice with everyone who is capable of community in law and agreement."[40] Moreover, Aristotle observes the wide range of affection that includes animal bonding and the validation of common humanity across cultural barriers.

> A parent would seem to have a natural friendship for a child, and a child for a parent, not only among human beings but also among birds and most kinds of animals. Members of the same race, and human beings most of all, have a natural friendship for each other; that is why we praise

friends of humanity. And in our travels we can see how every human being is akin and beloved to a human being.[41]

Aristotle hardly emphasizes being a philanthropist, a friend of humanity, though the generalities he proposed in his *Ethics* were not intended to be only locally helpful. They represent a normative distillation of observations and reflections based on his wide travels, study, and discussion. Indeed, the very enterprise of classical philosophy carried an implicit nisus toward a humanitarianism that would come to center stage in the Stoics.

THE COSMOPOLITAN GOLDEN RULE OF STOICISM

The universal scope of the golden rule in Stoicism was based on the affirmation that human beings are the offspring of God (Zeus), the universal *logos* (principle, reason) governing the entire cosmos. Within each person is a spark of divinity making it possible to realize cosmic truth; and the Stoics equated the divine spark with reason, an equation that has been the hallmark of philosophic rationalism.[42] To do the will of God, therefore, is to be true to one's nature and to act in accord with right reason.[43]

Golden rule thinking appears a few times in the writings of Seneca (4 B.C.E.–65 C.E.), the Stoic philosopher and assistant to the emperor Nero. Seneca's *On Anger* rehearses at length the cruelties and follies of anger, its deceptive rationalizations, its causes, and strategies for its cure. One's tranquillity of soul is too valuable to be squandered in anger. The text is full of the wisdom of psychological and social and historic experience. It is in the context of this perspective of seasoned reason that Seneca advocates imaginative perspective taking:

> Let us put ourselves in the place of the man with whom we are angry; as it is, an unwarranted opinion of self makes us prone to anger, and we are unwilling to bear what we ourselves would have been willing to inflict.[44]

In another text, Seneca brings the golden rule into tacit paradox in discussing how to do good to others. The rationality implicit in moral practice should not hinder spontaneity:

> Let us consider, most excellent Liberalis, what still remains of the earlier part of the subject; in what way a benefit should be bestowed. I think that I can point out the shortest way to this; let us give in the way in which we ourselves should like to receive. Above all, we should give willingly, quickly, and without any hesitation.[45]

The paradox of the golden rule is that many situations leave nary a moment for rational reflection, so the rule cannot succeed as a compulsive mental exercise; it must be forgotten to be fulfilled.

Seneca applies interpersonal moral comparison to the question of the treatment of slaves:

> I do not wish to involve myself in too large a question, and to discuss
> the treatment of slaves, towards whom we Romans are excessively
> haughty, cruel and insulting. But this is the kernel of my advice: Treat
> your inferiors as you would be treated by your betters.[46]

Questions about Seneca's character have raised doubts about the genuine-
ness of his extension of the golden rule to the question of the treatment
of slaves. It has been argued that Seneca's stand on slavery was not very
advanced for his time but was merely a collection of platitudes and cli-
chés.[47] While Seneca did promote the cause of humane treatment of
slaves, his stand was based an ambiguous combination of appeal to principle and warning about the dangers of slave revolt. He advocated neither
the abolition of slavery nor the large-scale freeing of slaves, though his will
provided for the manumission of his own slaves, and he was never accused of treating his slaves abusively. Although, as the teacher and friend
of the emperor, he is credited with influence on the early and worthy
phase of Nero's reign, Seneca's hypocrisies, obvious and alleged, occupy
his historians.[48] Proclaiming the virtues of poverty or moderation in material goods, he amassed luxurious wealth. Apart from the question of Seneca's sincerity, it is noteworthy that golden rule appeals had become platitudes. Whether or not people adhered to the rule or realized its
implications, people had come to recognize it as a worthy standard. And
those who cared about their reputation (or who, like Seneca, were in
charge of creating a good reputation for their employers) could press the
golden rule into service.

   If Seneca's golden rule pronouncement on slavery lacked credibility,
that of Epictetus, the freed Roman slave, did not: "What you avoid suffering, do not attempt to make others suffer. You avoid slavery: take care
that others are not your slaves."[49] Free of anger, Epictetus administers a
personal moral teaching with elemental moral logic. That logic is not only
a formal affair of deducing a specific application from a general law. The
moral logic of this golden rule teaching (and the negative formulation is
proper here) is precisely what is implied in the experience of suffering
under oppression. The Greeks had long held that wisdom comes from
suffering, and here we find a morally powerful pronouncement of the
golden rule from someone who has experienced the harm in question.

CONCLUSION

Is the golden rule, then, sophistic? Yes, if it is asserted in opposition to
philosophy. Yes, if it consorts with a partisan spirit. The rule is undoubtedly heard on the lips of modern-day sophists; but such a condition
hardly suggests the rule's higher potentials.
   Plato finds golden rule thinking occasionally useful for engaging the
mind in the first steps toward philosophic insight. If Socrates and Plato

rouse us from a complacent mediocrity, Aristotle protects us from extreme idealism. It is far easier with Aristotle to imagine a normal, social practice of the golden rule. If Aristotle had ever confronted a generally formulated golden rule proposed as a universal rule, he would have pointed out that the golden rule needs a way of articulating human similarities such that direct application of the rule would be justified (e.g., giving food to a starving person). Moreover, in order to work with the rule one needs a way of adjusting to situations in which one faces someone whose desires are unknown or different from one's own. Aristotle had just the flexibility needed to apply the rule. He understood that his principles would not have the character of mathematical principles—true for every conceivable application.[50]

The Stoics began to affirm the golden rule as a universal moral law, but their overemphasis on character achievement—ordering the self in harmony with reason—affected the outworking of their humanitarian insight. Excessive focus on the inner citadel of the soul tended to dissolve any profound sense of relationship and to distract the impulse to social service.[51] Their cosmopolitan concept of humanity expressed itself, rather, in philosophy of mind and philosophy of law, giving rise to the notion of human rights. Stoicism remained a philosophy, not a religion. Its recognition of human kinship was a fire waiting to be lit.

four

A Jewish Rule of Wisdom

In the Jewish literature of the Second Temple period, the golden rule arose during the second century B.C.E., and it quickly advanced from a marginal position to one among the central religious teachings. Indeed, its rise provides a case study showing the very sense of what a moral principle is traditionally understood to be. This chapter explores a segment of the history of Jewish ethics culminating with Rabbi Hillel, who flourished between 30 B.C.E. and 10 C.E. Upon being asked for a summary of the Torah, he replied, "What is hateful to you, do not do to your neighbor; that is the whole Torah, while the rest is commentary thereon; go and learn it."[1]

GOLDEN RULE THINKING IN THE HEBREW SCRIPTURES

To seek the origins of the golden rule in Judaism leads to the root of Judaism itself, the affirmation of God as the Creator of the heavens and the earth, who proposed, "Let us make man in our image,"[2] the God who made a covenant with Abraham, and who, through the leadership of Moses, brought the Hebrews out of bondage and gave them the Torah, including the Ten Commandments, for the guidance of his people.[3] The golden rule will emerge as a summary of the Torah only after centuries during which isolated examples of golden rule thinking would arise, momentarily and unsystematically. In the simplest sense, golden rule thinking may here be characterized as recognizing moral implications in the fact that others are like oneself.

In the earliest Hebrew example, we see how golden rule thinking, in the hands of a clever prophet, can successfully challenge a king on a most sensitive moral issue. After the Hebrews had settled in Palestine, their united kingdom flourished briefly, and a story from this period relates an encounter between the prophet Nathan and King David (tenth century). David, desiring the beautiful Bathsheba for himself, had sent her husband to fight in the front lines; after the husband was killed, David brought her to his house. Nathan then went to David and told him a story to get him to imagine a situation similar to his own, in which analogous wrongdoing would elicit the king's righteous indignation.

> "There were two men in a certain city, the one rich and the other poor. The rich man had very many flocks and herds; but the poor man had nothing but one little ewe lamb, which he had bought. He brought it up, and it grew up with him and with his children; it used to eat of his meagre fare, and drink from his cup, and lie in his bosom, and it was like a daughter to him. Now there came a traveler to the rich man, and he was loath to take one of his own flock or herd to prepare for the wayfarer who had come to him, but he took the poor man's lamb, and prepared it for the guest who had come to him." Then David's anger was greatly kindled against the man; and he said to Nathan, "As the Lord lives, the man who has done this deserves to die; he shall restore the lamb fourfold, because he did this thing, and because he had no pity."
> Nathan said to David, "You are the man!"[4]

After Nathan pronounced the retributive judgment of God on David, we read, "David said to Nathan, 'I have sinned against the Lord.' " David thus acknowledged that the judgment he had made on the rich man applied by implication to his own, similar case as well.

It is possible that the golden rule in its first clear, general formulation entered Palestine from Mesopotamia.[5] The Babylonian legend of Ahikar is at least as old as the fifth century B.C.E., though the Armenian translation containing the golden rule is from 450 C.E.; thus the golden rule may be a late interpolation in this text. The legend conjoins familiar motifs of advice to a son and advice to a king. "Son, that which seems evil unto thee do not to thy companion."[6] The irony is that the king's minister—who gives this counsel to his nephew (adopted for lack of an heir), on the expectation that the nephew will succeed him and become king—finds himself terribly mistreated by that nephew when the roles are reversed and the nephew does come to power. In the end, however, justice is done. There is a generality in this formulation of the rule in that it covers all conduct toward someone, not just a particular act. The scope of the application of the rule, however, remains restricted. Only conduct to one's companion is mentioned here.

WISDOM AND LAW

What sort of "rule" is the golden rule? Is it a piece of worldly wisdom or a command from a sovereign and mysterious God or what? The early contexts of the rule give a clue to how it was perceived. The early literary home of the golden rule in Palestine was Jewish wisdom literature, which shared perspectives with other traditions in the Near Eastern and Mediterranean world.

Wisdom had long been a highly cherished virtue, closely associated with righteousness. Proverbs 8:22–31 celebrates Woman Wisdom as the first creation of God and the partner in subsequent creation. A common pose assumed in wisdom literature that of a wise man advising a king. Though wisdom is to be prized by all, it is especially important that the king be wise to interpret the law domestically and to conduct international relations; King Solomon was esteemed as the paradigmatic wise man. Common in wisdom literature was the literary form of the proverb, a brief, pithy saying useful for human living; a proverb (mashal) is "a word-group connoting 'rule' or 'power.' "[7] Proverbs harvest from human experience lessons for living prudently and "walking in the way of the Lord."[8] They are lessons that generalize about nature and human conduct and exhort one to righteousness, for example, "Pride goes before destruction, and a haughty spirit before a fall";[9] "Better is a dinner of vegetables where love is than a fatted ox and hatred with it."[10] Righteousness is not mere conformity to an external demand; it is the way of life that proves itself in human experience. Promises of rewards and punishments convey the message that there is identity between the long-term best interest of the individual and the command of God. Those whose "delight is in the law of the Lord" are "like trees planted by streams of water which yield their fruit in its season"; whereas "the way of the wicked will perish."[11]

Since wisdom and law are related, the question arises whether the golden rule could ever be regarded as having a place within Jewish law. Its generality, like that of the "law of love," is exceptional for a Jewish legal text. Joseph Blenkinsopp writes of the blending of the legal and wisdom ("sapiential") traditions in Israel, with the result that

> the law can no longer be considered as a purely objective and extrinsic reality. . . . On the contrary, the "sapientializing" of the law implies that it is to be internalized by an activity which unites learning and piety in the pursuit of a common purpose: "You will seek Yahweh your God, and you will find him if you search after him with all your heart and with all your soul."[12]

Given this background, we are prepared to assemble the blocks of literary history that lead directly to Hillel's use of the rule.

THE RULE IN SECOND-CENTURY TEXTS

Each of the texts that express golden rule thinking adds a specific, new point. The first theme, expressed in the Ben Sira text (190–175 B.C.E.), is that golden rule thinking in Judaism expresses a logic of fairness and consideration, predicated on the recognition that others are like oneself.[13] This book, a discourse of forty-two chapters on wisdom, rises to a celebration of the works of God in nature and in history. It culminates with a hymn of thanksgiving and a poem narrating the author's persistent pursuit of wisdom and his habits of wise conduct; finally it exhorts the reader to follow in the same way. Ben Sira commends many virtues and specifies exemplary conduct for a variety of life situations. One golden rule passage begins with a teaching about the divine reward for human forgiveness:

> Forgive your neighbor the wrong he has done, and then your sins will be pardoned when you pray. Does anyone harbor anger against another, and expect healing from the Lord? If one has no mercy toward another like himself, can he then seek pardon for his own sins?[14]

According to golden rule logic, it is inconsistent to engage in selfish praying.[15] Ben Sira also uses golden rule thinking as the key to being considerate. Realizing that others' needs are like one's own has implications for table manners:

> Are you seated at the table of the great? Do not be greedy at it, and do not say, "How much food there is here!" Remember that a greedy eye is a bad thing. What has been created more greedy than the eye? That is why it sheds tears for any reason. Do not reach out your hand for everything you see, and do not crowd your neighbor at the dish. Judge your neighbor's feelings by your own, and in every matter be thoughtful.[16]

The specifically religious sense of the golden rule is evident in the Letter of Aristeas (127–118 B.C.E.), which recommends a golden rule of consideration on account of the model of God's way with humankind. The rule arises without fanfare in a context that portrays a king asking weighty questions of philosophers. The king has just appreciatively received brief and conventional answers from two philosophers, who are his guests at a banquet:

> He cordially approved this answer and looking upon another said, "What is the teaching of wisdom?" And the other replied, "As you wish that evils should not befall you, but wish to partake of all that is good, you should act in this spirit to your subjects and to offenders. For God, too, leads all men by gentleness.[17]

That the The Letter of Aristeas puts the golden rule in the mouth of philosophers strengthens the hypothesis that the rule entered Jewish culture from Greece. Note also that this text combines both negative and positive aspects of golden rule thinking.

The book of Tobit (compiled near the end of the second century B.C.E.) contains the golden rule in a clear, general formulation, in a context of worldly wisdom and divine reward for serving God.[18] The book tells the story of Tobit, a blind man whose life stretches over much of Israelite history from before the division of the kingdom (931 B.C.E.) until more than two centuries later. This man of exemplary righteousness and his daughter (who had had seven bridegrooms killed) long for death, but God brings solutions to their problems. Tobit mentions the rule as advice to his son alongside more or less specific maxims regarding family life, faithfulness to God, the rewards for righteous living, almsgiving, being a good employer, and the quest for wisdom. Here is the rule in its immediate context.

> Do not keep over until next day the wages of those who work for you, but pay them at once. If you serve God you will receive payment. Watch yourself, my son, in everything you do, and discipline yourself in all your conduct. And what you hate, do not do to anyone. Do not drink wine to excess or let drunkenness go with you on your way.[19]

Various considerations mingle here: rigorous fairness, personal interest in divine reward, a prudent sense of proportion. One may observe the moral ambiguity of this passage without suggesting any betrayal of moral integrity, any criticism of its particular moral rules, or a denial of the promised divine reward. Nevertheless, such a variety of commingling considerations raises a question whenever we observe it: What is the center of gravity of the golden rule in a given context? Is it self-interest, or conformity to the demands of divine righteousness, or some other possible center of gravity? The author of the text celebrates Tobit as a man of unquestioned righteousness, so it is all the more understandable that no need is felt for an explicit discourse to prioritize these considerations.

THE RULE AS A SUMMARY PRINCIPLE

Once the golden rule had entered Jewish literature, it became associated with the promulgation of the two great rules commanding the love of God and neighbor. The first half of the Ten Commandments, concerned primarily with the worship of God, was sometimes regarded (at least by the second century B.C.E.) as being summarized in the command "Hear, O Israel, the Lord is our God, the Lord alone. You shall love the Lord your God with all your heart, and with all your soul, and with all your might."[20] The second half of the Ten Commandments, concerned with moral prohibitions, was sometimes regarded as summarized in a teaching, from the "Holiness Code" of Leviticus 17–26 (named for its exhortation, "You shall be holy, for I the LORD your God am holy"[21]): "You shall love your neighbor as yourself."[22] Although the context in Leviticus envisions primarily obligations to fellow Israelites, every human being—including in particular the poor, the widow, and the stranger—is a potential beneficiary. What reason is given for extending generosity in this way? The people's memory of their suffering. "The alien who resides with you shall be to you as the citizen among you; you shall love the alien as yourself, for you were aliens in the land of Egypt; I am the Lord your God."[23]

To love God meant keeping the commandments.[24] These two great commandments were regarded as the sum of the law, and both were expressed as virtues: piety (*eusebeia*) and righteousness (*dikaiosune*), with the commandment to love God taking precedence over the commandment to love the neighbor. This priority differs from that (e.g., in Plato's *Euthyphro*) where piety is a specific type of justice. To subordinate piety to justice (where justice is made the subject of a "purely rational" discourse) tends to make religion irrelevant to philosophical ethics. To subordinate justice to piety makes justice a religious trait.

The twofold summary of the Ten Commandments—as the love of God and the love of neighbor—occurred first in the Book of Jubilees (150 B.C.E.).[25] At other times the summary was even more compressed: the law of love for one's neighbor stood on its own as a summary of all the Ten Commandments. How could this be? For the pious Jew, to be engaged in loving the neighbor is simultaneously to be engaged in loving obedience to God. Loving the neighbor is evidence of sincerity in loving God, so love of the neighbor serves as a test of one's love for God. Therefore, both intentions of love could blend, and both commandments could be summarized in terms of love for the neighbor.

The golden rule functioned as a partial summary of the decalogue in a manuscript found among the Dead Sea Scrolls, "The Two Ways," which contrasted the way of light and life with the way of darkness and death. After quoting the two Great Rules, the text juxtaposes the golden rule with the commandments to love and then uses the latter portion of the Decalogue to explicate the golden rule.

> The way of life is this: First, you shall love the Lord your maker, and secondly, your neighbor as yourself. And whatever you do not want to be done to you, you shall not do to anyone else. And the interpretation of these words is: Do not kill, do not commit adultery, do not bear false witness, do not fornicate, do not steal, do not covet what belongs to your neighbor.[26]

There are differences between the golden rule and the law of love; the second is not an imperative in Hebrew;[27] it tells how things *shall* be (in the future that God is establishing). In addition, the golden rule does not mention love.[28] These differences, however, did not prevent the golden rule from being used to explain the law of love for one's neighbor. In a first-century B.C.E. commentary, the golden rule is evoked to explain Leviticus 19:18: "Be not revengeful, nor cherish hatred to the sons of your people; but you shall love your neighbor; what is hateful to yourself you shall not to do him; I am the Lord."[29] In another text, the golden rule is substituted for Leviticus 19:18: "I command you to fear only the Lord, to worship him and to cleave to him . . . and that no one shall do to his fellowman what he does not want done to himself."[30]

The golden rule thus became part of a venerable tradition of expressing the law in summary form. One account of this tradition was given by Rabbi Simmlai (third century C.E.):

> Six hundred and thirteen precepts were imparted to Moses, three hundred and sixty-five negative . . . and two hundred and forty-eight posi-

tive. . . .[31] David came and established them as eleven, as it is written (Ps. xv): Lord, who shall sojourn in thy tent, who shall dwell in thy holy mountain? (i) He that walketh uprightly and (ii) worketh righteousness and (iii) speaketh the truth in his heart. (iv) He that backbiteth not with his tongue, (v) nor does evil to his neighbour, (vi) nor taketh up a reproach against another; (vii) in whose eyes a reprobate is despised, (viii) but who honoureth them that fear the Lord. (ix) He that sweareth to his own hurt, and changeth not; (x) he that putteth not out his money to usury, (xi) nor taketh a bribe against the innocent. . . . Then Isaiah came and established them as six (xxxiii.15): (i) He that walketh in righteousness and (ii) speaketh uprightly; (iii) he that despiseth the gain of deceits, (iv) that shaketh his hands from holding of bribes, (v) that stoppeth his ears from hearing of blood, and (vi) shutteth his eyes from looking upon evil. Then came Micah and established them as three (Micah vi.8): What doth the Lord require of thee but (i) to do justice, (ii) to love mercy, and (iii) to walk humbly with thy God? Once more Isaiah established them as two (Is. lvi.1) (i) Keep ye judgment, and (ii) do righteousness. Then came Amos and established them as one (Amos v.4): Thus saith the Lord, Seek ye me and ye shall live, or (as R. Nahman b. Isaac preferred): Habakkuk came and made the whole Law stand on one fundamental idea (Habakkuk ii.4): The righteous man liveth by his faith.[32]

Such principles, statements of the law, simplify tradition, giving the mind a more unified, manageable focus. A summary rule is a kelal in Hebrew, a rule or principle.[33] A principle, whose sage brevity goes to the heart of the matter, gives generality, and also emphasizes spiritual teachings over ritual requirements.

HILLEL'S INNOVATION

Having noted the experiential quality of the golden rule as articulated in Jewish tradition thus far, its simplicity, summarizing function, generality, and spiritual tendency, we are in a position to appreciate Hillel's use of the rule. This conservative rabbi, renowned for his patience, was once approached by an importunate prospective convert to Judaism who had been turned away by Shammai, the leader of the school competing with that of Hillel.

> On another occasion it happened that a certain heathen came before Shammai and said to him, "Make me a proselyte, on condition that you teach me the whole Torah while I stand on one foot." Thereupon he [Shammai] repulsed him with the builder's square which was in his hand. When he went before Hillel, he [Hillel] said to him, "What is hateful to you, do not do to your neighbor: that is the whole Torah, while the rest is commentary thereon; go and learn it."[34]

Here the golden rule summarizes not only the Ten Commandments but the whole Torah. Hillel might have cited the love of God and neighbor, but he neither quotes from the Torah nor mentions God; in these two ways, he presents a nontheologic philosophy of living to the proselyte. Renouncing the authority of scripture, Hillel responded to this questioner free of sanctimonious piety, legalistic defensiveness, and commentarial intricacies. This particular liberty in the use of the golden rule was less available once the rule had become canonical.

In his reply to the request for a summary, Hillel furthermore presents the golden rule as a principle standing on its own. The Torah is proposed, at the end of the reply, as commentary, not source. The word which is translated commentary is perusha, which also means specification; and if we emphasize the latter sense, the golden rule seems nearly ready to function as the leading axiom in a system of ethics. Hillel suggests that the rest of the Torah involves specifying or working out the particulars of the golden rule. Similarly, when Matthew says that the rest of the law and the prophets depend on the golden rule, the language suggests the metaphor of parental relationship; the other moral rules of the Torah are regarded as descendants of the simplifying golden rule.[35] One Ebionite Jewish-Christian text began to work out the derivation of the second half of the Ten Commandments from "one unique saying as transmitted to the God-fearing Jews":

> What we do not want done to us, we will not cause to be done to others; if you do not want to be killed, do not kill anybody; if you do not want anybody to commit adultery with your wife, do not commit adultery with anyone else's wife; if you don't want anything of yours stolen, do not steal anything that belongs to someone else.[36]

The specific commandments are carefully expressed here in hypothetical form, though there is a clear assumption that "you" do not want to be killed or have your spouse taken or your property stolen.

Rabbinic tradition would follow the precedent of Hillel's summary of the Torah in one principle.[37] In the following story Rabbi Akiba responds as Hillel did:

> It happened that one came to R. Akiba and said to him, "Rabbi, teach me the whole Law all at once." He answered, "My son, Moses, our teacher, tarried on the mountain forty days and forty nights before he learned it, and you say, Teach me the whole Law all at once! Nevertheless, my son, this is the fundamental principle of the Law: That which you hate respecting yourself, do not to your neighbor. If you desire that no one injure you in respect to what is yours, then do not injure him. If you desire that no one should carry off what is yours, then do not carry off what is your neighbor's."[38]

HUMANITARIAN IMPLICATIONS

The term "neighbor," used by Hillel in stating the golden rule, had evolved to include every human being. According to Edward Schillebeeckx,

"The neighbour" in the Old Testament underwent all sorts of changes of meaning. In the earliest texts it is the compatriot or social peer; later on, the poor or the lowly, less important and socially inferior fellow-countryman, needing protection; finally, all members of the nation are for every Israelite like the "weak man," entitled to help: all are brothers. According to the final redaction of Deuteronomy, the way one should behave in practice towards the poor is to be extended to all one's fellows within the nation; that is to say, above and beyond all law and justice, love of one's neighbour is a brotherly, protective, loving attitude towards each member of God's people. Then at last what is called for is an inward disposition of love and kindness. . . . In secular Greek ["neighbour"] means the "person next door," the nearest people around, ultimately the other person you happen to meet. Thus neighbourly love was extended by the Jews of the Diaspora to become universal: it included everybody. "My neighbour" is each and every person I meet (a consequence of the Diaspora Jews becoming adapted to their Gentile surroundings, and partly of an intensified faith in the God who creates everything and everybody).[39]

CONCLUSION

The golden rule, aligning with Jewish philanthropy, manifests the simplicity, generality, and spiritual tendency of the principles developing in first-century Judaism. By the time of Hillel, the rule is God's teaching, the Torah, wisely summarized; indeed, it is even taken as the quintessence of the Torah, and it is beginning to functioning as an axiom in the derivation of specific rules. However, even though the golden rule has a self-evident appeal of its own, its heritage as a summary principle conserves the moral and religious formation presupposed in its promulgation.

The point of calling the golden rule a principle is not to claim that it is the only satisfactory formulation of personal morality (replacing others, e.g., "You shall love your neighbor as yourself"). Rather, the implication is, I believe, that there is a unity to the moral life, and that the golden rule is one way of stating that unity.

Wisdom and righteousness, piety and justice, are the virtues most prominently associated with the classical Jewish golden rule. There is no confusion with principles of reciprocity or retaliation, no worry about extreme, perfectionist standards; even when God is proposed as the paradigm of golden rule conduct, the rule does not become a heavy burden. It has a close bond with the comparable maxim "Love your neighbor as yourself," and it governs the way the righteous individual treats each and every other person.

Theologically speaking, the emphasis on God as *Creator* has especially favored the theme of universal humanity. Moral rules are taken as commands proceeding from the Creator's love for all men and women as his creatures; God wants all to live, and he has shown us the way. From this perspective, the division of humanity into two classes—the wise, who pursue goodness and walk in the way of life, and the foolish, who pursue evil, sin, and iniquity, the way of death—has a logically secondary, derivative status, contingent on human decision. In first-century Jewish thought, there were two ways of prioritizing to revolve the apparent tension between "philanthropy"—imitation of God's love for all human beings—and critique based on the separation between the two ways.[40] The alternative to philanthropy assigns primary emphasis to difference—the difference between the wise and the foolish. This emphasis prevails in apocalyptic discourse, where themes of punishment and reward dominate the religious consciousness, reinforcing self-interested and exclusivist attitudes. Where difference is understood as subordinate to love of humankind, warnings occur in a context of encouragement. The choice that the individual faces at the parting of the ways is a choice illumined by invitation, patience, just chastisement, mercy, and welcome.

five

A New Testament Rule of Divine Love

Jesus is a controversial figure partly because the records of his teachings juxtapose intuitively appealing statements with controversial ones. The golden rule, for example, is associated with more problematic teachings. Therefore, whoever would take the initial, obvious sense of Jesus' golden rule as its final sense faces a challenge when interpreting the rule in context. Matthew's Sermon on the Mount (chaps. 5–7) and Luke's comparable Sermon on the Plain (6.20–49) may appear to associate the rule with inferior standards: Give to others, or face the punishment of God (Matthew), and Give generously in order that you may receive abundantly (Luke). But these contexts also associate the rule with a high standard, including the command to be perfect and to love your enemies. Thus, two main questions arise about the New Testament golden rule: How does the rule relate to notions of reciprocity? And how does the rule relate to the high standard of the Sermon on the Mount and the Sermon on the Plain, a standard some have called unreasonably high? It is necessary to sort things out in some detail to show that a progressive, reasonable, and high standard emerges from the rule in Matthew and Luke.

First, a word about reciprocity. The term is often used imprecisely to express the gist of the golden rule, and different ideas associated in the first century C.E. with reciprocity make it necessary to distinguish the rule from four other ideas with which it is sometimes confused:

1. The rule of reciprocity in a restricted sense: repay favors done to you; be friendly to those who are friendly to you.
2. The rule of retaliation: repay harm with harm; "an eye for an eye."
3. Repayment ethics: a combination of reciprocity and retaliation, such that justice means doing good to friends and harm to enemies.
4. A principle of social and cosmic realism: acts have consequences in normal social interaction, in the course of nature, and in the life to come. If we do good, we can, on the whole, expect good in return; if we do evil, we can expect to suffer ("As you sow, so shall you reap").

INTERPRETATION AND THE NEW TESTAMENT

The New Testament Gospels present memories and traditions, written and oral, fashioned in order to tell stories that the authors and redactors (editors) regarded as supremely important. Many scholars today emphasize the differing theological agendas of the various evangelists and so suspend judgment on the veracity of their narratives. Some scholars hesitate to ascribe the golden rule to Jesus, since the rule was already part of popular Jewish and Hellenistic culture and could have been inserted into the texts from sources other than the teachings of Jesus. There is a certain boldness in speaking about Jesus, instead of, say, Matthew's Jesus or simply Matthew, since we seem to have only a text and no way to verify independently the correctness of the text. How to solve this problem? Hegel somewhere remarks ironically about interpreting according to the spirit, namely, according to reason, namely, according to common sense (one's own opinion).

One may, to be sure, hope for inspiration to comprehend what is written and to help fill the gaps that are necessarily part of the text. If we understood Aramaic and could watch a videotape of Jesus and hear his voice and see his gestures, we would recognize how much we as readers fill in the *feeling* dimension of the text with our own emotions, perhaps projecting a note of unrealistic sentiment into a word of mercy or a note of fury into a warning. How something is said communicates even more than what is said.

Without appealing to a revealed, factual record or to spiritual experience, it is possible to explicate the coherence of the text, trusting it unless there is convincing reason to do otherwise. My interpretive hypothesis is that some tensions between different Gospel narratives or within a given narrative are consequences of the many-sidedness of Jesus' teaching. Furthermore, on the assumption that Jesus' life reflects his teachings, my hope has been, as far as possible, to reconcile these tensions by trying to grasp the unity in his life.

A many-sided teaching is especially vulnerable to distortion when people who differ intellectually, emotionally, and spiritually emphasize certain themes at the expense of others. A common observation, for example, is that the author or last redactor of the "Gospel" according to Matthew was addressing a Jewish audience familiar with Jewish law, and thus highlighted Jesus' rigorous moral teachings more prominently than did the writers of the other narratives.[1] Nevertheless, Matthew includes a fair sampling of other sides of Jesus' teachings, such as, "Come to me, all who are weary and are carrying heavy burdens, and I will give you rest. Take my yoke upon you, and learn from me; for I am gentle and humble in heart, and you will find rest for your souls. For my yoke is easy, and my burden is light."[2] The Gospel according to Matthew thus indicates a redactor committed to the full spectrum of the memories of Jesus rather than to a smooth theological blanket. Most interpreters of the Sermon on the Mount try to strike a balance—aiming to acknowledge the rigor of its standard without falling into an external legalism; to take the sermon seriously without falling into a literalism that ignores the illustrative character of its examples (turning the other cheek, going the second mile); to give full recognition to the primacy of the spiritual dimension without ending in an extreme ethic of attitude lacking a concrete norm for action; to interpret reasonably without merely accommodating the Sermon to today's culture.[3] A wide range of teachings are collected in the Sermon on the Mount, including tender encouragements (the Beatitudes)[4] and challenging warnings (e.g., about anger as the inner equivalent of murder). This complex matrix is the key, I propose, to understanding Jesus' golden rule. While it is common to find great literary sophistication in Jesus' parables, which put dynamic spiritual teachings in commonplace images, there has been a tendency to read Jesus' moral teachings, stated in equally commonplace terms, as univocal and dogmatic; but the golden rule is more complex than it appears.

THE GOLDEN RULE IN MATTHEW

Matthew 7.12 reads, "panta oun hosa ean thelete hina poiousin humin hoi anthropoi, houtos kai humeis poieite autois; houtos gar estin ho nomos kai oi prophetai."

> All things [panta hosa]
> therefore [oun]
> which you want/wish/will [ean thelete]
> that [hina] people [hoi anthropoi]
> do [poiousin] to you [humin],
> do [poiete] thus [houtos kai] to them [autois]
> for [gar] this [houtos] is [estin]
> the law [ho nomos] and [kai] the prophets [ho prophetai].

The plural "you" in the third line suggests that the golden rule is given not only to the individual but also to the community. Intuitive notions of wanting/wishing/willing and of doing are invoked. In the phrase "what you want people to do to you" the verb thelete carries no specific connotations. It can be translated by "wish," "want," or "will." There may be some contrast with boulomai, which connotes choice following upon reflection. The appeal, therefore, is to an intuitive sense of how one wants to be treated. A certain faith in humankind is expressed by inviting people to take their own desires for being well treated as a clue for how to treat others. The point is not that one's religious heritage and personal reflections do not shape intuition, nor that one will never need to retire "to the wilderness" to deliberate and formulate one's great decisions. The point rather is that the golden rule provides only an implicit guide to the maturing/transformation of one's willing, namely, the path of experience that follows upon engaging oneself in treating others as comparable to oneself. A similar remark can be made regarding *poiein*, to do or to make. There is no implied philosophy of action here, for example, along the lines of the Greek distinction between actions undertaken merely as a means to some further end, versus actions regarded as intrinsically valuable in themselves. The only implication for the philosophy of action is that action is understood, first and foremost, as interpersonal, as interaction.[5]

The Matthean context of the golden rule, however, introduces another level of meaning. The rule is given immediately after the remark about the good gifts that the Father in heaven gives to those who ask.[6]

> Ask, and it will be given you; search, and you will find; knock, and the door will be opened for you. For everyone who asks receives, and he who searches finds, and for everyone who knocks, the door will be opened. Is there anyone among you who, if your child asks him for bread, will give him a stone? Or if he asks for a fish, will give a snake? If you then, who are evil, know how to give good gifts to your children, how much more will your Father in heaven give good things to those who ask him! In everything do to others as you would have them do to you; for this is the law and the prophets. Enter through the narrow gate; for the gate is wide and the road is easy that leads to destruction, and there are many who take it. (Matt. 7.7–13)

Placing the golden rule in the context of fatherly love (Matt. 7.7–11) gains for it a new level of meaning. The rule might seem to fit oddly as directly appended to a lesson on prayer. Luke, logically, puts the lesson on prayer with other teachings on prayer.[7] One can understand why some scholars have construed the Sermon on the Mount as amplifying the memory of a single discourse with many additional teachings. It might have been smoother to position the rule, say, after the teaching about removing the log from your own eye before you try to remove the speck from someone else's eye;[8] this would have strengthened the customary association of the rule with brotherly fairness between equals, whose relations tend to be spoiled by selfish distortions of perspective.

Matthew is after something more than a rule of equity. To love in this context means to love as the Father loves, and that means doing the Father's will. "Not every one who says to me, 'Lord, Lord,' shall enter the kingdom of heaven, but only the one who does the will of my Father in heaven."[9] While it may be said of the Creator, "As the heavens are higher than the earth, so are my ways higher than your ways and my thoughts higher than your thoughts,"[10] in the immediate context the Father's love is simply presented as being at least as good as human parental love, and no heroic measures are called for.

THE FULFILLMENT OF THE LAW AND THE PROPHETS

Fatherly love and the golden rule in Matthew are best interpreted in terms of Matthew's overarching theme of Jesus as the fulfillment of tradition. "Think not that I have come to abolish the law and the prophets; I have come not to abolish but to fulfill."[11] That Matthew then refers to the golden rule as "the law and the prophets" attributes a special status to the rule and suggests a link between the golden rule and Jesus' mission: Jesus will demonstrate a new fulfillment of the golden rule. "The law and the prophets" was a twofold designation of the entirety of the Hebrew scriptures. Later, when Matthew cites the great commandments of the love of God and neighbor, he adds, "On these two commandments hang all the law and the prophets," and he thus suggests a link between the golden rule and these other summary principles.[12]

What could it mean to fulfill the Torah? In the Sermon on the Mount, fulfillment involves a combination of continuity and discontinuity. In the first place, fulfillment involves *preserving* the achievements of tradition (e.g., regarding the universality of moral obligation). The golden rule governs relations with all people (*anthropoi*), not just relations within the fellowship of believers.[13] Just as God makes the sun shine on the good and the evil and the rain fall on the just and unjust, so the love of the followers of Jesus cannot be restricted to an exclusive group.[14] The point is strengthened by Jesus' parable of the good Samaritan, not only because the Samaritan is not a member of the approved religious group, but also because the Samaritan had neither the need nor the opportunity to inquire about the religious status of the one he helped, the beaten-up, half-dead man by the side of the road.[15] Jesus told the crowds, "Call no one your father on earth, for you have one Father—the one in heaven."[16]

Fulfillment involves *adjustments* to make room for emerging facts and meanings and values. Both Matthew and Luke present the golden rule as adjusted from the previous negative formulations (e.g., "Do not do to others what you do not want others to do to you") to positive formulations. This change has absorbed a disproportionately large share of commentators' attention. First of all, there is an argument in favor of a negative formulation: one primal function of moral law is to demarcate boundaries that must not be trespassed. The need to promulgate respect for these boundaries is as urgent today as it was during the time of Moses.[17] Second, it seems that few first-century writers cared much about the verbal difference; negatively formulated expressions of the golden rule are more frequent in both pre-Christian and early Christian documents.[18] Finally, there are reasons in favor of a positive formulation: it calls the one who would follow the golden rule to be morally active; it is psychologically more effective to command the good than to prohibit evil; and positive expressions, such as the law of love, are more directly expressive of the values that are presupposed by prohibitions.

Fulfillment also involves a *deepening* of the commandments. "You have heard that it was said to those of ancient times, 'You shall not murder'; and 'whoever murders shall be liable to judgment.' But I say to you that if you are angry with a brother or sister, you will be liable to judgment."[19] God looks into the heart. Although the phrase "But I say to you" is unique in the literature of the period and expresses what scholars regards as an undoubtedly authentic presentation of Jesus' authority, this deepening of the commandments was familiar in contemporary Jewish preaching. Attaching the golden rule to a teaching about fatherly love deepens the rule.

Fulfillment can also involve change that *overturns* what was previously held. For example, as we shall see in a moment, the Sermon on the Mount instructs the hearers not to return evil for evil. This overturning does not justify a simplistic distinction between "a New Testament of love and mercy" and "an Old Testament of law and retribution."[20] Although the Hebrew scriptures command repayment in kind for an injury[21], they also counsel kindness to an enemy[22] and proclaim a God of mercy.[23]

In sum, though the golden rule was not part of the written Torah, it may be said to be fulfilled in Jesus' life and teachings. The traditional golden rule is preserved, adjusted from a negative to a positive formulation, deepened in context, and associated with the overturning of the principle of retaliation.

RECIPROCITY IN MATTHEW

Tradition had promised the blessings of nature for the righteous and ruin for the unrighteous.[24] No small proportion of wisdom literature emphasized rewards of good conduct and penalties for bad conduct. Regarded as generalizations about human interactions, they have a certain plausibility. What is more normal than to respond to love with love? What is more natural than to retaliate in response to harm? Tobit recommends giving alms as a protection against a time of need (4.10). Clement of Rome, in his First Epistle to the Corinthians, chapter 13 (which may chronologically precede or follow the Gospels), includes a rule of prudence: "As you treat others, so shall you be treated."[25] It may seem as though repayment thinking was common in society and religion and in the golden rule as well.

According to Bruce J. Malina, in the social world of first-century Palestine, reciprocity was a normal and prominent practice, in the sense of doing favors in the expectation of receiving favors in return and repaying favors previously received. Perhaps every society practices reciprocity in this sense.[26]

Although someone might associate the golden rule equation of self and other with the custom of exchanging favors, Jesus' responses to good and evil do not follow a policy of doing favors only for friends and getting even for injuries. He insists that beneficence not be restricted to returning favors: "If you greet only your brothers and sisters, what more are you doing than others?"[27] Nor does Jesus condone the popular notion that one may accumulate merit with God by performing enough good deeds to outweigh smaller sins.[28] In the Sermon on the Mount, Jesus dismisses the principle of retaliation. "You have heard that it was said, 'An eye for an eye and a tooth for a tooth.' But I say to you, Do not resist an evildoer. But if anyone strikes you on the right cheek, turn the other also."[29] Jesus rebukes the disciples when they wanted to retaliate by calling down fire from heaven on a Samaritan town that had rejected them.[30] To put things in perspective, recall that the "law of talio" was no maxim of wrathful vengeance. It was originally conceived as a *limitation* on vengeance: an eye for an eye—and nothing more;[31] Jesus nonetheless made it clear that his apostles were not to participate in this practice.

Jesus clearly calls for a standard higher than returning favors and retaliation, and yet there is a persistent impression that repayment ethics haunts the New Testament Gospels.[32] For example, the golden rule in Matthew is immediately followed by a remark contrasting the narrow way that leads to life and the broad way that leads to destruction. To untangle this issue requires probing topics remote from the leading edge of the Gospel, the heartening Beatitudes, or the golden rule. Does talk of reward and punishment indicate the persistence of repayment thinking in Matthew? The Sermon on the Mount concludes with a parable contrasting a house built on rock that will stand, with a house built on sand that will fall.[33] One who "invests" too tentatively the talents he or she has received gains a lesser reward than one who has been fully consecrated.[34] The link between sowing and reaping does not presuppose an arbitrary, intervening hand. Nor would a responsible teacher omit mention of the consequences to his or her hearers of the choices before them. Realism is not repayment thinking.

Talk of "rewards," such as the assurances given in the Beatitudes, are given to those who trust God, so that they will not need to think about things balancing out when they face a situation where much is at stake. The assurance received enables the individual to act in a crisis in a self-forgetting manner where there is no prospect of return from the other. Luke relates that Jesus prayed and received assurance in Gethsemani[35] and then went through the Crucifixion attentive to the needs of others.[36]

Jesus prescribes punishment in the context of the efforts of mercy to rehabilitate a wrongdoer. Consider the structure of the lesson on forgiveness given in Matthew 18.12–35, a social procedure framed by two parables. Jesus first tells the parable of the shepherd who goes in search of the lost sheep. The purpose of the shepherd's quest is to reintegrate the lost one into the vital circuits of the community of faith. Next comes the three-stage procedure that a member of the community is obliged to take if another member sins against him or her. If a series of efforts (e.g., from private one-to-one conversation to small group encounter to community meeting) do not succeed in rehabilitating the member, then, at the limit, the unrepentant, persistently willful, and disruptive individual is to be disfellowshiped. Just when the hearer/reader imagines himself/herself sitting in judgment upon someone else, a concluding parable challenges selfrighteousness with an application of golden rule thinking. The servant owed his lord a great debt and was about to be thrown into prison, but he begged for mercy and was forgiven. However, he was merciless in demanding punishment for one who owed him much less. When the lord discovered the harshness, he threw the unforgiving servant into prison.[37] Jesus' teachings on forgiveness combine a personal, spiritual attitude and a concrete social procedure. In the spirit of recalling how much we have been forgiven, believers are to undertake the necessary activities of retrieval and community maintenance. The Matthew 18 lesson illustrates the integration of spiritual and practical dimensions in loving a disruptive member of one's congregation, and an analogous integration surely applies in loving an enemy.

Forgiveness, in brief, can be accepted or rejected; and a human life, finally, falls on one side or another of a great divide. There comes a parting of the ways (cf. Joshua: "Choose this day whom you will serve").[38] As ambiguous as our lives may be, with our generosities and our stumblings and sin, there is an overall direction. From the standpoint of one who could see through the in-betweenness of immaturity, Jesus said, "Every good tree bears good fruit, but the bad tree bears bad fruit."[39] After this life comes either resurrection or "the destruction of the soul."[40] For the one who forever and finally rejects the divine offer of salvation, it can be said, "From those who have nothing, even what they have shall be taken away."[41] It is for divine judgment to discern when such a mortal has thoroughly identified with the antithesis of reality.[42] Judgment is not the reactive vengeance of an offended Deity, but an act that embodies the recognition of when the cup of iniquity has become full. It is not retaliation, nor exactly retribution; it is the consequence of iniquity in a universe ordered toward advancing goodness. Matthew shows us that Jesus was fully capable of being militant. There is some analogy to final, negative judgment in Jesus' last temple discourse[43] condemning the sin of those religious leaders who determined that he be put to death. The denunciation illustrates the exhaustion of patience when many appeals have been rejected.[44]

The narrowness of the repayment ethic is not implied by the normal connection between act and consequence, nor by the necessary procedure of a group to deal with incorrigibly harmful individuals, nor by the denunciation of murderous hypocrisy. The difference between the repayment ethic and divine love is that the repayment ethic is narrowly partisan, whereas divine love responds generously to good and mercifully to evil and judges righteously if and when mercy is finally rejected. The repayment ethic is oriented to short-term material advantage, and divine love is oriented to the heavenly kingdom.

Matthew's golden rule, then, should not be linked to the ethics of repaying favors and injuries. It is a pivot between (1) a summary of the law and the prophets and (2) Jesus' teaching of fatherly love and the progressive requirements of discipleship.

THE HIGH STANDARD OF THE SERMON
ON THE MOUNT

The link between the golden rule and the high standard of the Sermon on the Mount has chronically raised the question of whether the rule thereby becomes unrealistic, even inhumane. Part of the sermon teaches that righteousness is, initally, a matter of the heart. An appropriate spiritual attitude is needed to motivate conformity with such traditional requirements as the prohibitions against murder and adultery. If genuine righteousness is spiritually motivated, the standard may be said to be high, but it cannot therefore be regarded as inhumane.

In addition, there are requirements that require a more complex analysis.

> You have heard that it was said, "An eye for an eye and a tooth for a tooth." But I say to you, Do not resist an evildoer. But if anyone strikes you on the right cheek, turn the other also; and if anyone wants to sue you and take your coat, give your cloak as well; and if any one forces you to go one mile, go also the second mile. Give to everyone who begs from you, and do not refuse anyone who wants to borrow from you. You have heard that it was said, "You shall love your neighbor and hate your enemy." But I say to you, Love your enemies and pray for those who persecute you, so that you may be children of your Father in heaven; for he makes his sun rise on the evil and on the good, and sends rain on the righteous and on the unrighteous. For if you love those who love you, what reward do you have? Do not even the tax collectors do the same? And if you greet only your brethren, what more are you doing than others? Do not even the Gentiles do the same? Be perfect, therefore, as your heavenly Father is perfect.[45]

The hearers of the Sermon were not to resist evil, not to use the courts to defend their property rights; they were to love their enemies, and to be perfect. Most of these teachings, properly understood, are applicable to the ordinary believer, though not all.

To sort things out takes some reconstructive interpretation. To what group was the Sermon on the Mount addressed? The practical importance of the question is that the golden rule is associated in the Sermon on the Mount with an especially high standard, raising the question: Is this standard equally binding on all believers?

There is much discussion about which audience—the twelve apostles or all the committed disciples or the diverse crowds—were the intended recipients of which portions of the sermon.[46] Matthew frames the sermon ambiguously: at the beginning, the reader is told that Jesus is not speaking to the crowds: "When Jesus saw the crowds, he went up the mountain; and after he sat down, his disciples came to him."[47] At the end, however, we read, "Now when Jesus had finished saying these things, the crowds were astounded at his teachings."[48] The proclamation, "You are the light of the world,"[49] would hardly fit in a sermon to the crowds. The form and the content of the Sermon on the Mount, on one reading, "point to a group of committed disciples who go apart with their teacher and are instructed by him concerning the meaning of the separated or sacred community that gathers around him."[50] Luke places the Sermon on the Plain right after Jesus calls the twelve apostles from among a larger group of disciples.[51]

Should we say that among the teachings gathered in the Sermon on the Mount are some that define extraordinary requirements for the twelve apostles, the standard-bearers of Jesus' mission? As representatives of Jesus, and as heralds of the present and future kingdom, their function was to exemplify not merely currently adequate standards, but heavenly standards, the standards that represent planetary destiny, a future-oriented, "eschatological" ethic.[52]

No textual argument can conclusively settle the issue, but if we assume that the Sermon on the Mount was addressed to the twelve to explain the requirements of their mission, a number of things fall into place. Although most of the Sermon presents teachings like the Beatitudes, suitable for the crowds, other aspects pertain specifically to the apostles.

Regarding nonresistance, observe that, despite the Roman occupation of Palestine, Jesus rejected the idea of pursuing "the kingdoms of the world."[53] He offered spiritual leadership as an alternative to military revolt (which eventually proved to be national suicide in the failed wars of liberation [66–70 and 132–135]). The apostles did not serve in the army, and many early disciples followed their example; similarly, the apostles were not to settle their disputes in court, and this later was urged upon believers generally.[54] Jesus' high standard is sometimes mistaken for weakness, supine submission, returning nothing for evil. But look at Jesus' bold, final entry into Jerusalem to bring spiritual power to confront the intellectual arguments and physical force that his enemies would muster.

"Nonresistance" is a negative formulation of a positive, imaginative, creative, and courageous activity: returning good for evil, to "turn the other cheek" in response to a blow, to "go the second mile" when forced to go one mile (by law the Roman soldiers could compel Jewish citizens to carry their packs one mile). The teaching is not legislation but illustration of a fearless and loving response in a situation where one's options are constrained. Nor can pacifism be deduced from the Sermon. The term "enemy" refers to personal enemies, not enemies of the nation. The golden rule is consistent with group defense by force of arms. How should one want to be treated if one is a member of an invading army that is raping and killing? Do I regard it as a requirement of love that I be permitted to continue such a spree until I am sated? One should want to be stopped, if need be, with whatever force is necessary.[55] Jesus never condemns the soldier's function, and (in Luke) he praises the great faith of the Roman centurion.[56] In short, nonresistance involves some aspects that constrain the apostles and some aspects that are constructive good sense for anyone.

The Sermon's call to abandon anxiety regarding one's economic welfare[57] is universally applicable, though the requirement to trust the heavenly Father for daily necessities and to have goods in common specifically constrained the twelve who were traveling with Jesus during the time that the crowds were supportive.[58] Thus, the rich ruler was required to sell his possessions;[59] but Jesus suspended the requirement as he prepared to leave them: "When I sent you out without a purse, bag, or sandals, did you lack anything?" They said, "No, not a thing." He said to them, "But now, the one who has a purse must take it, and likewise a bag."[60] W. D. Davies remarked of the early church, "The primitive experiment in 'communism,' so-called, was short-lived; soon it became necessary to send money to the 'poor' of Jerusalem who had used their capital unwisely."[61]

The call to be perfect (teleios) is addressed to all, not in the sense that apostles or disciples are expected to have completed their personal growth, but in the sense that every believer is expected to be wholehearted. As Joachim Jeremias clarifies, we need not "take teleios in a perfectionist sense; rather, Matthew will have understood telios in the sense of the Old Testament tamim ('intact,' 'undivided') as the designation of who belongs to God with the totality of his life."[62] "You cannot serve God and wealth."[63] Abandoning anxiety, the disciple is to "strive first for the kingdom and his righteousness," and is to trust God for other essentials.[64]

The specific constraints on the apostles must of course not be substituted for the Gospel message itself and taken as legalistic requirements for anyone seeking to enter the kingdom; the Sermon itself refutes this view: "Blessed are the poor in spirit, for theirs is the kingdom of heaven."[65] Such an attitude of humility enables a genuinely childlike entrance into the kingdom.[66] Nevertheless, having entered, each believer must grow; and growth ultimately involves having one's entire life transformed by the relationship with God. Lest it be imagined that this view of a higher standard of morality for apostles entails a dangerously lax standard for others, consider that Jesus, before his final entry into Jerusalem, clarified the cost of anyone's following him: "If any want to become my followers, let them deny themselves and take up their cross and follow me. For those who want to save their life will lose it, and those who lose their life for my sake will find it."[67]

Jesus' eschatological presence sets up a gravitational attraction that strictly holds the apostles in a close orbit; partly similar requirements hold for the seventy who were also commissioned to preach the gospel; and other disciples and the crowds are accelerated into its vortex of righteousness.[68] The presence of Jesus generates a movement of desire and commitment to live like him: the core of his new community is to share his specific requirements, while teachings such as the golden rule function spiritually to help a morally diverse humanity to live in an increasingly God-like way.[69]

BEYOND RECIPROCITY: LUKE'S GOLDEN RULE

The Gospel according to Luke (joined with the Acts of the Apostles) presents Jesus as bringing the kingdom of God through abundant forgiveness, with a special welcome for the poor. Jesus heals, preaches, and teaches in the power of the Spirit, which, poured out upon all flesh at Pentecost, enabled the heroic work of Stephen and Peter and Paul, and which continues to bless believers in their outreach to the world.

As in Matthew, the golden rule is placed within a cluster of teachings, referred to as the Sermon on the Plain. Luke 6.31 reads, "kai kathos thelete hina poiousin humin hoi anthropoi, poiete autois homoios."

> And [kai]
> as [kathos]
> you want [thelete]
> that people do to you [hina poiousin humin hoi anthropoi]
> do thus to them [poiete autois homoios].

Luke's wording begins, "*As* you want people to do to you." This wording highlights not *what* is done as much as *how* it is done. Matthew's phrasing, "*All things* that you want people to do to/for you," implied individuated actions that, presumably, may be outwardly characterized. Both aspects of action, to be sure, are important in each Gospel. The context surrounding the golden rule in Luke pointedly raises the issues about a high standard and reciprocity.

> But I say to you that listen, Love your enemies, do good to those who hate you, bless those who curse you, pray for those who abuse you. If anyone strikes you on the cheek, offer the other also; and from anyone who takes away your coat do not withhold even your shirt. Give to every one who begs from you; and if anyone takes away your goods, do not ask for them again. Do to others as you would have them do to you. If you love those who love you, what credit is that to you? For even sinners love those who love them. If you do good to those who do good to you, what credit is that to you? For even sinners do the same. If you lend to those from whom you hope to receive, what credit is that to you? Even sinners lend to sinners, to receive as much again. But love your enemies, and do good, and lend, expecting nothing in return. Your reward will be great, and you will be children of the Most High; for he is kind to the ungrateful and the wicked. Be merciful, just as your Father is merciful. Do not judge, and you will not be judged; do not condemn, and you will not be condemned. Forgive, and you will be forgiven; give, and it will be

given to you. A good measure, pressed down, shaken together, running over, will be put into your lap. For the measure you give will be the measure you get back. (Luke 6.27–38)

Again the paradigm of the Father is invoked. Luke contrasts the golden rule with the ethic of reciprocity and identifies the rule with generosity to the poor and love of enemies, with being merciful as our Father is merciful; the one who gives abundantly will receive abundantly from the Father.[70] The thought of reward for giving is not altogether absent, though the overflowing generosity that is called for is hardly possible without self-forgetfulness. The teaching, therefore, is fulfilled, not by keeping its promise in mind, but by devotion to the needs of others.

There are at least three possible relations between the golden rule and the love that Jesus exemplified and called his hearers to share. First, the golden rule is an important traditional summary principle, but it falls short of the love of Jesus. Second, Jesus' love is so radical and so little adjusted to this world that it needs the golden rule of fairness to guide its expression in daily life. Third, the golden rule receives an ideal interpretation in terms of the love that Jesus exemplified.

The first conception, namely, that the golden rule is inferior to the command to love, has some plausibility, inasmuch as the golden rule, in its verbal formulation, is easy to associate with reasonable beneficence, rather than overflowing love; it is also easy to imagine judicious balance conflicting in some cases with a loving generosity. Nevertheless, Luke's golden rule is connected to the love of enemies; and it is even harder in Luke than in Matthew to restrict the meaning of the golden rule to past tradition: "The law and the prophets were in effect until John; since then the good news of the kingdom of God is proclaimed."[71]

The second conception, which holds that love needs the golden rule for its wise application, is appealing if we think of love as a delight in the other and a desire to do good to the other, a desire that functions to motivate agents to learn about their recipients' concrete situation and to balance generous impulses with a proportionate awareness of competing demands. This conception, however, risks implying that love is a tendency to do foolish things. If love is conceived as impulsive and undiscerning, then it is the more understandable that a complementary principle of golden rule equity is needed for daily living.

Paul Ricoeur, whose thought figures significantly in chapters 11 and 12, has argued for a combination of the first two conceptions. To show how Luke's context for the golden rule transcends repayment thinking, Ricoeur describes a move from the "the economy of exchange and its logic of equivalence" to the "economy of gift and its logic of abundance" and its associated "rhetoric of paradox." Because a gift has been previously received (from God), one is to be generous toward others, even in situations in which it cannot be expected that they will repay one's generosity.

Generosity supplants the motive of doing good in order to get future benefits in return. "The Golden Rule is not merely quoted here, it is integrated into a new ethics. This would be unthinkable if it could not be reinterpreted according to the new logic of superabundance sealed by the love of enemies."[72] Noncalculating love of enemies, for Ricoeur, is an ethical paradox that is "intended to disorient for the sake of reorienting, as many commentators have said about the parables."[73] The love of enemies suspends and transcends ethics altogether, according to Ricoeur. The golden rule emerges, on the other side of this disorientation to reorient social interchange.

Despite this analysis, Ricoeur interprets the golden rule, finally, as expressing the principle of social/economic/political equity that is needed for social stability in the wake of the revolutionary, noncalculating love of enemies which closes the old order and inaugurates the new. What is essential, according to Ricoeur, is to retain the "tension" between, on the one hand, a bilateral principle of justice and fairness that preserves reciprocity and, on the other, a unilateral love of enemies.[74] One must ceaselessly keep reinterpreting radical love from the perspective of fairness and fairness from the perspective of radical love. In another article touching on the same theme, however, Ricoeur allows that the golden rule may "lean toward one direction or toward the other, according to the interpretation it is given."[75] The abundance of the economy of giving is dramatized in the verse "Give, and it will be given to you; good measure, pressed down, shaken together, running over, will be put into your lap. For the measure you give will be the measure you get back" (6.38). He presents this comment as his conclusion: "The lack of measure is the good measure. Such is the poetic transposition of the rhetoric of paradox: superabundance becomes the hidden truth of equivalence. The Golden Rule is repeated. But repetition means transfiguration."[76]

Clearly, one may recognize the useful moral practice of comparing agent and recipient and a love which transcends this. To distinguish between these two levels is no reason to confine the golden rule to the lower level. In the Sermon on the Plain, Jesus does not propose the golden rule just to remind his followers to keep their feet on the ground and be fair-minded in their social relationships. Luke does not synthesize a spiritual love that is blind to actualities with a secular principle of fairness. Rather, he implies integrated conceptions of the golden rule and of love such that they involve each other.

The question of the reasonableness of the high standard arises again with the Sermon on the Plain. Does the love of enemies entail neglecting prudence, inviting abuse, turning oneself into a victim, embracing pacifism? As we have seen, nothing in Jesus' religious teaching to the individual proscribes the right to use force in national self-defense.

In economic affairs, to argue the reasonableness of Jesus' ethic is not to bless the status quo. The Sermon on the Plain is flatly incompatible

with a complacent response to economic inequality. Luke emphasized
Jesus' attention to the poor and the dangers of wealth.[77] In Jesus' society,
notes Joachim Jeremias, " 'almsgiving' is not a support for beggary, but the
dominant form of social help."[78] Luke's point about the poor is not that
each person is required to relinquish his possessions. It was with satisfaction that Jesus addressed Zacchaeus, who had pledged just half his goods
to the poor.[79] The poor, fundamentally, are those who are distressed and
afflicted. According to Malina, "A poor person seems to be one who cannot maintain his inherited status due to circumstances that befall him and
his family, like debt, being in a foreign land, sickness, death (widow), or
some personal physical accident."[80] Jesus did engage in healing; but he
would not let his sensitivity to material needs divert him from his specific
mission. When the crowds who had seen Jesus heal the sick sought for
him in the hope that their wonder-worker would stay in the area, Jesus
moved on: "I must proclaim the good news of the kingdom of God to
the other cities also; for I was sent for this purpose."[81]

The love that Jesus called for is neither impossible, nor impractical,
nor is his language a figure of speech designed primarily to jolt the hearer
out of conventional attitudes. Luke portrays Jesus as a man of prayer,
whose spirit enables believers to imitate him, to continue living in his
way: "Everyone who is fully qualified will be like the teacher."[82] The seventy evangelists found that they, too, could perform wonders.[83] Stephen,
"full of the Holy Spirit," preached boldly, paid for it with his life, and died
like Jesus, commending his spirit to the Lord and praying for forgiveness
for those who put him to death.[84] For the author of Luke and Acts, the
spirit that Jesus lived so fully is given to believers today to enable them to
live in continuity with that original inspiration: "How much more will the
heavenly Father give the Holy Spirit to those who ask him?"[85]

The overflowing, universal love of the golden rule in Luke is linked
with basic religious teachings. Jesus taught that "the kingdom of heaven is
within you";[86] and he portrayed God going forth in search of every "lost
sheep," awaiting the return of every "prodigal son," unwilling that any
should perish.[87] Luke teaches, finally, that the spirit has been poured out
upon all flesh.[88] He presents a God who loves each of us with a bound-
less love.

CONCLUSION

In context, then, Jesus' golden rule remotivates the normal practice of
exchanging favors, and it excludes retaliation. The New Testament shows
how talk of reward and punishment can be free of repayment thinking.
The high standard associated with the rule encompasses two sorts of
teachings: some that pertain specifically to the apostles as representatives
of the present and future kingdom of God, and other teachings that, when
reasonably interpreted, remain high, yet accessible, since every follower is
spiritually equipped to grow into them.

The flexibility of a rule that remains widely accessible and reasonable while conveying a high standard can be understood as engaging the hearer/reader in a movement through several levels of interpretation.

1. *The Golden Rule of Prudence:* Do to others as you want others to do to you . . . with realistic attention to the consequences of your choices for the long-term welfare of your recipient. This rule must be distinguished from a pseudo–golden rule of self-interest: Do to others as you want others to do to you . . . with an eye to avoiding punishment and gaining rewards for yourself. It is altogether legitimate that one have a prudent eye to the long-term welfare of one's own soul; prudence "counts the cost" of a proposed commitment or course of action. And it is altogether fitting that Jesus gave warnings about the consequences of selfish living and gave assurances to calm the fears and intrigue the imagination of those who are open to choosing the way of love and service. Jesus' promise of eternal life to all who will receive it in faith subverts natural concern about doing what is right at significant earthly cost to oneself. The prudent course is to do the will of God, and that is to act with golden rule regard for one's neighbor. But it is equally prudent for the neighbor to do the same, so the faithful person will act not only to satisfy the other's immediate needs but also to facilitate the other's growth in the golden rule. Prudence combined with the golden rule thus involves the next level.

2. *The Golden Rule of Neighborly Love:* Do to others as you want others to do to you . . . as an expression of consideration and fairness among neighbors, where the scope of the term "neighbor" extends to all without regard to ethnic or religious differences. Since the neighbor can be the enemy, however, fulfilling a "conventional ethic of fairness" can require extraordinary love, which involves the next level.

3. *The Golden Rule of Fatherly Love:* Do to others as you want others to do to you . . . imitating the divine paradigm. The rule has its paradigm in the way the Father loves, giving good gifts and being merciful, and in the life of Jesus, which shows that love is not without its severe disciplines.

These three levels are implied and blended in Jesus' teachings. His authoritative teaching gave assurance that those who upgraded neighborly love to fatherly love—loving enemies, giving generously, being a peacemaker, enduring persecution, and so on—would not thereby sacrifice the eternal welfare of their souls. A due appreciation of the spirit of Jesus' golden rule, I believe, comes from the recognition that he made use of the best of scriptural and oral tradition, which he invested with new meaning by virtue of his other teachings and by his life.

By the same reasoning, the intention to express the parental love of God must avoid falling into the trap of adopting a superior and condescending stance. Rather, what is fitting is the same attitude of service that one would welcome if one were the recipient of someone else's divinely parental love in like circumstances.

six

A Theological Principle

What difference does the presence or absence of religious faith make in the practice of the golden rule? While the question focuses on personal experience, the discussion of the question is not insulated from social and political issues. As theologians labored during the medieval period in Europe, the Christian church sought and eventually gained dominant cultural power. In that process, theologians and philosophers were occupied with efforts to integrate Christianity intellectually with Greek philosophy and politically with unbelievers. These aims affected interpretations of the golden rule. Theologians affirmed that faith had a transforming effect on the practice of the rule, even though the rule as a datum of common reason could serve as a principle for believer and unbeliever alike.

The West learned the universal scope of the golden rule as much from Stoicism as from classical Judaism and Christianity, since exclusivistic notions of "the chosen people" and "the church of the saved" complicated otherwise clear humanitarian messages about the need to extend welcome and concern to strangers, widows, and orphans; lost sheep and prodigal sons; Jew and Greek; slave and free; male and female.[1] The emphasis on the golden rule as a leading ethical principle, however, derived primarily from the New Testament repetition of Hillel's teaching that the golden rule is the quintessence of the law and the prophets.

PHILOSOPHIC AND BIBLICAL ORIGINS OF CHRISTIAN ETHICS

How is it that ancient Mediterranean philosophical and religious traditions could ever start to blend? Stoicism already contained the concept of God as the universal *logos* (reason), the source of intelligible principles; it had also begun to recognize the golden rule. The way was therefore open for the intellectual affirmation of the golden rule as a cosmic truth, a "law of nature," accessible to every human mind. At the same time, Jewish and

Christian writings affirmed that all people, nonbelievers included, know something of God's truth. While rabbinic ethics emphasized reflecting on the details of particular cases, Christian natural law theologians, as researched by Hans Reiner, gathered several ideas from the Old and New Testaments.[2]

1. According to the Hebrew scriptures, all people have a knowledge of good and evil. "God knows that when you eat [the fruit of the tree] your eyes will be opened, and you will be like gods, knowing good and evil" (Gen. 3.4).

2. Even before Moses' presentation of written law, it had been possible to recognize the righteousness of pious Jewish patriarchs. Abraham put his faith in God, and God counted his faith as righteousness. (Gen. 15.6)

3. Moses said that the commandment was written in the hearts of his people: "Surely, this commandment that I am commanding you today is not too hard for you, neither is it too far away. . . . No, the word is very near to you; it is in your mouth and in your heart for you to observe" (Deut. 30.11–14).

4. The golden rule had, moreover, been presented as a summary of religious law. "Whatsoever you will that others should do to you, do you also to them; for this is the law and the prophets" (Matt. 7.12).

5. Paul's letter to the Romans had affirmed that the Gentiles, too, had the law inscribed in their hearts:

> When Gentiles, who do not possess the law do instinctively what the law requires, these, though not having the law, are a law to themselves. They show that what the law requires is written on their hearts, to which their conscience also bears witness; and their conflicting thoughts will accuse or perhaps excuse them. (Rom. 2.14–16)

6. The golden rule was found to be implicit in Paul's critique of condemning others for doing what one does oneself: "In passing judgment upon another you condemn yourself" (Rom. 2.1).

The golden rule thus proved to be a meeting ground for philosophical and biblical ethics. During the period when Christian beliefs were first being systematically organized, Justin Martyr argued that a negatively formulated golden rule is universally known and acclaimed, since people feel guilty about doing to others what they would not like done to themselves.[3] Tertullian used positive and negative forms as equivalent and as a formulation of natural law.[4] Only the grace of God, however, could insure that the rule would be fulfilled in a person's actual conduct.[5]

There was a tendency during this period for Christian writers, partly on the basis of a simplistic contrast between the Old and New Testaments, to think in terms of several polarities and to map them onto one another: (1) justice versus love or charity; (2) action conforming to standards expected of everyone versus conduct proceeding from a soul infused with

divine grace; and (3) the negatively formulated golden rule versus the positively formulated golden rule. As a result, the negatively formulated rule
tended to become a principle of justice requiring the virtue of self-
restraint in all human beings, while the positively formulated rule became
a principle of love, requiring beneficence, a virtue that could flourish only
as a fruit of the spirit.

A RULE ADDRESSED TO THE WILL, FULFILLED
BY GRACE: AUGUSTINE

Establishing Christian doctrine during the decline of the Roman Empire,
Augustine (354–430), the North African bishop of Hippo, recognized the
golden rule as a popular proverb, and used a negative formulation of the
rule as a summary of natural law. Complaining that people worry more
about obeying the rules of grammar than obeying the rules of God, Augustine insisted, "And surely there is no literary knowledge more interior
than the writing of conscience, that he is doing to another what he himself
would not suffer."[6]

Although the rule is written in the conscience of every person, for
Augustine, those without faith have only limited capacity for virtuous conduct in accord with it. In the light of his own vivid experience of struggle
prior to his conversion, Augustine allowed that unbelievers are capable of
civic virtue and of outwardly correct conduct. Conduct truly pleasing to
God, though, is possible only by grace, the gift of God.[7]

Thus in Augustine we again meet the claim that the wholehearted,
spiritual fulfillment of the golden rule is a fruit of the spirit. It is well
known that Augustine engaged in the most vigorous literary combat with
his theological opponents, which only encourages the suspicion that such
a claim is a power play, a move to condemn, an authoritarian ecclesiastical
barrier, a defensive and prideful stance. Without attempting to eliminate
our suspicion (and without assuming that a religionist should be embarrassed to be found exercising power and engaging in conflict), we may
consider the possibility that Augustine's claim—connecting wholehearted
moral living with spiritual faith—bears witness, above all, to the author's
personal history and his observation of others. If so, Augustine's seem-
ingly "exclusive" claim about spiritual faith and the replete practice of the
golden rule seems not so much narrow and hostile as frank and helpful,
at least in its dominant motivation.

It was by considering a counterexample to the golden rule and providing two ways of handling it that Augustine's treatment of the rule broke
new ground.

> If someone wished something wicked done to him and for this purpose
> would allege this text [Matt. 7.12]; for example, if a person wished to be
> challenged to drink immoderately and to swill himself in his cups and
> first practiced this upon the person by whom he wished it to be per-
> formed upon himself: it would then be ridiculous for such a person to

suppose that he had lived up to this prescription [i.e., to the golden rule]. Therefore, inasmuch as this caused some apprehension, I suppose one word was added to clarify the matter; so that in the statement: *All things, therefore, whatsoever you would that men should do to you*, there was inserted the word "good." Now, if this is lacking in the Greek copies, they also ought to be amended; but who would venture to do this? It is to be understood, therefore, that the statement is complete and quite perfect even without the addition of this word. For the expression used, "whatsoever you would," should not be taken as spoken in a broad, general sense, but with a restricted application: that is to say, the will is present only in the good; in evil and wicked actions cupidity is the word, not will. Not that Scripture always speaks in a restricted sense; but where it must, it so restricts a word's meaning that it suffers no other interpretation of it.[8]

According to Augustine, then, the true meaning of the rule is expressed by saying, "All *good* things, therefore, whatsoever you would that men should do to you. . . ." He supported his interpretation by drawing on a later manuscript of Matthew containing a clarified wording of the golden rule.[9] At the same time he provided a second way, a conceptual distinction, to handle the counterexample of the Bacchanalian reveler. Interpreted on the level of the flesh, the golden rule appeals to mere human desire, and invites one person simply to gratify another. In fact, the rule appeals to what one *wills* ("whatsoever things you will [*vultis*]"). Augustine distinguished will (*voluntas*) from selfish, corrupt desire (*cupiditas*).[10] God created Adam and Eve with a well-functioning will, intrinsically oriented toward the good, toward happiness centered in God. The consequences of the fall of Adam and Eve are such that we now need divine grace to restore the original power of the will.

Augustine may have been defending the golden rule from contemporary objections, but he was surely not engaging in the enterprise of rehabilitating a remnant of antique piety by providing a reformulation to satisfy the demands of a secular rationalism. He presented the variant reading in order to clarify, and clarity for Augustine connoted the light of the divinely illumined human intellect. He commented further that the precept in Matthew 7.12 is given in the context of teachings that enjoin "singleness of heart," that is, that a man should bestow something on another "without expecting any temporal advantage from him." "Therefore, once the eye has been cleansed and made single, it will be fit and capable of beholding and contemplating its own interior light."[11] In this exposition, then, it is not that the natural intellect first grasps the precept and then performs its duty; rather, through steadfast attention to the precepts the "interior light" would be discerned. "A certain strength and ability to walk in the way of wisdom lies in good conduct persevered in until the heart's cleansing and its singleness are achieved."[12]

In one additional way, the golden rule for Augustine is not restricted to relationships between human beings. It is not that believers should contemplate treating God as they want God to treat them. Rather, they should realize that there is an analogy between the situation in which they bring their needs to God and the situation in which beggars bring needs to them. He cites the warning about reciprocity: "Whoso stoppeth his ears, saith Solomon, to the cry of the poor, he also shall cry himself but shall not be heard" (Prov. 21.13). Augustine continues:

> That he [God] may own us his beggars, let us in like manner look upon ours; and that we may know what we ought to bestow on our neighbor asking of us (begging alms of us) to the intent that we in like manner may be heard in what we crave of God, we may consider from this, what we would that others in a like case should bestow upon us.[13]

Thus, if believers desire to have their prayers heard, they must respond to others' needs as they would like to be treated.

LATER MEDIEVAL ETHICS AND THE THOMISTIC SYNTHESIS

Special emphasis on the golden rule as the summation and root of natural law began with Lactantius (early fourth century).[14] According to Reiner, in the early Middle Ages Christian thought lost the dynamic tension between the present age and the end times to come; as a result, the golden rule was mustered into the service of "a static ethic of order."[15] Gratian in the *Decretum gratianum* (ca. 1140) identified natural law with the golden rule. He placed special emphasis on the rule, and stimulated continuing reference to the rule in the writings of Magister Rufinus (whose *Summa decretorum* appeared around 1158), Anselm of Canterbury (1033–1109), William of Champeaux (d. 1122), Peter Lombard (d. 1160), Hugh of St. Victor (1096–1144), John of Salisbury (ca. 1115–1180), Bonaventure (1221–1274), Matthew of Aquasparta (ca. 1235–1302), and Duns Scotus (ca. 1270–1308).[16] Peter Abelard (1079–1142) stipulated that the golden rule should be understood, in the light of the Christian doctrine of love, to prescribe that we do to others only the good, not the evil, that we would be willing to receive from others.[17]

As the corpus of Aristotle's works entered northern Europe from Islamic centers of study and translation study during the twelfth century, it became necessary to resynthesize Christian tradition with the best available science and philosophy. A leader in this movement at the University of Paris, Thomas Aquinas (ca. 1225–1274) wove threads of Augustinian tradition together with new Aristotelian threads. On the topic of the golden rule, he followed Augustine, interpreting the rule as pertaining to the will (directed toward the good) as distinguished from mere desire.[18] He also continued the tradition of connecting the golden rule with the law of love. But he also used Aristotle's notion of friendship (the relation to those "dear" to one) to help interpret biblical teachings.

> We read in Aristotle that *acts of love for another are the outcome of acts proceeding from a man's love for himself, that is to the extent that a man regards another*

in the same light as that in which he regards himself. The directive, there-fore, *All things whatsoever you would that men should do to you do you also to them* represents a certain rule for loving one's neighbour which is also con-tained implicitly in the commandment, *Thou shalt love thy neighbour as thyself.* Hence it is, in a certain sense, an explanation of this commandment.[19]

To Aristotle's concept of self-love, Thomas added primarily the thought that love (*caritas*, charity, translating *agape*) is infused into the soul by the divine spirit.[20] Although Thomas considered the objection that love im-plies a relation between at least two persons, he insisted that the unity of the self with itself is a paradigm for the union toward which friendship strives.[21] He was careful not to say that one extends charity to oneself but rather that one is to cherish (*diligere*) oneself from love (*caritas*) as one who belongs to God. This notion of cherishing appears to include some of the meaning of Platonic *eros*, an attraction for what appears to be of value. Where Hebrew and Greek scriptures had used a single term for love, whether it was directed to God or the neighbor, Thomas reserved *caritas* as a unique term to denote the incomparable relationship between man and God.

Friendship with God allows us to become "partakers of the divine nature."[22] As a result, the logic of what we do for the neighbor becomes clear. "Our likeness to God precedes and is the ground [*ratio*] of the like-ness we bear to our neighbor."[23] The fact of one's own participation in God is the primary motive for loving others.[24]

A RULE OF RELIGIOUS AND SECULAR ETHICS: MARTIN LUTHER

The writings of Martin Luther (1483–1546) show a striking and complex evolution in the interpretation of the golden rule. Perhaps Luther's first sermon as an Augustinian monk (1510 or 1512) was on the rule, and he drew from it an extreme and religiously terrifying moral demand. Empha-sizing the importance of the positive formulation of the golden rule, he reasoned that we cannot conform to it merely by avoiding evil. It is neces-sary for our salvation that we do good, indeed, that we do all the good we can. He concluded that if we fall short, we are condemned to eternal punishment.[25]

As Luther came to a personal experience of salvation by grace through faith, he began to see the meaning of the golden rule through a new con-cept of love. Though in this life sin is never altogether extinguished—the believer is "always justified, always sinner"—faith enables one to receive, alongside the old human nature, as it were, the new humanity, akin to the original condition of Adam before the fall into sin.[26] Love for God and the neighbor is the dominant theme of religious living, and even the sense of rule or law is transformed by spiritual experience. Scripture may no longer be taken as a locus of laws prescribing meritorious works that the pious, conscientious mind can perform. Instead, scripture is a medium of communication between God and humankind, full of commands and promises, especially the promise that faith—the gift of God—and faith alone is the means of our salvation. The sinner who is willing to trust in the promises of God emerges into joy and liberty.

For Luther, then, the faith-practice of the golden rule can hardly be comprehended as rule following in a conventional sense. Good works are to spring from the believer as from a fountain of gratitude.[27]

The golden rule tends to connote some sort of equality between self and others, and this connotation finds specification in two egalitarian themes of Luther's religious ethics: religious vocations of monks and priests have no priority over those of workers and housewives;[28] and the believer is in bondage to none and servant of all.[29]

What for Luther is the status of the golden rule? He regards it both as a part of the natural law recognized by all men and also as a radical requirement for self-transcending love.[30] The rule calls us radically to transform or abandon all selfish love, as Jesus did on the cross. We are to identify with God's will for the true needs of the other person, and God enables the person of faith to do that. The implications of the golden rule are infinite, and they transcend the level of law in the ordinary sense of the word. Human nature (the old Adam) reacts through compulsion and minimally, according to Luther, while the true Christian fulfills the golden rule voluntarily and wholeheartedly.[31]

How does Luther integrate talk of natural law with the Christian appeal to the cross? Ever primarily the theologian, Luther regards natural law as promulgated by God. In the light of his doctrine of the unity of the law, Luther interprets the golden rule in Jesus' teaching, not as new legislation, but as recovery of the original Adamic phase of law, which had been developed in the Ten Commandments of Moses and in the twofold commandment of love and in the Sermon on the Mount.[32] Moreover, eternal law gains content through the concrete situation, in which, as part of continuing creation, God continuously indicates his will in the heart.[33] The golden rule thus functions as a teaching that provides for the ongoing situational interpretation and application of the eternal law of love.

In his later teachings (1520–1525), according to Jorma Laulaja, Luther used the golden rule as the key to social, economic, and political life. As part of his criticism of the ascetic idealism at the heart of the monastic movement, Luther interpreted the golden rule as situating human beings in relationship and community—not in an isolated, unserviceable, cloistered existence. The mutuality of the rule points to social fulfillment, typically including family life. In the economic realm, the rule prohibits taking unfair advantage of others, and requires moderate living, since others are in need. Regarding politics, Luther found that the rule requires the individual to make utilitarian compromises for the good of the community. The golden rule requires that judges be impartial and interpret not legalistically but according to equity, recognizing exceptions and individual characteristics. Peaceful settlements are to be preferred, but judgment needs to be enforced in order to be effective.[34]

In a 1530 sermon, Luther returns to Matthew 7.12, taking the golden rule as a condensed sermon. Luther's discourse is free from anxiety about salvation. Real peace with God no longer requires as a precondition that the believer attain altruistic perfection, though it remains true that disobedience is punished and that the rule, applied with an honest conscience, can oppress and drive one to stop every form of wrongdoing. Luther's moral critique targets the inconsistency and unfairness of abusing women and of taking unfair advantage of others in one's economic endeavors. The rule does not address one's relationship with God but refers rather to "whatsoever you wish that men would do to you." It synopsizes the commandments that deal with human relationships and the myriad inferences that can be drawn from these commandments. Luther presents the rule as moral teaching, but now the emphasis is not on the strictness of its standard but rather on the easy accessibility of its clear and sufficient moral teaching.

Luther's sermon gives assurance that it is no longer necessary for a person to rely on legal books and moral experts to know what Jesus requires, since the hearer's sense of how he or she wants to be treated serves as a continuous fountain of teaching and preaching. The problem is that our environment and our old nature do not let us "ponder what He says and measure our lives against the standard of this teaching."

> I am convinced . . . that [the rule] would be influential and productive of fruit if we only got into the habit of remembering it and were not so lazy and inattentive. I do not regard anyone as so coarse or so evil that he would shirk this or be offended at it if he really kept it in mind. It was certainly clever of Christ to state it this way. The only example He sets up is ourselves, and He makes this as intimate as possible by applying it to our heart, our body and life, and all our members. No one has to travel far to get it, or devote much trouble or expense to it. The book is laid into your own bosom, and it is so clear that you do not need glasses to understand Moses and the Law. Thus you are your own Bible, your own teacher, your own theologian, and your own preacher.[35]

Luther thus ends on a word of generosity and hope.

CONCLUSION

Despite moments of peace such as Luther's 1530 sermon on the golden rule, a great divide was brought into the open by theological discussions of the importance of faith for moral practice. The practice of the golden rule could be an external affair or an inward experience. Outwardly described, the actions might be "the same," whether or not they were motivated by living faith. Inwardly, however, the actions could hardly be considered identical. Actions of faith express fruits of the spirit, qualities of character that are not the product of self-disciplined habit formation, but the reward of cooperation with the invisibly present God. Despite the difficulty of determining the motive for a given action, theologians affirmed the radical difference between the works of the flesh and the works of the spirit. The continuity of the golden rule as a common principle for believers and unbelievers was obscured.

A cosmopolitan philosophy of mind tried to mediate this divide. Since all human beings share a universal endowment of mind, the golden rule could function in moral theology and in political theology and philosophy to provide a medium in which ancient Greek and biblical traditions could blend; the rule would also be a minimal but effective ethic for promoting social order and welfare. But conflict between spirit and flesh would persist and would invade the space of mind that was envisioned as a neutral zone. In addition, religion was a focus for unregenerate material emotions. Before the end of the sixteenth century, religious inflexibility, intolerance, and war betrayed the hope that the golden rule would mediate the interactions of a divided humanity. A generous and positive religious understanding of human capacities would not come to prominence for centuries.

seven

Modern Objections and Responses

From the Religious to the Secular

For centuries the golden rule had enjoyed favor as a principle in both religious and philosophical ethics. The honeymoon ended as philosophers exercised their critical freedom to reformulate traditional teachings in a manner more satisfying to the requirements of reason. The drama of the golden rule during early modern European ethics was the emergence, in response to philosophical critique, of the three alternative responses: retaining and revisioning the rule, using critique to clarify its meaning; retaining the rule in some reformulated version; and rejecting the rule or replacing it with a newly constructed principle designed to capture everything of value in the rule and to avoid the rule's handicaps.

The stage was set by the outbreak of religious wars, international wars, and civil wars in Europe and by the response of Thomas Hobbes (1588–1679), who used the golden rule as a basic principle of a peaceful society. For Hobbes, human motivation is predominantly egoistic, and in a "state of nature" (prior to the establishment of government), which is a war of all against all, each person has a right to defend himself by any means whatsoever. But there is also an obligation to seek peace, to enter a "civil society," in which peace is secured and contracts enforced by a sovereign power with a monopoly on the use of force. In giving up unlimited individual sovereignty, what rights should the individual seek to retain in the social contract establishing the new order? One should "be contented with so much liberty against other men, as he would allow other men against himself," a principle that Hobbes equated with the golden rule.[1] Hobbes's frank portrayal of human self-interest and hostility anticipated the concern of social Darwinism about the validity of the golden rule during the earlier stages of sociomoral evolution. However, instead of a gradual evolution to the full flourishing of the golden rule, Hobbes proposed the rule as a mark of the radical transition from anarchy to order. His writings would arouse protests and stimulate further reflection on the golden rule.

THE RULE IN SEVENTEENTH-CENTURY ENGLISH
RELIGIOUS WRITING

Given the wealth of classical thought, scripture, philosophy, and theology relevant to the golden rule, it is not surprising that books should emerge on the topic. Four seventeenth-century Englishmen wrote such books and gave the golden rule its name.[2] The first of these, the only one I will discuss in detail, is a book-length treatise, *The Comprehensive Rule of Righteousness, Do as You Would Be Done By* (1679), written by "the Reverend Father in God William Lord Bishop of St. Davids" of the Church of England (Bishop William). The second is a 1683 sermon by George Boraston (born c. 1634) entitled *The Royal Law, or the Golden Rule of Justice and Charity*," printed in response to requests from hearers. Boraston defended the rule as showing the harmony of natural notions and revealed religion—against Hobbes's idea of the primitive human estate, and against the Deists' displacement of revealed religion.[3] The third is *The Golden Rule; or, The Royal Law of Equity Explained,* by John Goodman (1626?–1690).[4]

Each of these three books uses the term "golden rule," though none explains why the color gold was associated with the first principle of morality. Though we may speculate about conscious and unconscious associations—metallurgical, financial, racial, and otherwise—that may have influenced the choice of this word, the word "golden" unmistakeably connotes supreme value, especially when used with the definite article (the golden rule). According to the *Oxford English Dictionary,* the term "rule" denotes a concrete standard, such as a carpenter's tool, a "ruler, used to establish a straight edge and to measure length."[5] By extension, it also denotes a moral standard or pattern or criterion. A rule can also be a guideline for doing something. The term itself brings to mind legislation, control, dominion, government, sway, mastery, fixed custom or habit; and thus connotations of rigidity and formality cling to the term. In sum, the associations of the term *rule* emphasize the notion of standard, strict governance, and general principle. The fact that the title, "the golden rule" is consistently juxtaposed with the parallel title, "the royal law" suggests the pairing of "golden" with "royal," implying a certain power, a certain sovereignty in the rule, reflecting the sovereignty of Christ the King and of God as lawgiver. The logic of the metaphors yields the image of the golden rule as the crowning principle of morality.

Bishop William, remarking that our actions do need to be ruled, gave several reasons why different people consider the law of neighbor love (which he identifies with the golden rule) a royal law: it is the law of Christ our king; it is the law of God.

Like the King's highway, 'tis plain, without windings and turnings, rubs and hindrances, common to all, and belongs to everyone in particular as well as to all: The Royal Law, lastly, say others, because of its latitude and

extent, upon which all other Laws depend, which takes in and comprehends all other Laws in itself.[6]

Addressing the "Christian reader," William draws widely on the Bible, on
"heathen" and Christian authors in Greek and Latin, especially on writings
of Augustine, Chrysostom, and Erasmus. William gives a new twist to the
association of the golden rule with Greek Sophists: "It was the saying of
Protagoras, and repeated again by Plato [sic], that man is the measure of all
things. . . . God hath made him the measure of his own actions towards
others, and referred him to himself as the standard of his duty."[7] William
later explains that the true self-love which is implied in the human measure is inconsistent with sin and with the love of the body, "for 'tis the
mind, and soul, and spirit which is principally the man."[8]

The first section of the text settles down to an eleven-page argument
that the word "therefore" in Matthew 7.12 links the golden rule to the
previous verse, that God gives good gifts to those who ask. The golden
rule instructs us what we should bestow upon our neighbors, as we in
prayer hope to receive from God. Indeed, the rule refers not only to what
other men do to us, but also to what Christ and God do to us. In Luke,
"the Divine Pattern" for us is God's being merciful. "We should all study
then to be such our selves towards others, as we desire to find God to
ourselves."[9]

The occurrence of the rule in the writings of several classical authors
"suffices to show that this rule of our blessed Saviour's is a clear branch of
the law of nature," which everyone may read in his own heart and conscience, if it has not been defaced.[10] In the comprehensive rule of righteousness the negative version is included in the positive. "Whoever commands the doing of any good, forbids at the same time the neglect of that
good, and the evil opposite to it."[11]

The commandment of love for the neighbor is set forth as "the soul
and life" of the golden rule. The definition of love follows Aristotle's Rhetoric: "to will such things to another as we conceive good, without self-ends;
and to promote and do the same according to our power."[12] The golden
rule requires "a considerate change of persons; that is, we must suppose
other men in our condition, rank, and place, and our selves in theirs."[13]

The rule is distinguished from several other principles that are criticized, including "Do you unto others all things whatsoever they would
have done to them." "All things whatsoever ye will, do ye unto others" is
to be avoided, as an open invitation to license. Nor is the rule a principle
of retaliation; many biblical passages forbid human acts of vengeance. One
who executes justice must take care to function simply and properly as an
agent of the law.[14]

William offered what John Locke would later demand: considerations
that declare "the foundation and reasonableness" of the rule. In addition
to the preceding, general considerations, he proposes three additional

particular ones. "Fellow-brethren of one and the same Father," "bearing the same divine image," "joynt possessors of the same earth," "we are all made and preserved by the same God," who "fashioned [our] hearts alike, so that we may well conceive what others would desire."[15] William speaks of "the actual equality of all men by nature and of Christians by grace."[16]

The second consideration that declares "the foundation and reasonableness" of the rule is our actual and possible experiences of role reversals. William discreetly warns about possible reversals ("we are all liable to a variety of changes in the world"); he observes other reversals (the parent has been a child, and the child may be a parent); and he recommends additional actual reversals (we "may profitably exchange relations and conditions with other men").[17]

The third and last consideration that grounds the rule as a reasonable principle is that we reap what we sow, from men and from God.[18]

The golden rule for William is a means for cultivating virtue. "The purpose of the Rule [is] to prevent or remove [the undue bias of self-love and self-seeking] which makes us swerve and decline from the particular precepts of order, justice, and charity."[19] The rule is designed to block hypocrisy. The golden rule conduces to thoughtful living, taking time to think about how we would like to be treated, neither indulging rashness nor engaging in "brutish labor."[20] The rule, conduces to "a well-ordered and regulate will, a will following on the dictates of right reason and religion, and consequently only conversant about things truly good and meet to be done." He quotes Grotius, "That we do unto others such things as reason dictates we should not unjustly desire from others ourselves."[21]

The author goes on to claim that all virtues may be deduced from the rule. He produces an extended discussion of virtues and their correlated vices, describing each virtue enough to make it vivid that this is how we desire to be treated, and each vice enough to make it vivid that this is how we do not want to be treated. The first four virtues pertain to personal standards in the conduct of private relations: (1) sincerity, not hypocrisy; (2) humility, not pride; (3) innocence, not harming others or inducing them to sin; and (4) making amends for the wrong we have done, not slander, rudeness, or gossip. The next virtue becomes the occasion for discourse on a social and political ethic of obedience to superiors: (5) "respective obedience and submission to all our superiors."[22] William then returns to personal virtues: (6) positive acts of justice, and (7) acts of love and charity unto others, including pity, compassion, sympathy, and fellow feeling with the afflicted and distressed; rejoicing with them that rejoice; forgiving; being merciful; expressing goodwill; praying for others; and doing your best for the benefit of others. He concludes his "induction" by quoting Paul's "heap of Universals" (Phil. 4.8) about thinking on whatsoever things are true, honest, just, and so forth: "reason your selves into these things, and that from the premises already laid down."[23]

The *Comprehensive Rule of Righteousness, Do as You Would be Done By* thus provides careful historical review and biblical exegesis, undertakes elements of epistemological and logical analysis, gives a threefold demonstration of the foundation and reasonableness of the rule, and shows how a multitude of virtues follow from the practice of the rule.

EARLY QUESTIONINGS BY JOHN LOCKE AND GOTTFRIED WILHELM LEIBNIZ

The modern critique of the golden rule began with John Locke (1632–1704), who attacked the philosophy of mind associated with natural law ethics: for Locke, there are no innate ideas, that is, ideas implanted in the mind by God and obvious to everyone. For Locke, the mind is originally a blank slate (*tabula rasa*), determined by experience alone. His emerging empiricism did not sever his bond with classical philosophy, however, since he was still willing to say that "pain of search" would enable eternal truths to become self-evident to the mind. Regarding ethics, he claimed,

> There cannot any one moral rule be proposed whereof a man may not justly demand a reason. . . . Should that most unshaken rule of morality and foundation of all social virtue, "That one should do as he would be done unto," be proposed to one who never heard of it before, but yet is of capacity to understand its meaning; might he not without any absurdity ask a reason why? And were not he that proposed it bound to make out the truth and reasonableness of it to him? [I]f it were [innate] it could neither want nor receive any proof. . . . [T]he truth of all these moral rules plainly depends upon some other antecedent to them, and from which they must be deduced.[24]

The project of deducing the golden rule would not be taken up until the twentieth century. The problem of showing "the truth and reasonableness" of the rule would lead Kant and others to leave the original rule behind in favor of more sharply defined principles.

The question about the golden rule opened by Locke was widened by Gottfried Wilhelm Leibniz (1646–1716), who contributed to philosophy as an avocation while he engaged in diplomatic efforts (for example, to promote the reconciliation of Roman Catholic and Protestant Christianity). While insisting, against Locke, on the concept of innate truths within the mind, Leibniz agreed in the main with Locke's assessment that the golden rule does not stand on its own as a rational, self-evident principle. The rule stands in need of proof and elucidation. It is a "practical truth" that is recognized instinctively, though in a confused way. In order to gain a clear and vivid understanding, we need to derive it rationally. It takes but a single counterexample to lead Leibniz to a stunning conclusion. Then he offers his interpretation of the true meaning of the rule: "One would wish for too much, if one were the master; do we therefore owe too much to others? Someone will reply to me that the rule assumes [*s'entend*] a just will.

But then the rule, far from being sufficient to serve as a standard [mesure], will need a standard. The veritable sense of the rule is that by putting oneself in the place of the other one gains the true point of view for judging equitably."[25]

Leibniz thus finally brings into focus the question of whether the rule furnishes or presupposes a standard for right conduct. The Judeo-Christian tradition of regarding the law as "depending" on the golden rule had seemed to make the rule into a supreme principle from which all other particular laws are to be deduced. However, once the problem arises that persons who want others to gratify their base desires might use the golden rule to deduce unacceptable conclusions, it becomes clear that proposing the golden rule as a supreme moral principle presupposes that the agent's desires are acceptable—or would become so adjusted during the reflective process of applying the golden rule. Particular laws specify what is not to be desired or done. If the golden rule is put forth as a summary of those laws, it cannot function as the sole source for their derivation.

A RULE OF REASON AND ETERNAL RELATIONS: SAMUEL CLARKE

Samuel Clarke (1675–1729) gave the golden rule an important but limited and clarified place in religious ethics. Though he did not explicitly respond to Locke or Leibniz in his adaptation of the rule, his discussion shows a modern care for precision. Clarke's religious ethics manifests a sense of cosmic order. In quest of what is fitting, we should seek to grasp "the same necessary and eternal *different relations* [that direct] the will of God . . . to choose only what is agreeable to justice, equity, goodness, and truth, in order to the welfare of the whole universe."[26] Our actions should be "for the good of the public" as determined impartially, that is, by considerations "antecedent to any respect or regard, expectation or apprehension, of any *particular private and personal advantage or disadvantage, reward or punishment, either present or future.*"[27] Our duty, he says, is

> that in *particular* we so deal with every man, as in like circumstances we could reasonably expect he should deal with us; and that in *general* we endeavour, by an universal benevolence, to promote the welfare and happiness of all men. The former branch of this rule, is equity; the latter, is love.[28]

This passage distinguishes equity or fairness from benevolence or love and connects the golden rule with equity.

For Clarke, the golden rule is a principle of reason. "Iniquity is the very same in *action*, as *falsity* or *contradiction* in *theory*; and the same cause which makes the one *absurd*, makes the other *unreasonable*. Whatever relation or proportion one man in any case bears to another; the same that other, when put in like circumstances, bears to him." Then comes his oft-quoted formulation of the golden rule: "Whatever I judge reasonable or unreasonable for another to do for me; that, by the same judgement, I declare reasonable or unreasonable, that I in the like case should do for him." The passage goes on to apply the rule, first, to symmetrical relations: "Were not men strangely . . . corrupted . . . it would be impossible, that universal equity should not be practised by all mankind; and especially among *equals*, where the proportion of equity is simple and obvious." Finally, Clarke addresses relationships marked by social asymmetry:

> In considering indeed the duties of superiors and inferiors in various relations, the proportion of equity is somewhat more complex; but still it may always be deduced from the same rule of doing as we would be done by, if careful regard be had at the same time to the differences of relation: that is, if in considering what is fit for you to do to another, you always take into the account, not only every circumstance of the *action*, but also every circumstance wherein the *person* differs from you; and in judging what you would desire that another, if your circumstances were transposed, should do to you; you always consider, not what any unreasonable passion or private interest would prompt you, but what impartial reason would dictate to you to desire.

The preceding observation enables Clarke to handle a notorious counterexample by clarifying the sense of the rule:

> For example, a magistrate, in order to deal equitably with a criminal, is not to consider what *fear* or *self-love* would cause him, in the criminal's case, to desire; but what reason and the public good would oblige him to *acknowledge* was fit and just for him to *expect*. And the same proportion is to be observed, in deducing the duties of parents and children, of masters and servants, of governors and subjects, of citizens and foreigners.[29]

For Clarke, then, the attempt to use the golden rule to discover what is fit by the standard of eternal relations and the good of the universe leads to a rational and empirical inquiry, a commitment to equity requiring wise and impartial judgment, grounded in a sensitive appreciation of the circumstantial details of the particular relationship at hand.

THE RULE REPLACED BY PRINCIPLES OF REASON: IMMANUEL KANT

Immanuel Kant (1724–1804) was reared in a pietistic atmosphere and worked for decades within the framework of traditional philosophy until David Hume's skeptical writings roused him, as he said, from his "dogmatic slumber."[30] Kant rejected not only theological ethics, however, but also the new empirical ethics of feeling; and he set forth morality as primarily an affair of rationally chosen universal principles, not desires, not even well-regulated or benevolent desires.[31] If Kant's ideas are correct,

both the golden rule (in its original formulation) and its religious foundation are obsolete.

He proposed three rational principles as formulations of one supreme
moral principle, "the categorical imperative" (unconditional command).
The first principle is that one should act only on principles that one can
rationally will for everyone to act on ("Act only according to that maxim
whereby you can at the same time will that it should become a universal
law).[32] The second principle affirms a certain respect for humanity: "Act
in such a way that you treat humanity, whether in your own person or in
the person of another, always at the same time as an end and never simply
as a means."[33] The third principle invites the agent to imagine himself as
a citizen of and legislator for a conceivable advanced civilization, a worldwide, even a universal community of truly moral agents; this principle
voices "the idea of the will of every rational being as a will that legislates
universal laws," that is, laws for a union ("kingdom") of all rational
beings.[34]

Kant's categorical imperative differs from the golden rule in at least
three ways. First, the categorical imperative focuses on principles of the
will rather than on actions we want to have done to us or on how we
want to be treated. Next, it focuses explicitly on the logical generality of
our decisions, on maxims or rules for action. Third, it focuses on a rational
criterion for judging those rules.[35] Not what you want, but what you rationally judge to be an appropriate universal law is the standard of duty.

To replace religious reasons for treating others well, Kant offered a
demonstration of the duty of respect for persons using a kind of golden
rule argument—deducing a duty toward others based on a major premise
expressing an insight I have about myself and a minor premise that others
are similar to myself:

> Rational nature exists as an end in itself. In this way man necessarily
> thinks of his own existence; thus far is it a subjective principle of human
> actions. But in this way also does every other rational being think of his
> existence on the same rational ground that holds also for me, hence it is
> at the same time an objective principle.[36]

What Kant does achieve here, in continuity with Stoic thought, is to affirm
the dignity of persons as free, rational agents capable of acting on principle. Kant furthermore correctly discerns that prereligious reason can
achieve that recognition of human dignity. Kant holds that each person
has moral reason, the capacity to act in accord with self-validated moral
law. Each rational being is to think for himself or herself and to exercise
self-determination—not to let external authorities or emotions determine
one's decisions and actions. The point is not that one is forbidden to get
ideas from others, or that emotions are evil, but that one must not act on
such ideas or motives unthinkingly. Only those maxims that reason has
validated are consistent with our functioning as autonomous agents. One

may never treat any person merely as a means to the happiness of oneself or society.

For the purpose of a later contrast between Kant's doctrine of universal rational laws and certain concepts of consistency in contemporary ethics, it is important to emphasize the meaning of rational consistency in Kant. The consistency of the putative sadomasochist or of a fanatical Nazi who is willing to be persecuted if he should be proved a Jew hardly satisfies Kant's requirement. The dignity of each free, rational, moral agent is such that everyone can determine his or her action on principle, rather than on the desires and fears that prevail on the level of material emotions, which are causally intertwined with the brain and its natural environment.

In the course of his discussion of respect for persons in the *Grounding of the Metaphysics of Morals*, Kant attached a notorious footnote criticizing the golden rule. He gives several reasons why the conventionally formulated rule cannot be the supreme principle of morality:

> Let it not be thought that the trivial *Quod tibi non vis fieri*, etc. [what you do not will to be done to you] can here serve as a standard or principle. For it is merely derived from our principle, although with several limitations. It cannot be a universal law, for it contains the ground neither of duties to oneself nor of duties of love toward others (for many a man would gladly consent that others should not benefit him, if only he might be excused from benefiting them). Nor, finally, does it contain the ground of strict duties toward others, for the criminal would on this ground be able to dispute with the judges who punish him; and so on.[37]

By referring to the golden rule in a footnote, by quoting it in Latin, by citing the rule in its negative formulation, and by using only a fragment of it, Kant minimized the clash with religious and political authorities. His critique is nevertheless thoroughgoing, and it touches the biblical formulations as well.

According to Kant, the golden rule cannot be a supreme moral principle, first, because the golden rule is *derived* from the perfectly general principle, the categorical imperative. This point refers to the scope of the duties implied by the rule. The categorical imperative pertains to laws of how everyone should treat everyone (including themselves), whereas the golden rule apparently pertains only to the way agents should treat their recipients.

The golden rule, moreover, is *incomplete*. A supreme moral principle would have to be one from which every type of duty can be derived. The simplest of Kant's objections is that the golden rule does not cover the category of duties to oneself, for example, the duty to cultivate one's potentials toward perfection or to respect oneself in one's actions.

Kant claimed that the golden rule gives no (adequate) ground for benevolence, since a person unwilling to do good to others could simply agree that he not be a beneficiary. This seems hasty, since everyone has, at least during early childhood, been the beneficiary of another's care, and it would be odd to interpret the golden rule so as to rule out the extension "We should treat others as we are grateful to have been treated." Nor does Kant's philanthropically lazy man follow the line of thinking suggested by a gradual unpacking of the golden rule, which would engage the man in considering, first, how he wants to be treated. The golden rule does not invite the agent to set up a negotiating situation. The lazy man plausibly does want to others to do good to him when his need for others' care becomes urgent.

Kant, unaware of Clarke's rejoinder, implied that if a judge were to follow the golden rule in sentencing criminals, it would lead to unjust leniency.[38] If the golden rule makes morality depend upon what the agent imagines he *would want* if he were in the other's situation, Kant insisted that morality depends rather on what the agent rationally *does judge* to be right (e.g., to punish the criminal). The very concept of moral duty, which all recognize, implies that duty is distinct from what one feels like doing, or from what one wants others to do to oneself. Not desire, but principled thinking determines what is right.

THE RULE AS THE SPIRIT OF UTILITARIANISM: JOHN STUART MILL

The reformist philosopher and legislator John Stuart Mill (1806–1873) defined right action in terms of the greatest good for the greatest number of those affected by the action; he further defined good in terms of happiness and happiness in terms of pleasure. Since the golden rule speaks of what the agent wants, it was easy for Mill to embrace:

> As between his own happiness and that of others, utilitarianism requires him to be as strictly impartial as a disinterested and benevolent spectator. In the golden rule of Jesus of Nazareth, we read the complete spirit of the ethics of utility. To do as one would be done by, and to love one's neighbour as oneself, constitute the ideal perfection of utilitarian morality.[39]

Mill does not here imply any religious conviction of his own. Whereas Kant had put his religious beliefs in the background when articulating his categorical imperative, Mill perhaps had no such background beliefs. Instead, his conviction was that religious beliefs, taken at their best, lead to a morality that converges with utilitarianism.

CONCLUSION

Regarding the golden rule, thinkers had three options. Like Bishop William, they could retain the rule as a general, "supreme" principle and let theoretical progress serve to enrich the conception of rule. Like Clarke, they could reformulate the rule as one important specific principle among others. Or they could criticize the rule—taken literally, in a traditional formulation, and in abstraction—as a poor candidate for membership in the club of principles as certified by current professional ethical discourse. The more influential philosophers of the Enlightenment followed the last path. By the end of this period, the golden rule, no longer something to cling to literally, would find some of its earlier meanings overshadowed as new philosophical interpretations advanced into prominence. Just as theocrats had tolerated unbelievers in the state, so long as they managed to live in conformity to common moral standards, so secularists would tolerate believers, so long as they managed the same.

Problems in several of the texts discussed here require comment. Bishop William, Boraston, and Goodman all understood the golden rule partly in terms of a pattern (or paradigm or standard or measure) in two senses whose tension never attracted comment. For Boraston and Goodman, the pattern for how we should treat others is, on the one hand, the way God treats people, on the other hand, what we desire for ourselves. To affirm the first sense implies that we know to a significant extent what God does to us and for us; it also implies that we welcome God's deeds. From a religious perspective, in the happy case, these conditions are satisfied. Pattern in the second sense, what we desire for ourselves, only harmonizes with pattern in the first sense if our desires are God-given and undistorted by selfishness. However, if the golden rule is needed as a guide for moral reflection, its mission may be in a particular case to balance one's concern for self and other so that one's own desires become moderated to fairness. The golden rule, then, is charitably understood not as exalting one's own desires as a pattern for conduct. It achieves its goal partly by serving as a reminder that others are extensively like oneself in how they want to be treated, and partly by engaging the agent with the genuine pattern, divine personality.

Next, Kant was not altogether content with simply affirming human dignity as an axiom, and his proof of human dignity may be challenged on three counts. First, the fact that I respect myself and the fact that you respect yourself do not, taken together, prove that I should respect you, even on the stipulation that we each have the same ground for our self-respect; since only by begging the question, by stipulating that the ground in question amounts to a rational foundation for self-respect, will the conclusion follow. Second, not everyone regards himself or herself with the superb self-respect implied in the premise of his argument; it would beg the question to reply that feelings of low self-esteem are be merely emotions, not the voice of reason to which each of us has access. Third, an affirmation of human dignity in terms of rationality tends to collapse to a weaker pair of affirmations: (1) all persons have the estimable *capacity* for reason, and (2) someone who lives in accord with reason, however rare such a civilized individual may be, is *actually* worthy of esteem.[40] Since it is always possible to doubt whether a particular action has been genuinely morally motivated, there is nothing that reason can certify as *actual* in any human being which gives grounds for respect.[41]

Finally, if taken merely as a principle of sympathy, the golden rule might raise worries about a vulgar utilitarianism, which would justify slavery as long as a small enough number of slaves were kept from suffering too much and as long as enough people were sufficiently pleased by the arrangement. Such an arrangement, however, intuitively violates the golden rule, since a self-respecting person does not want to be sacrificed for the gratification of a hypothetical multitude, and so would reject any interpretation of the golden rule that might require such sacrifice. Utilitarianism lacked a developed philosophy of the agent, but clearly the more profound the dignity ascribed to the individual, the stronger the bulwark against vulgar utilitarianism will be.

Aspiring to articulate a conception of the golden rule by finding consistency in various perspectives from Western theology, philosophy, and psychology, a mid-nineteenth-century optimist might have proposed the following synthesis. The golden rule is a revealed principle, appropriated in love of the neighbor, which acquires new meaning through contact with reason and is reflected in the normal operation of human sentiment (no matter what religious beliefs may or may not be associated with it in the mind of the agent). However, it would have been impossible to win agreement for such a synthesis, since the standards implied by various conceptions of the golden rule and its successor principles differed so widely. These standards ranged from human desires, to sentiments informed by keen judgment about human affairs, to rational standards separate from feeling and religious authority, to the paradigm of divine action and the eternal patterns chosen by the divine will. Unanimity prevailed only on the idea that the morality of the golden rule includes all humankind as its beneficiaries. Dispute continued, of course, about what it means to be a human being and about what kinds of experience are required to fulfill human moral potentials. A pessimist would have regarded the golden rule as a porous basket preserving the facade of an odd and merely formal unity among the disputants.

Indeed, the consensus fell asunder. A concept of morality based upon a continually updated synthesis of science, philosophy, and religion—pioneered by Philo and Augustine and Aquinas—was eclipsed during the Reformation and the Enlightenment. Religion would pull apart from science. Science, in modern psychology, would pull apart from religion and philosophy. Philosophy would pull apart from religion and science. An apparent counterexample, Hegel's synthesis of science, philosophy, and religion, would truncate religion and submerge the golden rule in the context of a ethic of social, corporate, and political organizations; Hegel compromised the golden rule's moral universality in order to avoid its postnationalist political implications. Nietzsche would then denounce the religious ethic of service as weak and submissive and animated by the very will to power that this ethic aspired to transcend. In the coming chapters, I indicate that contemporary scientists, philosophers, and religious thinkers, functioning separately, tend to make up tacitly for the grand synthesis they had apparently left behind. How could anyone write about morality without making assumptions and assertions, empirical, philosophical, and religious (or antireligious)? And how can the full, vital spectrum of meanings in the golden rule be rehabilitated without a team effort to synthesize threads of science, philosophy, and religion?

eight

The Golden Rule of the Fatherhood of God and the Brotherhood of Man

The late nineteenth and early twentieth centuries in America were times of great economic expansion and inequality, opportunity and abuse, times of American power and of world war. Early scientific doctrines of evolution were being used to gain understanding of the human species and social life, and the result was a profound challenge to traditional religion. Does religion render a person less fit for the rigors of competition, or does real religion empower a person to deal in a progressive way with those very challenges? As that debate went on, America was a center of a dynamic, religiously motivated golden rule movement, affecting society, politics, economics, business, and interfaith relations. Many enthusiastic individuals chose the rule as their motto; a popular literature on the rule arose; many a store was called "Golden Rule Store"; it was the custom to bestow on exemplars of the rule the nickname "Golden Rule." Authors expounding the maxims for the exercise of a given craft would dub their principles "golden rules," and many books carried titles such as *Golden Rules of Surgery*. A Golden Rule Brotherhood was formed with the intention of unifying all the religions and peoples of the world. During this period the golden rule came to symbolize a wholehearted devotion to the service of humankind.

This movement, which spread beyond the boundaries of Christianity, held the conviction that all men and women are brothers and sisters in the family of God, and they formulated the essentials of religion in the gospel of the fatherhood of God and the brotherhood of man. The phrase "brotherhood of man" was used to include, not exclude women. Since the struggle to synthesize religious idealism with scientific realism had become especially urgent, the golden rule became caught up in the debate.[1] Does living by the rule render the individual needlessly vulnerable to rugged, evolutionary competition and conflict, or is the rule itself a vehicle of evolutionary progress?

There had been a growing sense that each individual is akin to every other human being. The fabric of humanity had been torn by religious

wars between Christians and Muslims during the Middle Ages and between Protestants and Catholics during the early modern period. Europe-
ans disgusted with the slaughter turned toward tolerance, especially since
it was clear that professing a religion was no guarantee of morality and
that some atheists lived highly moral lives. In the eighteenth century,
Hume had proclaimed that every person has a spark of benevolent sentiment toward humanity, and Kant and others attempted to distill universally acceptable basics of religion and morality. In the nineteenth century,
at all levels of culture, religious and secular humanitarianism flourished.
Beethoven's Ninth Symphony used Schiller's "Ode to Joy," which reads,
in translation: "Joy, beautiful divine spark, . . . your magic binds together
what convention had strictly divided; all men become brothers where
your gentle wing rests." Leo Tolstoy (1828–1910) abandoned the life of a
Russian nobleman and the privileges of literary success for a life in some
ways like that of a peasant. He defined art in terms of its capacity to arouse
the feeling of the fatherhood of God and the brotherhood of man.[2] His
radical application of the Sermon on the Mount and his critique of luxury
and oppression stimulated the idealism of many others throughout the
world.

Among German theologians, Albrecht Ritschl (1822–1889) drew on
Kant for a conception of the kingdom of heaven as the organization of
humanity through moral action inspired by love;[3] Ritschl's influential student Adolf Harnack (1851–1930) used historical study with the aim of sep-
arating the kernel of original Christianity from the husk of associated
Greek philosophic dogma. Painstaking scholarship enabled Harnack
boldly to read between the lines of the New Testament text and to discover afresh Jesus' persistent tendency to speak of religion in terms of
family life. He presented the teachings of Jesus as, in sum, the fatherhood
of God, the brotherhood of man, and the infinite value of the individual
soul. With this conception of religion, the golden rule would find new
meaning and historical vitality.[4] In interreligious relations, the new conception of religion reached an historic high-water mark at the World's
Parliament of Religions, organized in Chicago in 1893 by Presbyterian minister Dr. John Henry Barrows in conjunction with the Columbian Exposition. It is not surprising that the most frequently mentioned principle of
morality at the parliament was the golden rule.[5] Praise for the rule came
from representatives of Confucianism, Judaism, and Christianity.[6] The
golden rule was perhaps the most widely shared commitment among all
the religions; and it came to symbolize the participants' commitment to
live the warm brotherly and sisterly unity that most of them had experienced together during their days of the parliament.

It is remarkable how many functions are performed by the combined
concepts of the fatherhood of God and the brotherhood of man. The
teaching implies the unity and personality of God. The concept of God as
parent preserves the thought that God transcends the believer yet suggests

that God is close, that we may experience the divine presence. The sequence of components in the slogan implies the primacy of the relationship of the individual with God. The phrasing excludes no religion, yet connotes the special emphasis given in Jewish and Christian thought. The brotherhood of man is the social consequence of the individual's relationship with the Creator. Talk of brotherhood addresses the special challenges of modernity, to dissolve the forces that tear the fabric of humankind: religious intolerance, nationalism, racism, sexism, economic and political injustice, and so on. And "the fatherhood of God and the brotherhood of man" sets forth those components of religion with the universal logic of family life.

The emerging movement of the golden rule was nourished by a romantic and democratic mood. Despite its capacity for purely nationalistic applications, the new mood did exalt the common man and the worthy sentiments of the human heart. Nineteenth-century America showed widespread tendencies toward belief in equality, an impatience with traditional social authority and with confining rules and regulations, confidence about the place of man within a vast universe, optimism about the human capacity for moral growth, a distaste for sophisticated theories, and a readiness of Everyman to be his own philosopher.[7] Appropriately, the golden rule champions of this era do not come from the ranks of philosophers and theologians; they are ministers, politicians, and businessmen.

THE GOLDEN RULE IN DOCTRINES OF SOCIAL EVOLUTION: HERBERT SPENCER

The golden rule ethic of brotherhood had to compete with a concept of evolution that was coming to occupy the center stage of scientific thinking, not only in biology, but also in economics and sociology. Proponents of the rule contrasted it with "the rule of gold," and loyalty to the golden rule implied a protest against the doctrine that social progress comes mainly through ruthless competition in the struggle for survival. Nevertheless, insofar as evolution was understood to involve the gradual mastery of competitive forces by moral motives, the golden rule could be regarded as a symbol of the social order that would one day prevail.

Herbert Spencer (1820–1903) was the leading theorist of social Darwinism, which applied an evolutionary biological model to society and history. Almost entirely self-educated, Spencer was perhaps the most influential writer in English in the late nineteenth century. He is best known for the doctrine that government should permit business competition to weed out inferior companies; the "survival of the fittest" will result in long-term benefit for all. Spencer also wanted the poor and the sick to be weeded out.

Spencer's vision of evolving civilization provided for the simultaneous growth and eventual harmonization of egoism and altruism (defined as "all action which, in the normal course of things, benefits others instead of benefiting self").[8] Egoism functions as a competitive principle for a being that needs to live if it is to do anything else at all, and also as a principle of recreation, a provision for gaining and sustaining a hearty zest (which the sickly Spencer sorely lacked), resulting in a life "brimming with energy," on "the rising tide of life," "radiating good cheer." "The adequately egoistic individual retains those powers which make altruistic activities possible."[9] In society, it is of course rational to practice altruism to some extent. As the need diminishes for conflict, which weeds out those incapable of advancing civilization, an altruistic age would evolve. But the extremes of altruism and egoism would disappear; a "more qualified altruism" would balance "a greatly moderated egoism."[10]

Consistent, presumably, with the evolutionary use of the golden rule, was the rhetoric and practice of John Hay (1838–1905), secretary to President Abraham Lincoln, and secretary of state to Presidents McKinley and Theodore Roosevelt. His aim was to use the golden rule to moderate the exercise of American diplomatic power, and he seems to have had some success in his efforts. A rhetorician and statesman in the tradition of the Greek Sophist Isocrates, he once summed up his approach to foreign policy in two phrases: the Monroe Doctrine and the golden rule.[11]

The increasing brutality of economic power in the late nineteenth century and the inroads against religion made by positivists and agnostics led to various religious responses.[12] One author predicted a moral interregnum—a time of moral chaos intervening between the fall of the morality of one age and the rise of a different social order.[13] One response to the intolerable aspects of the time was to minimize one's involvement with the cultural changes, either through defensiveness or by adhering to the older ways that continued to suffice in rural settings. Another response was the development of "social Christianity" in the form of increased involvement in various projects of charity, or in agitation either for reform aimed at the evils of urban life or for radical socialist reconstruction. The preaching of the social gospel of Washington Gladden (1836–1918), Lyman Abbot (1835–1922), George Herron (1862–1925), J. E. Scott (1836–1917), Walter Rauschenbusch (1860–1918), and others aimed to make explicit the social, economic, and political implications of the fatherhood of God and the brotherhood of man. Opinions varied, of course, regarding what sort of economic change the rule required.[14] Some regarded state socialism as the obvious requirement of the rule, but most dissented from the doctrines of Karl Marx, since they neither accepted class conflict nor revolutionary methods in pursuing their goals.

THE GOLDEN RULE BROTHERHOOD

It is not enough, of course, to have speeches about religious unity and humane conduct. One must actually do something. Civilization must be transformed. On March 26, 1901, a meeting was held in Calvary Baptist Church in New York City to inaugurate the Golden Rule Brotherhood. The meeting was held under the auspices of its predecessor organization, the Baron and Baroness de Hirsch Monument Association, which had been founded by George E. Bissell, a New York sculptor. Recognizing philanthropists Baron and Baroness de Hirsch as Jewish examples of the best Christian virtues, Bissell proposed to construct a symbol of the golden rule, dedicated to them, in Central Park, "where a commanding site has been assigned to it."[15] The first project of the new Golden Rule Brotherhood would be to complete this monument, but that was only one of their goals. They envisioned the time was ripe for their organization to bring about the ecumenical unification of Christianity, harmony between Judaism and Christianity, and eventually the unity of humankind.

Some organizations languish, it appears, for lack of powerful connections. The Monument Association was not one of these. Its president was a former postmaster general of the United States. Vice presidents of the association included former U.S. president Grover Cleveland and the president of Columbia University. Directors included Theodore Roosevelt, John Hay, and the presidents of Harvard, Princeton, and Johns Hopkins Universities. Alfred Dreyfus, Mark Twain, and Mary Baker Eddy had written letters of commendation for the association. It was not the sort of association one could turn down. The meeting to inaugurate the brotherhood opened with the reading of letters from President William McKinley and vice president Theodore Roosevelt. One person recalled the story of a United States senator who was defeated for reelection for having expressed the opinion that "the hope of the dominance of the Ten Commandments and the Golden Rule in American politics, was an iridescent dream impossible of realization."[16]

The narrator of these events, the secretary of the Golden Rule Brotherhood, was Theodore F. Seward. At the World's Parliament of Religions, Seward had gathered twenty-one members for a new organization, the Brotherhood of Christian Unity, to perpetuate the spirit of unity of the parliament and to "begin the federation of the new world" on the basis of "the declaration of love to God and man under the leadership of Christ."[17] Seward wrote that the inaugural meeting of the brotherhood "was felt by all who were present to be one of the most important and significant occasions that the world has seen."[18] It was an interfaith gathering, with speeches from Jewish, Confucian, and (mostly) Christian perspectives. One minister expressed the common feeling: "We have all been on a Holy Mountain tonight. We have been transfigured as we have each looked upon our different leaders and teachers, and perceived in them a greater still, the God of Love, the Universal Father."[19]

In addition to the monument to be placed in Central Park, the formally constituted Golden Rule Brotherhood of Man projected a variety of activities, including instituting Golden Rule Days during the year in churches, synagogues, and schools; working for the humane treatment of animals; and providing a membership card and a badge—a one-inch ruler, marked off in tenths, with "Golden Rule" written on it.

A map of the statues and monuments in Central Park indicates nothing that could be a monument to Baron and Baroness de Hirsch. Rather, one discovers the story of the energy with which the management of the park had to fight off the multitude of "benevolent" organizations that wanted to contribute their statue or monument to the park.[20] There is no evidence of the continued function of the Golden Rule Brotherhood after the adoption of their constitution.

What happened? The influential supporters of the earlier Monument Association may well have been embarrassed by the naive ambitions of the successor organization. In addition, participants fell into the temptation to attribute to their slogan the dynamic qualities of the persons who best exemplify it. During the March 26 inaugural meeting, one minister had claimed, "This motto will secure the safety and protection of the humblest citizen."[21] The golden rule had become a fetish. Another clue to the organization's failure comes from Rabbi Joseph Silverman's remarks during their inaugural meeting. He explained that religion had failed for thirty-five centuries to unite man. Atheism had tried "on other bases— upon ethics, philosophy, science, art, literature." But culture emphasizes inequalities. The work of impassioned reformers led so often to violence. Failures were based on two false premises: "First, that the universal brotherhood did not exist, that it had to be created by human effort; secondly, that the solution of the problem consisted in the formation of a universal church or ideal social state."[22]

THE RULE APPLIED WITH CHARISMA AND POLITICAL POWER: SAMUEL JONES

One of those who earned the coveted nickname was Samuel Milton ("Golden Rule") Jones (1846–1904). Born in Wales, he came to the United States at the age of three, and worked hard from the age of ten. Those who most influenced his thinking were Leo Tolstoy, Walt Whitman, and Congregational minister George Herron. Brotherhood would be the leading theme of Jones's life after he discovered Herron's teaching that the phrase "Our Father" implied that all men are brothers.[23] Along with Walt Whitman, he wanted the nation to be "a land of comrades," indeed a family—not on a disciplinarian model but in "the all-for-one, one-for-all spirit."[24] Working as an oil well pumper, he invented a superior method of pumping oil and, on the basis of his inventions, founded the Acme Sucker Rod Company in Toledo, Ohio. Touched and outraged by the pitiable condition of the unemployed begging for work, he dedicated his own company to the practice of the golden rule.

Those seeking employment were not questioned about their religion, morals, or habits, and did not have to submit to a physical examination. This action tended to facilitate the complexity of personnel problems since no effort was made to hire the most reliable or trustworthy applicants. Nevertheless, discipline was established on the cooperative principle. . . . With his sister Ellen, he established Golden Rule House, a community center, and incorporated a free kindergarten.[25]

Jones wanted to make factory conditions so "attractive and beautiful to men as to lead them to live beautiful lives."[26] He established a Golden Rule Park next to his factory and opened it to the public. Well-known lecturers addressed the public there, including Jane Addams of Hull House, Dr. Kellogg of Battle Creek, Michigan, and social gospel preacher Washington Gladden. Jones was radically committed to an open forum at which all ideas could be expressed. The platform was open to agnostics and atheists and radicals of every sort, and the park became the social and intellectual center of town.

Jones, along with his closest friend, Nelson O. Nelson, aspired to the radical courage to live the teachings of the Sermon on the Mount according to the utopian, agrarian model of Tolstoy. Said Jones, "We must all understand the gospel of DO. I know well enough how to practice the Golden Rule; the difficulty comes in my unwillingness to do it entirely, with my half-way doing it."[27] But he found himself increasingly engaged in business and city politics. In 1897, "Golden Rule" Jones was elected mayor of Toledo (chosen to run by the Republicans after many ballots). He was reelected as an independent in 1899, ran for governor and lost, was returned as mayor again in 1901, and died during his fourth term in office in 1904. Jones engaged in many hard political fights along his path of reform. His major issues were "(1) insistence on non-partisanship; (2) home rule; and (3) the campaign to bring the public utilities and street car company under strict public control."[28] He achieved brief national prominence, but like Whitman, he rejected accepted notions of decency and conformity. He replaced the policemen's clubs with lighter canes and insisted they function helpfully, not aggressively; his enforcement of the law was criticized for laxness.[29] "Golden Rule" Jones fell far short of bringing his dreams to reality.

> In legislative matters . . . Jones was a failure because of insurmountable political constraints. His reform measures were deeply hindered by State eminence, powerful pressure groups, and his own non-partisanship. Even if such variables had not interfered, Jones might have had difficulty in implementing his cooperative commonwealth since he had not previously drawn a clear distinction between free enterprise and public ownership. Also his limited knowledge of economics would have caused a breakdown in the transition from a competitive to a cooperative state.[30]

Nevertheless, Jones was regarded as the champion among the Christian social reformers of his day for his personal forcefulness, courageous spontaneity, and for making a real difference within the tumultuous realm of industry and politics.

FROM RELIGIOUS ETHICS TO BUSINESS ETHICS: ARTHUR NASH

Two sides of the American golden rule movement are represented by Arthur Nash (1870–1927) and J. C. Penney (1875–1971) respectively. Each wrote an autobiography from the perspective of a successful Christian business leader offering advice concerning the practical, moral, and spiritual principles of living that had proven themselves through years of personal experience in the competitive arena.[31] Nash, whose story is recounted here in more detail, participated in the social drama of urban Christianity during the years surrounding World War I, and his application of the rule is religiously motivated from the start. Penney, by contrast, was a traditional, rural and small-town man who followed the golden rule as a moral principle and achieved success in business without religious motivation until his evangelical conversion later in life.

Is religion a sphere apart from business activity, or should there not be continuity between one's religion and the way one conducts one's business? As a bridge of continuity between religion and business was being built by those whose primary motivation was religious, it was found that the bridge could be traversed by others whose primary motivation was economic. In some cases, the intertwining of religious and business ideas resulted in an ambiguity that has lent itself to cynical interpretation. If Jesus could be popularly portrayed as the greatest advertiser and salesman in history in Bruce Barton's 1924 bestseller *The Man Nobody Knows*, business writers could also promote religion as a tonic that would inspire an individual to conduct relationships in a way that should conduce to prosperity. Many unwitting secularists painted a veneer of religious idealism on their enterprises.

Although Arthur Nash had some tendency to let the rise and fall of his business affect his confidence in the evident, practical worth of religious principles, he remains one of the most sincere of the exponents of the golden rule as the guide to business relationships. Nash was born in a log cabin in Indiana in 1870, the eldest of nine children of strict Seventh-Day Adventist parents. He referred to his parents as having a "stern, rigid, uncompromising" faith and "great and sterling character."[32] He was educated in Adventist schools and seminary and was sent to Detroit as an instructor in a school for Adventist ministers and missionaries. His refusal to conform to denominational boundaries led to conflict and the first of his two breaks with Christianity.[33] He left Detroit and did not return for years. When he did, however, he was touched by the plight of the unemployed there, and with the help of others was able to open a laundry in which he was able to provide many jobs for poor people. Church people began to send him their business, and he met the Christian woman who

would be his wife and the mother of his three children, and who convinced him that his objections to Christianity were not to the religion of
Jesus but to the very lack of it. Inspired again, he reentered the ministry
with the Disciples of Christ. But when in a funeral service he eulogized a
man of considerable character who had no professed religion, he was
asked to resign his ministry. He then found work to support his family
selling clothing—and did very well at it. In 1909 he moved to Columbus,
Ohio, started manufacturing men's clothing, began to prosper, but lost
nearly everything in the flood of 1913. He then moved to Cincinnati and
was able to organize the A. Nash Company in 1916 with sixty thousand
dollars in capital, making made-to-order suits for individual clients. A
short while after the Armistice was concluded, he acquired ownership of
the small shop that had been making his garments under contract.

Then came the breakthrough, the pivot of this narrative. Nash took
over the limping business of a man who had leased floor space in the
building of the A. Nash Company. The tenant had run a sweatshop in the
depressed clothing manufacturing industry of Cincinnati. When payroll
time for his new employees came around, Nash realized that some fine
and vulnerable people were only earning four dollars per week. He had
recently become impressed with the kind of world that could result if
people would only practice the golden rule, and he had been giving
speeches to that effect. He thought of raising wages substantially, but his
son, freshly disillusioned from having participated in the war in Europe,
resisted the idea. They had lost four thousand dollars during the previous
fiscal year, but Nash decided he would close up shop rather than exploit
people to stay in the clothing business. The stockholders agreed to close
the company, and Nash agreed to make up their losses, but he decided
to pay a living wage until they went out of business; he would put whatever capital remained as a down payment on a farm where he would at
least have the satisfaction of honest earnings. He went in to announce
the decision to the small group of workers. The speech is worth quoting
in full:

"Friends, you have heard no doubt that we have bought this shop, and I
have come in to get acquainted with you. No doubt, too, you have heard
a great deal about the talks that I have been giving during the War about
Brotherhood and the Golden Rule, while pleading the cause of Christianity and its affiliation to my conception of true Democracy. Now I am
going to do a bit of talking to you. First, I want you to know that Brotherhood is a reality with me. You are all my brothers and sisters, children of
the same great Father that I am, and entitled to all the justice and fair
treatment that I want for myself. And so long as we run this shop [which
to me meant three or four months longer], God being my helper, I am
going to treat you as my brothers and sisters, and the Golden Rule is
going to be our only governing law. Which means, that whatever I would
like to have you do to me, were I in your place, I am going to do to you.

Now," I went on, "not knowing any of you personally, I would like you to raise your hands as I call your names."

I read the first name. Under it was written: Sewing on buttons—$4.00 per week. I looked straight before me at the little group, but saw no hand. Then I looked to my right, and there saw the old lady I have referred to holding up her trembling hand. At first I could not speak, because, almost instantly, the face of my own mother came between that old lady and myself. I thought of my mother being in such a situation, and of what, in the circumstances, I would want someone to do for her. I hardly knew what to say, because I was aware that when I went into the shop, that after agreeing to stand all of the loss entailed by the liquidation of the company, I could not go too far in raising wages. It seemed to be my obvious duty to salvage something for the boys who were coming home from military service, and for the daughter just entering the university. But as I looked at that old lady, and saw only my mother, I finally blurted out: "I don't know what it's worth to sew on buttons; I never sewed a button on. But your wages, to begin with, will be $12.00 a week."[34]

Nash continued through the list, giving equal 300 percent raises for those earning the least, and raising the highest wages from eighteen to twenty-seven dollars. It was not a move made out of ecstasy, but in blunt lucidity about what it would subtract from the money he would have to invest afterward in a farm. For months thereafter he gave little attention to the clothing business, but when he needed to see how it was doing financially, he was surprised: their little business was putting out three times the quantity it had done the previous year. He then learned that after his little speech the Italian presser had concluded that if he were the boss and had just spoken like that to his employees and raised their wages, he would want his employees to "work like hell." And that is exactly what they did. Soon the shop had more orders than it could handle. Encouraged, Nash turned his business into a laboratory for the application of the golden rule, and the business prospered greatly.[35]

Nash's leadership with the golden rule led to many changes in his business.[36] He proposed a profit-sharing plan; the workers chose to take their benefits in the form of higher wages. By 1923 the workers owned nearly half of the company stock. The best-paid employees petitioned to extend the distributions based not on the wages but on time worked. "The higher-paid workers, therefore, on their own motion thus relinquished their claim to a considerable sum of money in order that the lower-paid workers, whose need was greater, could be better provided for."[37] Nash continued to raise wages, limited the profit of capital to 7 percent, and reinvested remaining profits in the extension of the business. He lived simply. When Nash proposed to withhold bonuses from those who had worked less than six months (since an employee had joined for a short time and left right after receiving a bonus), the workers insisted that the golden rule indicated assuming sincere motivation in every employee—and they prevailed. Nash and the workers agreed that the consumer should play a role in the setting of prices, and consequently their prices were drastically cheaper than others' (sixteen to twenty-nine dollars for a suit instead of fifty to a hundred). They also agreed to return extra profits to the customer in the form of better goods and extra trimmings. And they proposed, during a time of unemployment, to take a wage cut and make additional work for the unemployed in Cincinnati. They had abundant sunshine and fresh air and a healthy vapor heating system, and they remodeled their plant according to a schedule that the group agreed to. The work week was reduced to forty hours, and Nash was resolutely opposed to overtime. Every change was either proposed by one of the workers or thoroughly discussed in a company meeting. Nash supported labor unions; his firm unanimously agreed to make no clothes for a firm fighting a union and looked askance at someone taking a striker's job; but he thought there was a better way to safeguard the rights of workers, and so he had no union in his plant. An experienced factory observer visited Nash's workers and concluded that he was watching piecework, so rapid was the labor; but those people were working for an hourly wage. In one room, however, workers were taking such painstaking care with their work, the observer was sure they were on an hourly wage; but they were in fact the only one's getting paid by the piece. Even during hard economic times they continued to grow from around $132,000 in 1918 to $3,750,000 in 1922.

Nash became widely known, and in 1923 he published an autobiography, proclaiming the golden rule as his cardinal principle, telling of his path to success, and reproducing two appreciative commentaries.[38] After writing the triumphant account of his spiritual, social, and material success, the former preacher finally had a national pulpit that could not be taken from him.

In a posthumous 1930 edition of his book, completed by an associate, we learn the rest of the story. As a result of his renown, Golden Rule Nash became overcommitted to travel and speechmaking, and during the last four years of his life his business, now grown quite large, began to weaken in sustaining its original spirit. As Nash came to employ not a few hundred but 140,000 employees, the service motive did not permeate as thoroughly as before. Previously he had estimated that 90 percent of his workers identified with the spirit of his undertaking, and the other 10 percent worked alongside them faithfully. But now some people began to take advantage of the looser system of control; some subordinate executives did not keep pace with their leader. Favoritism, discrimination, and poor workmanship became noticeable, and morale slackened as Nash was away much of the time on speaking engagements with dinner clubs, lodge and church conventions, and chambers of commerce.

Nash's resolution of the problem led to an expansion of his management philosophy. At first he approached a group of ministers and invited them to examine every phase of his operation and to report any situation where the teachings of Jesus could be more truly put to work. They refused, deferring to his greater experience in business. At length he decided to turn to a union. Previously, despite his sympathies with the union movement, Nash had endeavored to treat his workers so well that they would feel no need for a union. The enmity between labor and management, especially in the clothing industry, had been strong during the previous decade; now, however, in December of 1925, he turned to the Amalgamated Clothing Workers Union, on account of its sustained dedication to the skills of the trade and to the welfare of the workers. The union's technical competence, which Nash had previously rejected as deadening, proved most helpful. New methods of accounting, inventory management, and finance were introduced. Thus many techniques of scientific management that he had scorned as mere mechanical substitutes for human cooperation were introduced, and he found that they in fact constituted the very extension and application of the golden rule itself. The business weathered a slump and emerged stronger than ever; sales for 1926 were fourteen million dollars. The workers owned most of the stock. It became evident that the supreme desire to apply the golden rule did not enable Nash to discover by himself every step of forward progress that he needed to take. He needed the union to show him that techniques he had opposed were in fact required by his own purposes. Nonetheless, it was by following the golden rule that he came to the union and thus to accept ideas he had previously rejected in the name of the rule.

He founded the *Nash Journal* as a forum for popular and inspirational tidbits of wisdom, business advice, editorials, news of the company and the world. In one of his rare forays in the direction of philosophy, Nash responded to an article in which his company's success was explained in terms of the golden rule plus other factors of business judgment. He challenged the separation of the golden rule from good business judgment.

> In order to perfectly live the Golden Rule, one in business, to begin with, would be compelled to buy his merchandise in such a way that he would be dealing with the seller on the basis of the Golden Rule, as well as buying for his customers on the basis of the Golden Rule. The thought I want to bring out, is that we have left most things religious and spiritual down in the boggy swamps of sentimentalism. The efforts of the church in the past have not been directed as much as they may be toward educating and equipping men and women to live large and full lives. Whatever success has come to the A. Nash Company in living the Golden Rule has come because there has been enough business knowledge to enable us to live it to just that degree, and whenever we have failed in exercising the very highest and keenest business judgment on a truly ethical basis, it has been because we did not have sufficient insight to understand our obligation measured by the Golden Rule. . . . In other words, perfect and infallible living of the Golden Rule would require infallible mentality and undaunted courage.[39]

Nash's book argued that religion is needed for the socially effective practice of the golden rule. Any acceptable economic success must be based not upon profit-hungry manipulation but upon good relationships between those involved. Acting in accord with the golden rule is required in order for a business enterprise to flourish in its social relations, since the rule stimulates improved service. The practice of the rule in business should not be regarded as suicidal; often it is an aid to success. Religious motivation is usually necessary to motivate the wholehearted practice of the golden rule. Therefore, religion is essential for the flourishing of business and consequently for the flourishing of society and of civilization. In sum, Nash used the rule as a symbol of his Christian ideals of brotherhood and service and as a method to discover new ways of treating his workers and his customers well.

FROM BUSINESS ETHICS TO RELIGIOUS ETHICS: J. C. PENNEY

J. C. Penney experienced the golden rule during his early years more as a symbol of the rigorous, edifying, and self-denying morality of his "good and dedicated" father rather than as a symbol of the spiritual example of his "unselfish and saintly" mother.[40] The son of a Primitive Baptist preacher (and the grandson of a preacher), the third child of twelve children (six of whom survived to adulthood), growing up on a farm, Penney recalls learning self-reliance by having to earn the money for his clothes beginning at age eight. He ran errands. He raised pigs. But when the neighbors complained about the smell, his father obliged him to stop raising pigs—an early lesson about the unwelcome implications of living by the golden rule. The boy turned to growing watermelons, spending the last nights before harvesting in the field with a dog and a shotgun to protect his crop. He took them to the county fair to sell them, and set up his wagon close to where the crowds were entering. Sales were becoming brisk when his father interrupted and ordered him to close down and go home. The lad had unwittingly broken the norm of selling along with other merchants who had set up inside the fair and had paid for a concession to do so. This was his second hard lesson about the implications of the golden rule.

The next phase of his life with the golden rule were his early years in business. He learned to sell dry goods. "I concentrated on two points: knowing the stock and exactly where everything was, and giving the customer the utmost in service and value, making only a small profit on each sale. I was particularly interested in the idea of keeping the store sold out of old stock."[41] He learned how "to add service and value from the woman's point of view."[42] He stayed away from the cities, feeling that he knew "how to get close to the lives of small town people, learning their needs and preferences and serving them accordingly."[43] He liked working where he and those who worked with him "understood our neighbors as readily as they could understand us."[44] In 1902 he opened a store in Kemmerer, Wyoming, with the sign: Golden Rule Store. He and his wife worked together without any help at first, working hard, too hard, as Penney recalls, from early in the morning to late at night seven days a week. They abided strictly by the golden rule, they were extremely frugal, and they made money. As they began to hire people, Penney never hired anyone who did not have a "positive belief in a Supreme Being"; he selected people with "character, enthusiasm, and energy."[45] He had large ambitions: "By our service to our customers we would create in them that spring of sparkling good will which would prompt them to want to help us to serve them."[46]

The last period of his life was marked by his religious conversion. Chronically troubled by his merely external engagement with religion, he had not been able to convince himself wholeheartedly that "it was enough for a man to lead a moral and upright life."[47] At the age of fifty-eight, having financially overextended himself in philanthropy when the Great Depression hit, this wealthy and successful man was brought to bankruptcy, alcoholism, and despair. Through an evangelical mission in New York City, he found God in a radiant and satisfying way and could then speak anew of the golden rule. "From our spiritual wellsprings come our capacities for unselfishness."[48] Penney proclaimed that the world must be transformed, would be transformed, and could only be transformed by the spiritually motivated practice of the golden rule, service to all people as one's neighbors.

> As civilization grew and horizons widened, the definition of "brotherhood" took on more exact meaning, and people came gradually to understand the golden rule as a basic principle, applicable to all relationships. In former periods business was identified as *secular*, and service as *sacred*. In proportion as we have discerned that between secular and sacred no arbitrary line exists, public awareness has grown that the golden rule was meant for business as much as for other human relationships.[49]

Thus Penney joined men like Nash and Jones in holding to a religious conception of brotherhood as the basis for the replete practice of the golden rule.

CONCLUSION

The golden rule has functioned to mobilize sympathies, to sustain human dignity, and to express religious experience on a diverse planet in need of unifying ideals. Despite the follies of some of its champions, the rule, interpreted through the gospel of the fatherhood of God and the brotherhood of man, has showed itself a sturdy player in the encounter between religious idealism and scientific realism.

Evolution means progress as well as struggle. Not only does idealism need realism to make its ideals effective, but realism also needs idealism in order to keep pace in a progressive world. The fact that the rule provided a focus for the experience of harmony among members of different religions and the fact that the rhetoric of the golden rule could be an effective lever of reform give hope for the moral sense within the human heart and an incipient spiritual community. How, then, shall the golden rule be applied in practice? There is no formula for finding the proportion of legitimate self-interest in a life dominated by the service motive. There is no formula for determining when a sacrificial deed will have great leverage. Nor is the golden rule a substitute for gifted leadership, though it can contribute the moral focus for inspired leadership and teamwork.

Simply to ridicule the follies of idealism or to expose the scandals of a narrow-minded realism may make people more cynical about the prospect of combining idealism with realism. Pointing beyond cynicism, the biographies summarized here show how some, daring to treat others as they would be treated, found their way. Arthur Nash discovered that his apparently self-sacrificing wage increases won a profitable response from his workers, and they gained national attention for joining religious and moral dynamism with business progress. J. C. Penney respected the rule as a moral constraint on profit seeking and as a guide to service, and in the end also wrote of religiously motivated brotherhood. Samuel Jones, despite relative economic and political success, continued to aim, sometimes unwisely, for social and personal objectives beyond his reach. His sense of the pathos of life's contradictions was much sharper than that of Penney or Nash. Nash and Penney showed that an individual and a company can flourish with a profound commitment to the rule. Jones, however, also showed that a society transformed by the practice of the rule is a long way off.

nine

In the Other Person's Shoes

No one will say that the emotional life is simple, nor the intellectual life, nor the spiritual life. Not only are they complex within themselves, but their interrelations also form a thicket that resists analysis. The business of psychology is to plunge into that thicket and to bring forth increasingly well-established results that help us comprehend ourselves and others. Surveying a century of psychological literature, one may observe that the major theorists are those who bring to light a previously neglected theme or cluster of themes, developed with enough systematic structure, empirical evidence, and philosophic and literary appeal to attract support and criticism; they focus discussion, affecting the shape of their discipline or subdiscipline for more than a decade. This chapter will first review the work of several such theorists who have explicitly written about the golden rule and then present selected results on sympathy, empathy, self-deception, perspective taking, and altruism that are helpful in applying the golden rule.

The reader should not be deceived by the occasional semblance of coherence in the account formed from the studies distilled here. The studies were designed to answer different questions, and they utilize different psychological methods: description of the researcher's own experience, psychoanalytic observation, observation of childrens' games, interviews with altruistic persons, interviews combined with moral problem solving, interpretation of biography, experiments with subjects unaware of the focus of the investigation, dramatic adventures in personal realization, and programs for professional development. Over a thousand studies have been done on empathy or altruism alone. There are studies that confirm their hypotheses strongly, studies that confirm their hypotheses weakly, inconclusive studies, studies that disconfirm each other, studies that reconcile discrepancies between previous studies, discussions about whether empathy or altruism have been rightly conceptualized, and discussions about how difficult it is to give operational definitions of such concepts so that hypotheses can be tested. The ship of psychology has steamed out of the harbor of intuitive understanding, but no port of scientific consensus is on the horizon, at least no agreed-upon general theory regarding the cluster of issues surrounding the golden rule.[1]

Future research may well affect how we apply the golden rule by examining the practical import of distinctions among experiences including the following: observing the other, imagining how one would feel in the other's situation, imagining what the other is feeling, imagining the world from the perspective of the other, imagining the effect of an action on the other, imagining how the fairness of an act would be judged by the other, and taking the other's perspective vividly into account in moral decision making. There are auspicious beginnings, but ambition for the full range of relevant research is not yet on the horizon.

Let it be noted that imagining oneself in the other's situation is not literally required by the golden rule, nor is it a necessary or sufficient condition for sound moral judgment. In other words, sometimes one performs the imaginative exercise but remains unenlightened through ignorance or self-deception, and sometimes one grasps intuitively what is to be done without any explicit act of imagination.

RECIPROCITY AND THE GOLDEN RULE IN CHILDHOOD DEVELOPMENT: JEAN PIAGET

Jean Piaget's writings, based on the observation of children, have proven very influential among psychologists of cognitive development. In The Moral Judgment of the Child (1932) Piaget set forth a conception of moral development, based on the notion of morality as conformity to rules. Following Emile Durkheim, he regarded morality as an affair of rules and regarded moral rules as products of society. He approached the study of moral development by observing children of various ages playing rule-governed games.

Piaget identified stages of growth by observing differences in how children relate to the rules of their games. He focused on experiences of reciprocity in the sense of "give and take," where roughly equal persons exchange roles, for example, taking turns being "it." Prior to the emergence of morality, during ages two through five, the child engages in egocentric imitation, playing according to the rules of elders, without understanding the rationale of the conduct he or she is imitating.[2] For the child at age five, "rules are sacred and unchangeable because they partake of paternal authority."[3] Next, two stages of morality emerge in sequence. The stages are a matter of proportion, and adults tend to emphasize one or the other of these two basic types of morality

1. *The Morality of Obedience to Rules.* Children of six to seven years have become capable of conforming to rules on the basis of understanding what the rules mean. At this age, children can exercise mutual control in applying the rules, together with an effective respect for obligations such

as the prohibition on cheating.[4] The child tends "to regard duty and the value attaching to it as self-subsistent and independent of the mind, as imposing itself regardless of the circumstances."[5] Retaliatory, retributive justice—repaying the offender in kind—is the norm. Respect is unilateral and hierarchal. According to Piaget, this moral attitude is associated with religious authoritarianism in adults.

2. *The Morality of Cooperation.* Children aged eleven to twelve are capable of a systematic understanding of rules, and they experience a new level of freedom and potential for cooperation: they understand that conventional rules may be modified by group consensus. They are ready to codify rules to cover all possible cases, though girls are less legalistic than boys.[6] Children can now cooperate as autonomous equals. For this later stage, "a rule is looked upon as a law due to mutual consent, which you must respect if you want to be loyal" although it is possible to change it by agreement.[7] Respect is mutual.[8] "Cooperation is really a factor in the creation of . . . the self that takes up its stand on the norms of reciprocity and objective discussion, and knows how to submit to these in order to make itself respected."[9] According to Piaget, "The norms of reason, and in particular, the important norm of reciprocity, the source of the logic of relations, can only develop in and through cooperation. Whether cooperation is an effect or a cause of reason, or both, reason requires cooperation insofar as being rational consists in 'situating oneself' so as to submit the individual to the universal."[10]

It is in connection with the topic of justice that Piaget referred to the golden rule. Put simply, there are two main types of justice, corresponding to the two levels of morality in the developing child. In the spirit of the game, reciprocity operates "without any false respect for tradition nor for the will of any one individual" and without factors such as "inequalities due to chance, excessive individual differences in skill or muscular power."[11] At the initial level of morality, reciprocity operates to enforce a type of retaliatory justice that exacts a punishment equal to the infraction. But retaliation leads to a cycle of responses that destroys the game. The higher notion of reciprocity as involving equity facilitates a cycle of responses that allow the game to be sustained. The play of reciprocity bound up with the initial sense of justice leads beyond itself to reciprocity in a higher sense of mutuality.

> In our view, it is precisely this concern with reciprocity which leads one beyond the rather short-sighted justice of those children who give back the mathematical equivalent of the blows they have received. Like all spiritual realities which are the result, not of external constraint but of autonomous development, reciprocity has two aspects: reciprocity as a fact, and reciprocity as an ideal, as something which ought to be. The child begins by simply practicing reciprocity, in itself not so easy a thing as one might think. Then, once he has grown accustomed to this form of equilibrium in his actions, his behavior is altered from within, its form

reacting, as it were, upon its content. What is regarded as just is no longer merely reciprocal action, but primarily behavior that admits of indefinitely sustained reciprocity. The motto "Do as you would be done by," thus comes to replace the conception of crude equality. The child sets forgiveness above revenge, not out of weakness, but because "there is no end" to revenge (a boy of 10). Just as in logic, we can see a sort of reaction of the form of the proposition upon its content when the principle of contradiction leads to a simplification and purification of the initial definitions, so in ethics, reciprocity implies a purification of the deeper trend of conduct, guiding it by gradual stages to universality itself. Without leaving the sphere of reciprocity . . . between the more refined forms of justice, such as equity and love properly so called, there is no longer any real conflict.[12]

For Piaget, then, morality is a matter of conformity to social rules, but there is a difference in the level of maturity between obedience to rules regarded as external impositions "from above" and cooperation with rules generated by one's own social group. Describing the process in almost mystical terms, Piaget affirms that the practice of exchanging roles in rule-governed situations promotes moral growth.

THE GOLDEN RULE IN STAGES OF MORAL REASONING: LAWRENCE KOHLBERG

Among psychologists, Lawrence Kohlberg was the primary advocate of the golden rule as an expression of the highest level of moral reasoning. Kohlberg found himself unprepared by his education for a dilemma he faced when he had a chance to escape from the Nazis after having been caught for getting a ship loaded with Jews to sail from Europe. Should he stay with the Jewish prisoners or escape to try to rescue others? Kohlberg's 1958 University of Chicago dissertation was based on his study of boys in a Chicago reform school, whom he asked to explain how they would handle a series of moral dilemmas. The point of using dilemmas, presumably, is to force one to subordinate some legitimate considerations to others, to clarify priorities, to make what is implicitly or explicitly a choice of principle. The best known of these puzzles is the Heinz dilemma. Heinz's wife is dying for lack of a two-thousand-dollar prescription drug that he cannot afford but can acquire only by stealing. What should Heinz do? Kohlberg classified the responses not in terms of the particular solution chosen, but rather in terms of the kind of reasoning used. According to Kohlberg, everyone goes through a universal and necessary sequence of stages (though many adults do not advance beyond stage 3 or 4). He found two *preconventional* stages: reasoning about how to act to avoid punishment (stage 1) or to gain the rewards that come from pleasing authority figures (stage 2). Next come two *conventional* stages: reasoning about how to act to satisfy the role expectations of one's immediate social relationships (stage 3), and then reasoning based primarily on respect for the law and order underlying one's society (stage 4). In the *postconventional* stages, individuals are capable of criticizing conventional standards. These stages are marked by reasoning that one must act according to agreements that result as different groups come together to establish a common framework of conventions (stage 5) and reasoning on the basis of universal moral principles (stage 6).[13]

Kohlberg reported that persons at various stages of moral reasoning have different conceptions of the golden rule. "We have systematically asked children who 'know' or can repeat the Golden Rule the question, 'If someone comes up on the street and hits you, what would the golden rule say to do?' Children at moral Stages 1 and 2 say, 'Hit him back. Do unto others as they do unto you.'"[14]

The golden rule comes into its own in conventional reasoning. "In contrast to Stage 1 and 2 concrete reciprocity, Stage 3 equates reciprocity with reversibility, with the golden rule. The golden rule implies (1) ideal role taking or reversing perspectives . . . , not exchanging acts, and (2) reversing perspectives in terms of the *ideal* ('What would you like in his place?'), not the real ('What would you do in his place?')."[15] A person in stage 3 has a conception of equity: "It is fair to give more to helpless people, because you can take their role and make up for their helplessness." A person at stage 3 is oriented to taking the initiative in "unilateral helping followed by gratitude, rather than to strict equal exchange." Nevertheless, morality tends to function, at this stage, only within the context of reciprocal relationships. "The sociomoral order is conceived of as primarily composed of dyadic relationships of mutual role taking, mutual affection, gratitude, and concern for one another's approval."[16] For Kohlberg, stage 3 is limited by its somewhat exclusive focus on one-to-one relationships, in comparative isolation from the social systems in which many ethical dilemmas arise.

Stage 6 reasoning is fully developed intellectually. It is based on a commitment to universal moral principles. For Kohlberg, the key insight is that "a moral judgment must be reversible, that we must be willing to live with our judgment or decision when we trade places with others in the situation being judged. This, of course, if the formal criterion implied by the Golden Rule: 'It's right if it's still right when you put yourself in the other's place.'"[17] Philosophers such as Immanuel Kant and John Rawls illustrate stage 6 reasoning. In order to handle complex situations where more than two persons are involved, Kohlberg proposes his own method of moral reasoning, which he calls "moral musical chairs."

1. The decider is to successively put himself imaginatively in the place of each other actor and consider the claims each would make from his point of view.
2. Where claims in one party's shoes conflict with those in another's, imagine each to trade places. If so, a party should drop his conflicting

claim if it is based on nonrecognition of the other's point of view.
. . . In moral musical chairs there is only one "winning" chair, which
all other players recognize if they play the game, the chair of the person with the prior claim to justice.[18]

Kohlberg also described a seventh stage, going beyond principles of
justice and involving religious faith either in a personal God or in a pan-
theistic, cosmic order.[19] Kohlberg had understood progress from one
stage of moral reasoning to another as motivated by the need for an increasingly adequate way to think through moral issues. Problems arise at
one stage that are resolved at the next stage. The question "Why be
moral?" however, is one that cannot be answered satisfactorily from
within the moral standpoint; one can answer it either reductionistically—
by reducing morality to a means to personal and/or group satisfaction—
or by moving into religious thinking. Confrontation with the apparent injustice of the course of the world provokes, in many people, a quest for
deeper meaning that culminates in new depth of discovery and conviction. A stage-7 person still uses universal moral principles when issues
of justice are raised. Characteristically, however, such a person responds
primarily on the basis of love for others as members in the family of humankind, fellow cosmopolitan citizens of the universe, or as beings in the
unity of life and love. Stage-7 persons engage in service that transcends
what justice and duty require. Just as logical development is necessary,
but not sufficient for moral development, so moral development is necessary, but not sufficient for the stage of agape or responsible love. Kohlberg
did not, however, identify a new level of the golden rule in describing the
highest religious stage.[20]

TWO CLARIFICATIONS PROMPTED BY FEMINIST
CRITICISMS: CAROL GILLIGAN

Insofar as Kohlberg presented the golden rule as, at best, an abstract principle of justice, it is relevant that Carol Gilligan criticized Kohlberg for
failing to recognize the importance of what she identified as women's
tendency to approach morally difficult problems by exploring the details
of the relational situation (the "women's caring orientation") rather than
by reasoning about how to apply abstract principles (the "men's justice
orientation").[21]

This criticism, whatever insight it may or may not express regarding
differences between men and women, calls for a clarification. A keen eye
for situational complexity and a clear grasp of principle should be mutually helpful. One wants to be treated with due regard for relevant situational details and with relational sensitivity, not on the basis of a blind
application of an abstract principle (whatever that would mean). Situational details are meaningful in terms of features that could be expressed
in language, and thus in general terms that could be applied to other situa-

tions. Moreover, principles are relevant only in terms of a particular description of a situation.

If Kohlberg's religious seventh stage had not been ignored in the Kohlberg–Gilligan debate, it would have been observed that Kohlberg's prime example of stage 7 is a woman (Andrea Simpson) who devoted herself extraordinarily to the care of her insane brother. More attention to that kind of example should lead to further understanding of the character of morality, the importance of religion, and the equality and difference of men and women.

Another feature of the golden rule becomes evident in response to a point raised by some feminists. Moral teachings have been used to keep women in their place within patriarchal systems. The reason for this, some say, is that morality is typically called upon as a bulwark against men's selfishness and egocentric aggression, whereas women's excessive responsiveness to others' demands and needs is a problem of comparable importance. A moment of reflection suffices to dispose of a false corollary to the golden rule: If I want to be treated kindly, does that mean that I must treat an abusive "superior" in a way he might regard as kindly? More to the point is this golden rule question: Would I want to be "served" by a person whose "good deeds" were prompted by deficient self-respect? If the rule is to function in the emerging age of equality between men and women, the rule must also be understood as an antidote to an undervalued, imploded self.

STAGES OF MATURITY AND THE GOLDEN RULE: ERIK ERIKSON

For Erik Erikson, the golden rule symbolizes a universal, humanitarian ethical orientation that presupposes many stages of growth. Life sets a typical sequence of challenges, and the mature individual acquires a constellation of ego strengths, or virtues, by meeting these challenges successfully. Each virtue lays the ideal foundation for acquiring the next one. In response to the experiences of the first year of life, trust should come to predominate over distrust. During the second and third years, the issue is whether *autonomy*, confidence in one's ability to assert oneself, will prevail over shame (being exposed before one is ready, revealing a vulnerability or deficiency felt to be intrinsic to the self). At age four to five, the issue is *initiative* (manifested differently by boys and girls) versus guilt (a reprimand may be overpowering in the child's mind). Next, in later childhood, one is challenged to acquire the virtue of *industry*: the "I can" attitude, a sense of competence about doing and learning and making a contribution, rather than developing a sense of inferiority by despairing of one's skills and status. Then, during the teenage years, one must struggle with a sense of *identity* versus role confusion. When identity is firm, one is able to commit oneself in fidelity to a friendship, a religion, a community. Next, sustained *intimacy* implies mutuality in sexual satisfaction and the virtue of love. The crisis of middle age is between *generativity versus stagnation*. Is one willing to invest oneself caring for the next generation (in child rearing and contribution to society) or will one be captured by self-centeredness? In later adult life one faces the challenge of ego *integrity versus despair*. After triumphs and disappointments, there arises a new love of self as part of a world order grounded in spiritual depth. The final virtue is wisdom, which refreshes courage, renews earlier visions of wholeness, and whose fearlessness toward death encourages children.[22]

Erikson uses the terms "moral" and "ethical" to name contrasting orientations: "I would propose that we consider *moral rules* of conduct to be based on a fear of *threats* to be forestalled. These may be outer threats of abandonment, punishment, and public exposure, or a threatening inner sense of guilt, of shame or of isolation. In either case, the rationale for obeying a rule may not be too clear; it is the threat that counts. In contrast, I would consider *ethical rules* to be based on *ideals* to be striven for with a high degree of rational assent and with a ready consent to a formulated good, a definition of perfection, and some promise of self-realization."[23] Thus, moral development begins as the child is restrained by means of threats, which instill in the unconscious vast "arsenals of destructive rage," which may lead in later life to moralism and cruelty.[24]

By contrast, maturity is achieved through interaction with others, since the individual participates in social actuality by activating others and by being activated by them. Each rouses and responds to the other in an invigoration largely "preconscious and subconscious."[25] In an intermediate stage, the developing person holds to some ideology as a tool for dealing with temporal uncertainty.

The golden rule embraces humankind universally, including people and groups that lesser levels of maturity exclude. The rule is not best interpreted as a counsel of prudence or as a maxim of sympathy, but as a principle of mutuality in which the agent takes initiative, "approaches an encounter in a (consciously and unconsciously) active and giving attitude, rather than in a demanding and dependent one." Action fulfilling the golden rule strengthens the doer and the other in "whatever strength is *appropriate to his age, stage, and condition*."[26]

In India, Erikson delivered the address "The Golden Rule in the Light of New Insight," and he took the occasion to express his sense of the dangers of international conflict and his respect for Gandhi. Commenting on various formulations of the golden rule from Hindu tradition, he observed that the maxim "Do not to others what if done to you would cause you pain" presupposes little maturity. More advanced is another formulation, "No one is a believer until he loves for his brother what he loves for himself."[27] Erikson recognized the most unconditional commitment in the teaching of the Upanishads, "He who sees all beings in his own self and his own self in all beings." He concluded, "At our historical moment it becomes clear in a most practical way that the doer of the golden rule, and he who is done by, is the same man, is man."[28] Erikson's almost mystical conception of the unity of humankind is based on the experience of mutual activation, in which each is "acting upon and being guided by what is most genuine in the other."[29] Clearly, for Erikson, the golden rule is a principle that persistently embraces all humankind, despite every device of narrow-mindedness to restrict the scope of considerate conduct to an in-group.

CONCERNS ABOUT STAGE SEQUENCES

Some psychologists have expressed the concern that sorting people according to "hierarchal" stages is harmful. In one sense, the objection refutes itself, since a nonhierarcichal approach would, presumably, be superior to the hierarchal approaches. Thus, there may be no way to extricate oneself from such thinking. But the concern is well taken, since there is a persistent risk of failing to respect those regarded as inferior, in some sense. Sequences of levels are dangerous. They risk obscuring the common humanity of the classifier and the classified. It is all too easy to stereotype others and to cease letting oneself be interrogated by them. To recognize that danger is not sufficient for safety, however, since pride can reemerge in one's sense of superiority over "those people who go around classifying, those dualists, those compulsive intellectuals who construct level schemes."

Expressing certain differences between people in terms of stages sometimes gives the impression of disrespect for those of us classified as being in the lower stages. For example, one kind of rationalist may regard material emotions as a lower-level nuisance. From a dialectical perspective, however, the lower stages are presupposed by and contribute to higher ones, which, in turn, transfuse the lower levels with new meaning and value. For example, a mammalian emotion of sympathy becomes an ingredient in a mature feeling of compassion. Spiritual growth infuses the emotions so that loving sympathy gradually pervades natural desires and fears; people incline to "bear one another's burdens"; as Isaiah wrote of God, "In all their afflictions, he is afflicted with them."[30]

In defense of stages, it should be possible to agree at least that two hypotheses are plausible: each step of personal growth should yield an enhanced sense of self and other, giving rise to an enhanced interpretation of the golden rule; and the practice of the golden rule conduces to personal growth. Moreover, objections to stage thinking has still less force when the stages are steps of progress in respect or caring or love directed potentially to any human being. The highest stage should be marked by integration of the entire personality rather than by departure from the achievements of lower stages. It seems more realistic to humanize the talk of stages than to try to eliminate it. A sense of proportion is also essential.

Distinguishing levels remains helpful for analysis, though it must be remembered that life *blends* what the intellect distinguishes, that the personality acts as a whole, and that a growing personality, at any stage, is a progressively *unified* personality.

A SKETCH OF THE DEVELOPMENT OF SYMPATHY

The golden rule instructs the agent to treat others "as you want others to treat you." The rule in its economy of statement does not make explicit that you need some understanding of the other person. But how shall that understanding be gained? Perhaps our most basic sense of others comes through feeling. Indeed, the conventional sense of the golden rule does seem to be, in effect, a principle of sympathy: "Be considerate of others' feelings as you want others to be considerate of your feelings." Sympathy—defined by Lauren Wispé as "the heightened awareness of another's plight as something to be alleviated"—develops through an interplay of affective and cognitive factors, and I would summarize some of the research by constructing a series of stages.[31]

1. The infant is not yet psychologically differentiated from the mother. Especially during the first few months, cries of distress from another child elicit cries of distress from the infant. Positive as well as negative feelings are contagious. This phenomenon continues in adults, who may be buoyed up by others' infectious enthusiasm or invaded by their depression.

2. The child spontaneously imitates the gestures of others. In addition, there is a developmental connection between perception and social awareness. The child begins to be able to move around and to identify objects—the same thing can be seen from here and from there. The very sense of the objectivity of perceived things involves the sense that others, from their perspectives, could confirm one's own perceptions. The child also shows an awareness of being able to be in another's place, for example, by being jealous that another child is in its mother's lap.

3. The child relieves the distress of another child by doing the same helping activities that a parent would do. Sympathetic behavior can occur before the second birthday.

> In her suburban home, 18–month-old Julie was excited when another baby, Brian, came for a visit. But Brian was less than pleased at being with strangers and soon began to shriek and pound his fists on the floor. Almost immediately, Julie's delight vanished, her body stiffened and she looked worried, startled and anxious.
>
> Julie's mom put Brian in a highchair and gave him cookies, but he continued screaming and threw the cookies on the floor. Julie, who usually tried to eat everyone else's cookies, put them back on the highchair tray. Brian's crying continued, and Julie tried to stroke his hair. She then went to her mom, grabbed her by the hand and brought her to Brian.[32]

This report shows sympathy operating prior to moral decision. The child can act in ways that satisfy rules but does not yet understand the meanings and values that the rules express.

4. As early as age four, and surely by age eight, perspective taking becomes a more cognitive activity, as distinguished from the predominantly affective experiences of emotional contagion and personal distress.[33] Comparatively individuated experience is gained as the developing ego becomes assertive about its desires and as intelligent volition appears. The child becomes capable of moral decision. The child can give some account of his or her action that indicates some understanding of the point of rules, some recognition of moral meanings and values. Sympathetic behavior can be motivated more by an interest in relieving the other's distress than by an interest in relieving one's own distress.

5. Advancing stages of moral experience and commitment emerge on the horizon. Thinking, feeling, and doing develop new capacities for living accord with the golden rule, and sympathy can grow into compassion.

THE PROBLEM OF SELF-DECEPTION

We typically assume that we understand others intuitively, that we empathize accurately, that our expressions of consideration are appropriate. Psychology tells us, however, that despite our customary reliance on empathy to inform us about others, our empathic sense of others is often misleading. The golden rule tells us to treat others as we want to be treated, thereby tacitly encouraging the assumption that there are important commonalities or similarities between self and other. Overreliance on commonalities can blunt sensitivities to difference just as much as being overly impressed with difference can blind people to kinship.

The problem of empathic error is obviously important for the practice of the golden rule. If the rule were taken to encourage complacency about understanding others, then the rule would appear to foster narrow-mindedness and treating others in an insensitive manner. One might be simply unaware of differences between oneself and another, a natural tendency, according to Sigmund Freud:

> Without any special reflection we attribute to everyone else our own constitution and therefore our consciousness as well, and . . . this identification is a *sine qua non* of our understanding. This inference (or this identification) was formerly extended by the ego to other human beings, to animals, plants, inanimate objects and to the world at large, and proved serviceable so long as their similarity to the individual ego was overwhelmingly great; but it became more untrustworthy in proportion as the difference between the ego and these "others" widened.[34]

Therapist Robert L. Katz has described the possibilities of error and self-deception in empathy. Superficial empathy is one source of error:

We recognize some parallels and vaguely apprehend some quality of the experience of the other and then proceed, quite without the necessary supporting evidence, to make inferences regarding the whole personality. It is a case of premature disengagement and a withdrawal of emotional energies before the meeting has actually taken place. We presume too quickly that we have overcome our strangeness and that we have understood the other person from within.[35]

Katz notes the obvious dangers. One needs to take care about imposing personal valuations on others and about the use of categories and language that reflect racial, cultural, gender, or class stereotypes.[36] Katz writes of the "evangelical empathizer," who is "confident that his values and his conceptions of what is normal are valid for himself and for all of his clients. He is more attached to his categories than to his clients."[37] When the therapist employs his own feeling and does not rely exclusively on concepts that are necessarily abstract and stereotyped, he understands more profoundly.[38]

There is of course hope. Three professors of nursing responded to studies showing that intuitive abilities do not enable even many helping professionals to demonstrate empathy in a way that is actually helpful to the client.[39] Conceiving of empathy as a skill, Jean R. Hughes, E. Joyce Carver, and Ruth C. MacKay, of Dalhousie University in Halifax, Nova Scotia, designed a successful training program to develop empathy through interpersonal interaction. They created programs for nurses in the Burn Unit of Victoria General Hospital, working with E. L. La Monica's three-stage definition: "Empathy . . . involves accurate perception of the client's world by the helper, communication of this understanding to the client, and the client's perception of the helper's understanding."[40] The nurses learned to recognize cues better, to show understanding of the patient through verbal recognition of both content and affective dimensions of the patient's message, and to be alert to the client's perception of the helper's understanding. Those participating in the study came to recognize that it is more difficult to understand others and to make oneself understood than we normally realize, and they learned "how misunderstandings could result from a series of small but inaccurate assumptions resulting from failure to validate client messages."[41] Though it was emotionally demanding to go through training concerning a matter that affects one's sense of professional and interpersonal competence, during the course of the training, the nurses moved from resistance and skepticism to commitment and personal initiative in seeking out supplementary materials relevant to their own felt needs. The twenty- to twenty-five-hour programs began with initial sessions with lectures and written exercises, moved on to role playing with partners, and concluded with videotaping and group review of role-playing exercises. The nurses reported improved understanding in their relations with their patients and with colleagues as well. The programs yielded consistent behavioral improvement throughout the group of nurses, with no decline after seven months. A major lesson of this program is that, in cultivating empathy to the level of service effectiveness, it is helpful to communicate and test one's perceptions in conversation.[42] Imagination is not enough.

DRAMATIC AND THERAPEUTIC ROLE REVERSALS

As Katz reported, in order to get beyond the limitations of imagining oneself in the other's situation, it may be necessary to *do* something:

> Trigant Burrow recorded a personal experience which made him sharply aware of certain built-in hazards in the therapist's position. . . . One of his patients had questioned his sincerity. He requested Dr. Burrow to change positions with him. He would take the chair of the therapist and the doctor would take the reverse position of being the patient. It was unprofessional and unorthodox, but Dr. Burrow acceded to his patient's request. Soon after yielding his own chair to the patient, Dr. Burrow gained new and painful insight into the professionalism and authoritarianism which had crept into his own therapeutic attitudes. He now recognized in himself certain tendencies toward self-vindication. *His awareness came into being only after he had changed places.*[43]

Burrow's adventure was a form of role playing, a technique which has been widely used in education. The term "role reversal" is fully appropriate since there was a (mutual) *exchange* of roles, not just a unilateral attempt to put oneself into the other's "role."

Deliberate role playing involves the imagination in what we may call the *dramatic role reversal.* Its use in a combination of psychology and theater was pioneered by Jacob L. Moreno and is employed in workshops conducted by Armand Volkas, a psychologist, drama therapist, actor, and director from Oakland, California. Volkas, a child of Holocaust survivors, brings together Jewish children of Holocaust victims and children of Nazis. In "Acts of Reconciliation," a two-day workshop, performed many times in Oakland and in Berlin, dramatic role reversals engage memory, perception, and imagination in improvisational acting. There is no script; the participants create the drama as they go through a sequence of exercises, which give participants an opportunity to experience the moral and emotional power that comes from the two groups resolving to remember the Holocaust together, to transcend stereotypes, and to build communication.

A few details that Volkas gives about some of the exercises indicate the place of the dramatic role reversal in the workshop. He begins by having each participant begin telling about himself by saying, "I am a German" or "I am a Jew," and each one shares the thoughts and feelings associated with stating this fact about himself or herself. They discuss their experiences and feelings as they arise. Working with groups of, say, ten Germans and ten Jews, he next gathers them into pairs of a German with a Jew to exchange life stories. Each then retells the other's story to the group in the first person, as if it were his or her own. In another exercise, participants take the positions of individuals in photographs of scenes from Nazi Germany.[44] Midway through the workshop, participants reenact an experience of a parent, for example, a man who had his wrists broken for stealing bread, having emerged from the sewer at dawn to find something to eat. There is an exercise in which pairs alternate playing the roles of master and slave, partly to discover "the potential Fascist in each of us." They create masks of the Fascist part of themselves. Each group enacts stereotypes of its own culture. At the end, there is commemoration. Each participant finds something in nature that represents hope for the future. Then they look forward to how the Holocaust may be remembered in two hundred years, and create a ritual of remembrance through mime, music, and poetry. Finally they take some action and make some public statement. Through these experiences, participants are helped to confront painful childhood memories, and they find themselves able to relate to their parents with new honesty. The role reversal, for Volkas, is at the heart of the therapy: "If you can stand in somebody's shoes, it's impossible to dehumanize them."[45]

Empathy is even used as a means of self-discovery by dramatist, theater professor, and performer Anna Deavere Smith. Her piece, Twilight: Los Angeles 1992, brings the audience to empathize with the wide spectrum of people involved in the riots following the trial of policemen involved in the Rodney King incident. On the basis of more than 170 interviews, Smith dramatizes on stage the pain in each of her characters. As a solo performer on stage, her primary purpose is clear. In an interview with John Lahr for a New Yorker article, she explained, "It's crucial that whites in the audience find points of identification . . . with themselves. To create a situation where they merely empathize with those less fortunate than themselves is another kind of theatre."[46] Lahr observed that "she creates a climate of intimacy by acknowledging the equality of the other. She waits out the anger. She accepts the contradictoriness. She cleverly notes the body language. And sometimes even her right to listen is tested."[47] Smith speaks about the horror of racism, of getting people to wake up: "The only way to master this fear of coming into consciousness is by coming into the consciousness of others, mimicking how other people did it, because it's terrifying to come into my own."[48]

IDEAS ON ALTRUISM FROM EXPERIMENTAL PSYCHOLOGY

A major reason for the interest in empathy, sympathy, and perspective taking is that they should promote helping behavior, actions in conformity with the golden rule. Experimental subjects instructed to take the perspective of another person are somewhat more likely to perform the helpful action than subjects who do not receive such instructions.[49] Nevertheless, there are qualifications, including the following noted by Dennis Krebs and Cristine Russell: "We can say that when people put themselves in the shoes of others, they may become more inclined to render them aid. But the shoes of others do not fit all people equally well, and getting into them is never enough. The path from role-taking to altruism is tortuous and indirect."[50]

There is some evidence that effective practice of the golden rule maintains focus on the person and situation that calls for response. A person who is actively involved tends to focus more on the situation, whereas the person who is simply imagining tends to focus more on the suffering person.[51] In other words, productive involvement sidesteps pity. A high degree of empathy can be associated with a counterproductive level of physiological and psychological arousal.[52] "Arousal" is an umbrella term that incorporates many factors. In an extreme case the individual may experience paralyzing fascination while witnessing a crime or panic at the scene of a horrible accident. In less extreme cases, the sense, "I ought to do something—what am I going to do?" can precipitate a shift of focus from the urgent situation to the self that needs to measure up to certain standards. A high degree of physiological arousal, associated with a strong feeling of personal distress, can reduce altruistic behavior.

Indeed, the fact that much apparently altruistic behavior can be explained as a way of relieving personal distress or repairing one's mood has stimulated the debate about whether people ever engage in altruistic actions without an "underlying," dominant motive of self-interest. The golden rule appears to call agents to act with the interest of the other ultimately in mind. The moral tone of the rule differs intuitively from the tone of a maxim of self-interest. But how far can psychology demonstrate the existence of true altruism, in this sense? Although it is not possible to extinguish every doubt, it has been possible to turn the tide of psychological opinion. The weight of evidence is now on the side of the view that genuine altruism exists. This shift is mainly due to a series of experiments carried out by C. Daniel Batson and associates, showing, for example, that empathy differs from personal distress, where personal distress is defined in terms of emotions such as "shock, alarm, disgust, shame, and fear"; while empathy is defined in terms of emotions such as "compassion, concern, warmth, and softheartedness."[53]

However, despite the evidence in favor of the claim that genuine altruism can be distinguished from behavior in which the dominant motive is self-interest, Batson, Patricia Schoenrade, and W. Larry Ventis have also carefully organized evidence for the sobering conclusion that many people characterized as religious do not exhibit altruism more than those characterized as nonreligious. In *Religion and the Individual*, following a social-psychological approach not biased against religion, they use three categories of religious attitude: religion may function as a vehicle of self-interest;

religious convictions may be regarded devoutly as truths of intrinsic value; and religion may be embraced as an ongoing quest. Only with the last category is there clear evidence of increased tolerance for socially marginalized people and increased sensitivity to the needs of others. Jesus' parable of the good Samaritan seems to convey a keen sociological generalization: many a religious person—when the cost of helping is high, when escape is easy, when one believes that one is unobserved by others—does not do more than the average.[54]

Experimental psychology has done little directly with the golden rule. A lone experiment, however, has addressed the question of how people respond differently to the positive and negative formulations of the golden rule. Ron B. Rembert asked sixth-grade students to make two lists, one list of actions they did not want others to do to them and another of actions they did want others to do to them.

> Their list of "Don'ts" was longer than their list of "Do's." For example, "hit," "steal," "laugh at," "snub," and "cheat" appeared in the list of "Don'ts" while "love," "respect," and "help" appeared in the list of "Do's." The list of "Don'ts" . . . included specific behaviors which are relatively easy to identify. This list of "Do's" . . . focused upon general attitudes and behaviors which are more difficult to define."[55]

The students concluded that the negative version of the golden rule would be easier to follow than the positive version.

CONCLUSION

Psychological research into empathy, sympathy, and altruism is just beginning to affect the understanding of the golden rule. However stages of development may be conceived, it is clear that those who think about the golden rule interpret the rule differently as they grow. The fact that empathy and perspective taking often fail to motivate altruism is in itself an important result, for it suggests that we look for moral motivation beyond sympathy. Furthermore, if religious motivation is claimed to be an answer or the answer, it is clear that such motivation must be spiritual in an uncommon degree.

It is also helpful to understand how deeply the practice of imaginative perspective taking is part of human development. Imagination makes difference understandable. Not that the mystery of the personality we recognize is reduced to something we can define or fathom intellectually. Not that the fluid, growing, changing individual can be pinned down by knowledge. But mind can understand mind; imagination, here, is not a playful departure from the actual, but an approach to understanding.

The capacity for identifying with others inheres in the mystery of personality. Each unfathomably unique person recognizes other persons. Each lives within the matrix of an ongoing interpersonal comprehension, and interpersonal experiences are double-sided; they involve the side of the agent and the side of the recipient of the action, and they are comprehended only as both sides are known: loving and being loved, hurting and being hurt, learning and teaching, growing up as a child and then, as a parent, helping someone else grow up. The mature practice of the golden rule involves an identification with others that includes understanding plus an appropriate level of shared feeling plus an appropriate practical response.

Clearly there is more to the golden rule than putting oneself in the other person's shoes. The human awareness of others' perspectives on oneself can even be intensely constraining. Consider the following from *The Souls of Black Folk* by W. E. B. Du Bois:

> After the Egyptian and Indian, the Greek and Roman, the Teuton and Mongolian, the Negro is a sort of seventh son, born with a veil, and gifted with second-sight in the American world—a world which yields him no true self-consciousness, but only lets him see himself through the revelation of the other world. It is peculiar sensation, the double-consciousness, this sense of always looking at one's self through the eyes of others, of measuring one's soul by the tape of a world that looks on in amused contempt and pity. One ever feels his two-ness,—an American, a Negro; two souls, two thoughts, two unreconciled strivings; two warring ideals in one dark body, whose dogged strength alone keeps it from being torn asunder.[56]

Thus not only sensitivity to the others' perspectives but also moral reason and spiritual insight are required for an appropriate sense of self and other.

ten

A Principle of Consistency in Moral Decision Making

When contrasted with the contextual richness of the golden rule in earlier philosophy, twentieth-century discussions of the golden rule in analytic philosophy seem to gain precision and a kind of clarity at the cost of spiritual and even moral impoverishment, as the golden rule is reduced to a principle of consistency. By the end of the twentieth century, however, a new development is beginning to find the macrocosm within the microcosm; in other words, the concept of golden rule consistency is now being expanded with logical skill in the direction of a more adequate ethics.

First, a word about the loss of an earlier fullness of meaning. A backward glance reminds us that, in the beginning of Western philosophy, Greek thinkers asked about the *arche*, the cosmic source/origin/beginning/foundation—or *archai*, if there was an irreducible plurality of primal opposites or elements. *Arche*, in Latin, became *princeps*, which became *principle* in English. For Judaism, a principle was the distilled wisdom of experience and scriptural tradition. From early Christian days, Jesus was regarded as a *princeps*, and a believer might aim to live in a manner consistent with the divine will or with the divine paradigm revealed for believers to imitate. For David Hume (1711–1776), "principle" had a double meaning; it was both a fundamental factor (a source or spring) within the human mind, and it was also a proposition. The second meaning came to predominate, and today talk of moral principles refers to propositions. According to current usage, propositions are principles if they are more general than the particular rules that exemplify them in a given system of thought; in addition, according to one standard, principles, unlike particular moral rules, apply in every case and never conflict with one another.

A *universal* principle, for the Stoics, was a rationally intelligible structure of the universe, something binding every human being—indeed any rational being. Some religious philosophers conceived of those universal principles as "ideas in the mind of God." Samuel Clarke preserved the sense of divine and universal pattern as he spoke of the fitness of things. Kant bracketed the notion of being consistent with universal patterns and represented moral principles as being consistent simply with reason itself, with the supreme dignity of every rational agent, and with legislation appropriate to an advanced civilization. In the twentieth century, the golden rule became attached to the career of universal principles, and it would be reinterpreted along with them. The universality of a principle was reduced to being simply a matter of consistency with other judgments the individual agent is prepared to make. The notion of universality had temporarily lost its cosmic, religious, metaphysical, and philosophical-anthropological connotations. There has been an attempt to use this reduced basis to retain everything worth conserving from the older tradition, and it is striking how much this approach has yielded.

This chapter and the following one are organized to present different approaches in contemporary philosophy, Anglo-American analytic philosophies and continental European philosophies, including phenomenology, existentialism, and "heterology," that is, the philosophical discourse on the other (person). (The geographic stereotypes are somewhat misleading, but they cause no problems for these chapters.) To understand this difference, it is useful to consider philosophy as mediating between science and religion. Philosophy, classically, considers the full spectrum of the human quest for truth, from science to spiritual experience. Analytic philosophy gravitates toward logical methods closer to those of scientific inquiry; this is evident even when analytic philosophers who happen to be believers discuss philosophy of religion. Phenomenology, existentialism, and postmodern writing gravitate toward thinking that is characteristically religious, bordering on the religious (philosophy that limits itself to what shared human experience can affirm), or postreligious (philosophy following "the death of God"). The purpose of this simplified scheme is to suggest that the "two" types of approach in philosophy are complementary. To be sure, interaction between methods is increasingly a feature of the contemporary scene, in all its chaos and promise. The present chapter examines the golden rule in the light of the analytic tradition, while the following chapter deals with German and French thought.

UNIVERSALIZABILITY AS CONSISTENCY AMONG ONE'S OWN JUDGMENTS

In the tradition of analytic philosophy—characterized by attention to clarity, the distinction between statements of fact and other types of statements, and logical reasoning—a number of ethicists have held that the golden rule states, in an intuitive way, something important that can be rationally reformulated to avoid counterexamples. The leading interpretation of the golden rule in twentieth-century analytic philosophy is that the rule is a rough expression of the requirement that all our moral judgments should be universalizable in the sense that we should be prepared to apply the same judgment in the same type of situation, no matter what individuals happen to be involved.

A clear statement of this interpretation of the rule is given by the utilitarian Henry Sidgwick:

> Whatever action any of us judges to be right for himself, he implicitly judges to be right for all similar persons in similar circumstances. Or, as we may otherwise put it, "if a kind of conduct that is right (or wrong) for me is not right (or wrong) for some one else, it must be on the ground of some difference between the two cases, other than the fact that I and he are different persons." A corresponding proposition may be stated with equal truth in respect of what ought to be done to—not by—different individuals. These principles have been most widely recognized, not in their most abstract and universal form, but in their special application to the situation of two (or more) individuals similarly related to each other: as so applied, they appear in what is popularly known as the Golden Rule, "Do to others as you would have them do to you." This formula is obviously imprecise in statement; for one might wish for another's cooperation in sin, and be willing to reciprocate it. Nor is it even true to say that we ought to do to others only what we think it right for them to do to us; for no one will deny that there may be differences in the circumstances—and even in the natures—of two individuals, A and B, which would make it wrong for A to treat B in the way in which it is right for B to treat A. In short, the self-evident principle strictly stated must take some such negative form as this; "it cannot be right for A to treat B in a manner in which it would be wrong for B to treat A, merely on the ground that they are two different individuals, and without there being any difference between the natures or circumstances of the two which can be stated as a reasonable ground for difference of treatment." Such a principle manifestly does not give complete guidance—indeed its effect, strictly speaking, is merely to throw a definite onus probandi [burden of proof] on the man who applies to another a treatment of which he would complain if applied to himself; but Common Sense has amply recognised the practical importance of the maxim: and its truth, as far as it goes, appears to me self-evident.[1]

This treatment epitomizes analytic discussions of the golden rule, in that it recognizes the vulnerability of the rule to the counterexamples of an agent with corrupt desires, and it distills from the rule an acceptable ethical and logical point.[2]

THE GOLDEN RULE AS DERIVED FROM A PRINCIPLE OF CONSISTENCY

Marcus George Singer, a University of Wisconsin philosopher, continued Sidgwick's use of Clarke and Kant in interpreting the golden rule. He began his book *Generalization in Ethics* (1961) by considering the question "What would happen if everyone did that?" (This question, he later says, is a generalization, of sorts, of the reversibility question, "What if someone were to do that to you?")[3] The question usually suggests the "generalization argument" that if the consequences of everyone's doing that would be disastrous (or undesirable), then "you" should not do it. Singer explores in what kinds of case this argument is valid. (The argument is invalid in certain types of case: for example, it would be disastrous for everyone to become a farmer, and it would also be disastrous for no one to become a farmer; in such cases, the generalization argument is said to be invertible, and then it does not apply.) He observes that the generalization argument rests on what has been traditionally known as a principle of fairness or justice or impartiality, which he calls the generalization principle: *What is right (or wrong) for one person is right (or wrong) for any similar person in similar circumstances.* The golden rule is a specification of the generalization principle. The generalization principle could also be regarded as a generalization of the golden rule.

What about the qualification about *similar* persons in *similar* situations? Is there a criterion for deciding what features of persons or situations are ethically relevant? If not, is it evasive to put in the similarity qualification? Does it beg the question or make the generalization principle trivial and shift substantive ethical inquiry to the question about relevant similarities? There is nothing evasive or trivializing about reference to similarity, says Singer. The similarity qualification is an invitation to list, in each particular case to be explored, the relevant factors that justify the particular moral judgment in question. On the basis of this list one can define a class of individuals to whom, or situations in which, the generalized judgment applies. A new, more specific principle results, not containing the term, "similar."[4] As an example, we might consider a man who leaves all the work of the kitchen to his wife. If he justifies this as the right of "the man of the house," the generalization principle shows that, by implication, he would be claiming that any husband, however lazy and unproductive, could justify leaving the work to his wife, however exhausted and pressed she might be. If he justifies leaving the work to his wife in terms of his emergency at work versus her comparative leisure, the generalization principle implies that he should be prepared to do the work whenever his wife's schedule is more demanding than his.

On the basis of his analysis of generalization, Singer published two influential articles on the golden rule in 1963 and 1976. He noted that the most contradictory claims have been made for the golden rule—that it is the solution to the world's problems, that it is misleading, false, or absurd; that it incorporates utilitarianism, that it supplies a principle of justice that is precisely lacking in utilitarianism; that it summarizes morality, that it requires a moral system for its application. Singer's testimony is that the golden rule is more than a handy reminder; it is "the most effective instrument of moral education that I know of."[5]

Regarding the debate over the merits of the positive and negative formulations of the rule, Singer argues that the formulations are equivalent (from a logical or moral standpoint as distinguished from a rhetorical or psychological standpoint), since any action can be described either in positive or negative terms:

> A want, wish, or desire formulated in negative terms can always be reformulated in positive terms. For example, there is no difference between not wanting others to lie to oneself and wanting them not to lie to oneself, wanting them to tell one the truth and wanting them not to fail to tell one the truth. In general, "A wants x to happen" is equivalent to "A does not want x not to happen," and "A does not want x to happen" is equivalent to "A wants x not to happen".[6]

In order to defend the golden rule from such counterexamples, Singer interprets it in terms of his theory of generalization:

> In any of its traditional formulations this rule is not only imprecise, but if taken literally would be an abomination. . . . Such literal interpretations of the rule are undoubtedly misinterpretations of what is intended by it. But what this shows is that as it stands the rule is imprecise and needs qualification. It neither says what it means nor means what it says. Stated precisely, the Golden Rule would be an immediate consequence of the generalization principle. Sidgwick remarks that Samuel Clarke's "rule of equity" ("Whatever I judge reasonable or unreasonable that another should do for me; that by the same judgment I declare reasonable or unreasonable that I should in the like case do for him") is "the 'Golden Rule' precisely stated."[7]

The golden rule is here defended by rejecting interpretations that are *logically* narrow. Singer argues that counterexamples to the golden rule apply not to the *general* interpretation of the rule, but only to the *particular* interpretation of it. For example, on the particular interpretation, the golden rule requires that I impose on others what, in particular, I want (e.g., some practice drumming at 3 A.M.) On the general interpretation, "One should act in relation to others *on the same principles* or *standards* that one would have them apply in their treatment of oneself" (e.g., not gratuitously do what is annoying).[8]

One must be careful, however, not to fall into what Singer terms the inversion of the golden rule—Do what others want—which leads to paradox if others have conflicting wants. The golden rule, rather, enjoins us to take into account others' interests, needs, tastes, wishes, desires. This guidance is problematic, since one's wishes and desires may conflict with one's needs and interests, and all those taken together may conflict with others' needs and interests. Singer's more precise ethical guidance comes, not from the golden rule itself, but from related principles.[9]

Singer does not acknowledge any enduring need for moral intuition. His appeal to the general interpretation of the rule shows that if a desire or an action is described in a way that is too particular, a golden rule argument based on that description will yield bad results. If an action is described at an appropriate level of generality, the golden rule argument should be valid. The distinction between the particular interpretation and the general interpretation is helpful as a start, but it raises the question of how to describe actions. What level of generality is appropriate? Is it one's sheer capacity for abstraction or one's moral intuition that guides one's formulations? Singer does not mention this problem in his articles on the golden rule, but in *Generalization in Ethics* he does recognize the problem. After doing some fine work to circumscribe the range of acceptable descriptions, he acknowledges that one cannot decide in the abstract the question of how to generate appropriate descriptions of actions, although in particular cases one surely can answer the question.[10]

THE GOLDEN RULE AS FORESHADOWING A THEORY OF MORALITY: R. M. HARE

The Oxford philosopher R. M. Hare developed the tradition of interpreting the golden rule as a principle of consistency among the agent's moral judgments, but whereas for Sidgwick and Singer the rule, properly formulated, was part of a larger theory of morality, Hare developed themes implicit in the golden rule as the basis for an entire theory of moral reasoning. The reasoning associated with the imaginative role reversal became the primary test for moral judgments. Given inclinations about how one wants to be treated plus an awareness of the facts of the case plus a vivid imaginative awareness of the recipient's actual or possible situation (if the action in question is performed), the test is whether the agent is prepared to prescribe the action, no matter which role—agent or recipient—he might occupy. Since his book *Freedom and Reason* (1963), combining a careful analysis of the tangles of ethical theory and the nuances of moral language with applications to practical moral issues, Hare has been more responsible than any other philosopher for the rebirth of discussion of the golden rule in recent analytic ethics.[11]

Two golden rule arguments from papers published in 1975 afford the easiest access to his thought. The first one was presented in a talk on euthanasia.

> I am not going to take the usual hospital examples (though I have such examples in mind). I am going to take what is perhaps an unusual case, but which did actually happen some time ago and was reported in the press. The driver of a petrol lorry was in an accident in which his tanker overturned and immediately caught fire. He himself was trapped in the cab and could not be freed. He therefore besought the bystanders to kill him by hitting him on the head, so that he would not roast to death. I think that somebody did this, but I do not know what happened in court afterwards.
>
> Now will you please all ask yourselves, as I have many times asked

myself, what you wish that men should do to you if you were in the situation of that driver. I cannot believe that anybody who considered the matter seriously, as if he himself were going to be in that situation and had now to give directions as to what rule the bystanders should follow, would say that the rule should be one ruling out euthanasia absolutely.[12]

The argument does not recommend euthanasia for a wide range of cases. In this context, addressing a Christian forum, responding to the objection that admitting euthanasia in one case takes one down a slippery slope weakening the general resolve against killing, Hare replies that the true answer to the problem of moral decay is to seek again "the roots of morality in the duty to love our neighbour as ourselves." In the past, the church, with an eye to pedagogical effectiveness, has taught overly simple rules. The fact that we are accustomed to simple rules should not prejudge the case at hand. Christian ethics, as Hare understands it, requires one to obey the commands of Christ, to love one's neighbor as oneself. Christ has directed us how to do that in the golden rule. So to use our best efforts of reason to follow the method of the golden rule is to fulfill Christian ethics. Hare refuses, though, to appeal to the notion that "all men are brothers," since facts, in and of themselves, do not enable us to deduce conclusions about how we *ought* to act; moreover, we need a criterion to determine who are our "brothers" in the relevant sense.

Abortion is another issue on which Hare has presented a golden rule argument. He derives from the rule the following principle: We should to do others as we are glad was done to us. The application seems straightforward: "If we are glad that nobody terminated the pregnancy which resulted in our birth, then we are enjoined not, *ceteris paribus*, to terminate any pregnancy which will result in the birth of a person having a life like ours."[13] By this move, Hare avoids asking the agent to apply the golden rule by imagining himself or herself, impossibly, in the position of the fetus. The qualifier, *ceteris paribus*, "other things being equal," directs us to seek relevant similarities in terms of "those things about our life that make us glad that we were born. These can be stated in a general enough way to cover all persons"—past, present, and future.[14]

How is it possible to arrive at substantive moral conclusions without relying on any substantive moral assumptions (e.g., about the equality and dignity of persons as free, rational, moral agents)? For Hare, golden rule arguments operate on the basis of the logic that is already implicit in moral language itself. Moral terms, such as "good" and "right" and "ought," have two logical features that guide the theory of morality. The first is *universalizability*. To judge that one student ought to attend class implies that any other student in exactly or relevantly similar circumstances should attend class. Moral terms, by their own "logic," carry implications for use in similar situations. The situations in which I use moral language have certain describable features on which my judgment is based. By making a moral judgment, I imply that in another situation that is like it in the relevant respects (the respects, namely, that I think entitle me to make the first judgment), I am prepared to make the same judgment again. In other words, universalizability is a feature of moral language, of how speakers are normally understood and expected to speak. Universalizability is therefore not equivalent to a moral thesis requiring that someone's conduct be motivated by the desire to conform with rules of a certain sort. The universalizability thesis merely prohibits an agent from affirming contradictory moral judgments.[15]

The other special feature of the logic of moral language is that it is *prescriptive*, or action-guiding. If I judge that I ought to pay my taxes, I am, according to Hare, implying a prescription—"Let me pay my taxes." By prescribing to myself, I commit myself to *doing* what my judgment requires. If no obstacle prevents me, I must act in conformity with my prescription, if I am to be a normal participant in the language of morals. Hare borders on saying that prescriptivity requires one's actions to be consistent with one's judgments. If I judge that you ought to pay your taxes, I imply a prescription, "Pay your taxes." I may judge that it is all right for you, my dinner guest, to refuse dessert. By prescriptivity, I thereby *consent* to your refusing dessert.

By universalizability, I am also committed to the prescription "You, too [if like me in relevant respects]: Pay your taxes" (though I am not committed to *telling* you to pay your taxes). Because of the two central features of moral language—that moral terms imply "universal" application to any relevantly similar situation and that moral terms are prescriptive—Hare calls his ethical theory "universal prescriptivism." The notion of universal prescriptions, it should be recalled, does not imply that one's moral rules need any high degree of generality; nor does the theory of universal prescriptivism generate any imperatives such as the golden rule.

Once the universalizability and prescriptivity of moral judgments are recognized, the strategy of golden rule argumentation follows. If I am considering doing something to someone, presumably I would judge that it is all right to do so. The universalizability of moral judgments implies that I judge that it would be all right for someone to do the same thing to me in an exactly or relevantly similar situation. The prescriptivity of moral judgments implies then for such a situation the prescription "Let the agent do this to me." If I cannot accept that prescription, then I cannot consistently affirm that it is all right for me to do the action in question to my recipient.

The challenge of the moral life, according to this conception, is to actually do what is prescribed by prescriptions that one has passed through the universalizability test. When deliberating about what one ought to do, one is to isolate the morally relevant features of the situation, consider similar situations, including situations where the roles are reversed, and then ask whether one is prepared to prescribe the action in

question for those other situations. Agents are to use imagination to consider what inclinations they would have if they were in the position of the
others; they are to be informed about the facts of the case (actual or supposed); and their preferences must be logically consistent. Faced with a
moral decision, then, given that we have inclinations about how we want
to be treated, all we need is to know the facts of the case (actual or supposed), to imagine ourselves in the positions of others, and to follow the
requirements of logic.

Hare clarified one point that has often muddled discussions of the
golden rule. Recall Kant's counterexample of the sympathetic judge, who
asked himself how he would feel if he had been convicted. The golden
rule, by contrast, pertains to one's *present* attitude toward a hypothetical
situation in which one is a prisoner.

Hare used his method of testing prescriptions to construct an example
of golden rule reasoning adapted from the parable in Matthew's Gospel
about the unforgiving creditor whose debts were forgiven but who refused to forgive, in turn, the man who owed money to him:

> The example is adapted from a well-known parable. A owes money to B,
> and B owes money to C, and it is the law that creditors may exact their
> debts by putting their debtors into prison. B asks himself, "Can I say that
> I ought to take this measure against A in order to make him pay?" He is
> no doubt inclined to do this, or *wants* to do it. Therefore, if there were no
> question of universalizing his prescriptions, he would assent readily to
> the *singular* prescription, "Let me put A into prison." But when he seeks
> to turn this prescription into a moral judgement, and say, "I *ought* to put
> A into prison because he will not pay me what he owes," he reflects that
> this would involve accepting the principle "Anyone who is in my position
> ought to put his debtor into prison if he does not pay." But then he
> reflects that C is in the same position of unpaid creditor with regard to
> himself (B), and that the cases are otherwise identical; and that if anyone
> in this position ought to put his debtors into prison, then so ought C to
> put him (B) into prison. And to accept the moral prescription "C ought
> to put me into prison" would commit him (since, we have seen, he must
> be using the word "ought" prescriptively) to accepting the singular pre-
> scription "Let C put me into prison"; and this he is not ready to accept.
> But if he is not, then neither can he accept the original judgement that
> he (B) ought to put A into prison for debt.[16]

Logically speaking, the merciless debtor cannot conclude that he ought
not throw his creditor into prison. He can only conclude (assuming prescriptions are universalizable) that to throw his debtor into prison is incompatible with his own inclination not to be thrown into prison. Logical
considerations alone do not tell him which element of the contradiction
to reject—his disinclination to be thrown into prison or his inclination to
throw his debtor into prison. The example shows that golden rule consistency (among one's own prescriptions) is not necessary for a particular

moral judgment to be correct. Nor is consistency a sufficent condition of correct moral judgment. We may observe, however, that it is a test of one's willingness to place oneself on a par with others. The problems surrounding this argument continue to be discussed in highly technical responses.[17]

If the golden rule is, initially, a moral principle regarding the conduct of an agent toward a single recipient, how is it to be applied in "multilateral situations," when more than one recipient is involved? Agents must consider the impact of their actions on all those affected, imagining themselves in the position of each, in random sequence. Hare claims that universal prescriptivism leads to utilitarianism.[18] On this theory, since the interests of all are ideally to be taken into account, the effort of moral thinking may be compared to attempting to take the perspective of an *ideal observer*, who would unite in him-or herself the concerns of all to be affected by the action in question.

The counterexample to his theory that Hare discusses most is that of a fanatical Nazi, who considers it right to persecute Jews.[19] (Hare, a prisoner of war in Burma during World War II, has been especially concerned to apply moral philosophy to undermine racism.) Suppose this fanatic were to perform the universalizability test and realize the implication that if he were a Jew then he should also be persecuted. Suppose furthermore that he is one of the rare ideologues who is prepared to accept this conclusion; if genealogical research should prove him a Jew, he is willing to undergo everything that he imposes on other Jews. Moreover, Hare says, the fanatic, by embracing an ideal that is indifferent to people's interests, can satisfy golden rule consistency and put himself beyond the reach of golden rule arguments.[20] Later, developing a more thoroughgoing utilitarianism in *Moral Thinking* (1981), since he had allowed that the intensity of the preferences is relevant to the calculation, Hare claimed that such a counterexample was practically impossible: how could the Nazi's preferences possibly be more intense than the Jew's?[21] Nevertheless, Hare's method judges by the preferences of all those affected. One is to imagine oneself in the position of each person affected by the action. If the population of Nazis were very large, their preferences very intense, and the population of Jews very small and sufficiently tranquilized, what would a utilitarian conclude? For such an implausible situation, Hare follows his theory and flies in the face of what is intuitively morally right.

Hare carefully distinguishes moral judgment from inclinations with which one may empathize; but he makes those inclinations the criterion for moral judgment. Hare wants a theory that could dispense with substantive moral assumptions, but is there not a substantive moral assumption in letting ethical questions be decided by totaling up preference intensities? If someone is prepared to universalize a prescription that seems immoral, Hare's theory gives him just three lines of reply: (1) the individual has failed to imagine vividly enough what it would like to be on the receiving end of such an action (the hurt, the shock, as distrust explodes trust); (2) the individual has failed to take into account the facts of the consequences of such a practice (weakening one's character, contributing to institutional decline); or (3) the individual is admitting a prescription that comes into logical conflict with another inclination that he has (the desire for esteem).

THE IMAGINATIVE ROLE REVERSAL

Responding to Hare, C. C. W. Taylor has objected that, on one interpretation, the role reversal seems to make no sense.[22] Am I required to imagine *being* the other person? To succeed in such an impossible undertaking would produce confusion. I would not know who I am any more. If I were you, I would not be me; but I remain intractably myself. Moreover, something about being you inevitably eludes me. I cannot coherently imagine that I *am* someone I am *not*. How, therefore, can I imagine myself in a hypothetical situation with all your properties? Taylor proposes to solve the problem by drawing distinctions between the first, incoherent interpretation of the imaginative role reversal and two coherent alternatives: I can try to imagine how I *would* feel if I *were* in a different situation; or I can try to imagine how *the other* person would feel. Thinking of how I would feel in a different situation gives an estimate of how the other would feel, though it may be difficult or impossible to imagine how someone very different from myself feels.

Willingness to rely on the imaginative role reversal to solve moral questions is challenged by Alfred J. MacKay, who alleges the following dilemma. On the one hand, where the difference between the agent and the recipient is small, the role reversal is not needed. Insofar as the other is assumed to be like me, I need no imaginative role reversal in order to know the other. On the other hand, where the difference is great, the role reversal cannot bridge the gap of strangeness. The intuitive, imaginative process does not inform me of how the other is likely to be affected. As MacKay put it, "I may as well ask questions directly about Jones as ask them about myself *under the supposition that I have Jones's reaction-relevant characteristics and not my own.*"[23] The consequence of this dilemma is to restrict the function of the imaginative role reversal to reminding oneself of what one already knows.

> When a Buddhist, in a morally difficult situation, is advised to think of what the Lord Buddha would do, the aim is normally to get him to attend to, consider, give due weight to, what he already knows but is likely to overlook. Likewise for putting yourself in someone else's shoes. It may be aimed at remedying the "process defects" of inattention, insensitivity, or bias, presuming that the information about the other's feelings is somehow already available but likely not to be used or used inappropriately.[24]

MacKay's dilemma—that the role reversal is either superfluous or impossible—may haunt, but does not defeat the imaginative role reversal. When one's recipient is familiar and extensively similar to oneself, is there not always the need to be alert to the other's changing needs and the indirect social effects of an action? When one feels oneself relating to the other across an abyss of difference, are imagination and understanding frozen in ignorance? These rejoinders, however, leave untouched MacKay's point about the cognitive value of the imaginative role reversal.

Hare is confident about the solution to problems of applying the role reversal to very different others:

> The difficulty of knowing what it feels like to be a Bantu is . . . one of the same kind as, and greater only in degree than, that of knowing what it is like to be James, my twin brother. The practical . . . difficulty of knowing what it feels like to be a Bantu on a farm is to be got over by a closer and more sympathetic acquaintance with individual Bantus on farms.[25]

The point is well taken. Personal acquaintance facilitates understanding. Hare's point is not that personal acquaintance is required in order to test prescriptions for their consistency with other moral judgments, but that personal acquaintance is needed for an adequate grasp of the facts of a situation and the consequences of a proposed action.

Nevertheless, the limits of a person's experience do pose a problem for the imaginative role reversal, a problem addressed by black philosopher and artist Adrian M. S. Piper:

> Forms of creative expression such as music, painting, poetry, fiction, and first-person narrative accounts enhance our ability to imagine . . . another's inner states, even if we have had no such first-personal experience ourselves. Fresh combinations of images, words, metaphors, and tonal progressions enable us to construct an imaginative vision that may in turn causally transform or enlarge our range of emotional responses. Claims that one cannot understand, for example, what it is like for a woman to be raped if one is a man, or what it is like for a black person to be the object of racial harassment if one is white, have the virtue of refusing to appropriate the singularity of another's experience into one's necessarily limited conception of it. But they are too often based on a simple lack of interest in finding out what it is like through exploring the wide variety of literary and artistic products designed precisely to instruct us about these things. It is not surprising to find a failure of . . . imagination of another's inner states preceded by a failure of curiosity about them or to find a self-centered and narrowly concrete view of others accompanied by a lack of interest in the arts.[26]

Piper advocates artistically enlightened imagination along with emotionally balanced empathy.

One current frontier in the practical extension of the golden rule is to go beyond imaginative role reversals to dialogue and cooperative decision and action.[27] The distinction between imagining and discussing how a rule is to be applied is emphasized in an article by Jürgen Habermas. The first way is to think "monologically, in a merely virtual way," that is, to think all by oneself, how the principle might possibly be applied.[28] Kant had asked what maxims everyone could will as legislation; T. M. Scanlon speaks of a system of rules for action "that everyone concerned can rationally represent as being the result of an informed, uncoerced, and rational agreement of all concerned."[29]

The second way to apply a rule is to conduct an "intersubjectively organized test." Incorporating ideas of George Herbert Mead and Lawrence Kohlberg, Habermas envisions a universal discourse, in which participants would engage in ideal role taking (i.e., would consider what they should ideally want in the others' positions). In case of a moral conflict, the self needs to begin with a sympathetic identification with another, in order to "be able to take the precise perspective from which [the other] could bring his expectations, interests, value orientations, and so forth to bear." Next, the project of role taking must be undertaken by both sides. Dialogue sharpens empathy, "the intuitive understanding that parties . . . bring to one another's situation."[30] Next, one moves from one-to-one relationships to relationships within a group. Now it is possible to test the universalizability of a particular action.[31] Habermas quotes Mead: "The universality of our judgments . . . arises from the fact that we take the attitude of the entire community, of all rational beings."[32] Such universality transcends the limited, ethnocentric fellowship based on sacrifice for the leader, as in Nazism.[33] Practical discourse "transforms ideal role-taking, which in Kohlberg was something to be anticipated privately and in isolation, into a public event, something practiced, ideally, by all together."[34]

Considering how his ideal of justice is to operate with persons who have various conceptions of the good, Habermas distinguishes two concepts of equality: "Equal respect for each person in general as a subject capable of autonomous action means equal treatment; however, equal respect for each person as an individual can mean . . . support for the person as a self-realizing being."[35]

Habermas has developed an ethical theory based on what would be required for individuals to communicate fairly in order to determine the actions that would affect them all. Discourse ethics articulates the conditions required for nondistorted communication between equals. What social conditions, for example, affect the ability of the participants to share knowledgeably in the discussion? Habermas does not advocate an abstract and heartless rationalism:

> Every requirement of universalization must remain powerless unless there also arises, from membership in an ideal communication community, a consciousness of irrevocable solidarity, the certainty of intimate relatedness in a shared life context. . . . Even in the cosmopolitan ideas of the close of the eighteenth century, the archaic bonding energies of

kinship were not extinguished but only refined into solidarity with everything wearing a human face. "*All* men become brothers," Schiller could
say in his "Ode to Joy."[36]

Habermas thus acknowledges the historic association of the moral ideal
with the feeling of humankind as a family.

The last problem with the imaginative role reversal that has attracted
discussion is the question of what aspects of the other person one must
identify with. Identifying with another person seems to be a global experience, not consciously differentiated into aspects. In a particular case, one
discerns intuitively what is relevant in terms of one's practical purpose.
When treating a guest to ice-cream, the host orders what the guest *desires*.
When a mother takes a young child for an immunization shot, she imaginatively identifies with the child's anticipated pain not in order to decide
what to do, but only to think how to best to help the child navigate the
experience; she identifies with the child's interest in being healthy in deciding to have the immunization done. When recommending a diet for a
patient, the physician considers what the patient *needs*. But what if the host
has scruples about chocolate that the guest does not share, or what if the
physician has religious beliefs about pork that the patient does not share?
Must a policeman identify with the beliefs of terrorists? When imagining
how a terrorist will react to being apprehended, the policeman imagines
himself with the terrorist's beliefs, but when judging what to do about the
bomb, he retains his own moral viewpoint: "I judge that, in the reversed
situation, in which I hold the terrorist's beliefs, even if I feel with maximal
intensity that my cause is right, I should be apprehended."

FORMALISM AND THE PROJECT OF MINIMIZING
RELIANCE ON INTUITION

Some analytic philosophers operate with a basic dichotomy between intuitive understanding, expressed in ordinary language, and an ideal rational
analysis. While there is a respect for the subtleties of ordinary language,
which preserves distinctions that philosophers have often neglected, and
while analyses are evaluated, to some extent, by their fit with "our intuitions," intuition is often regarded as equivalent to a naive and uneducated
hunch. Isolated intuitions, the "plain person's" way of taking things, however necessary they may be for daily life, are often regarded by philosophers as standing in need of translation into a more adequate vocabulary,
and in need of the context of some sort of general theory.

Thus many philosophers criticize the traditional golden rule for being
vague. "Treat others as you want to be treated" is not as precise as say, the
"rational core" that can be distilled from the rule, as in the reformulations
of Clarke, Sidgwick, Singer, or this one by Bruce Alton: "If A is rational
about rule R, then if there are reasons for A to think R applies to others'
conduct toward A, and A is similar to those others in relevant respects,

then there are reasons for A to think R applies to A's conduct toward others."[37] Alton argues that the golden rule must be understood as a formal principle stating a requirement that any particular moral rule (e.g., about reciprocating favors, acting fairly, or being loving) must satisfy in order to qualify as a *rational* moral rule. The golden rule cannot be *equated* with any particular moral rule, though it is often *associated* with one or more such rules. In this context, the formality of the golden rule has not to do with any intimidating symbolic notation, but with the fact that it is a constant throughout the variation of particular rules that are used in practically applying the golden rule.

The most thorough formal treatment of the golden rule as a principle of consistency has been worked out by Harry J. Gensler, developing key ideas of Hare in a new book, *Formal Ethics*.[38] Gensler's intuitive formulation of the rule is this: "Treat others only in ways that you're willing to be treated in the same situation." His precise formulation (setting aside the symbolic logic formulation) is this: "Don't combine (1) acting to do A to X, and (2) not consenting to the idea of A being done to you in an exactly similar situation."

Logic furnishes the first part of Gensler's concept of consistency. Logic requires that we be consistent in our beliefs, that is, that that we not embrace contradictory beliefs, and that we not accept a belief while rejecting another that logically follows from it (with the qualification that the person is, or should be, aware of the logical relationships). Logic is helpful in forcing us to be clear and to spell out our presuppositions. Gensler uses a broad rationality axiom, which runs, intuitively worded, "One ought to think and live consistently with logic and the other axioms of formal ethics."

In addition to logical consistency there is practical consistency (my term), or conscientiousness, which has several components. This sort of consistency is violated if our willing is inconsistent; if our desires, resolutions, and actions conflict with each other; if we will the end but not the required means; or if we do not live in harmony with our moral beliefs. Gensler claims that to accept an imperative is to act (when nothing prevents our doing so). So there can be consistency or inconsistency between willing and acting. Gensler sets forth a twofold "weak prescriptivity" axiom: "If you ought to do A, then do A. If it's all right for you to do A, then you may do A." He uses this axiom to prove that it's inconsistent to prescribe an action that one judges not to be all right. Consistency in our willing also includes not accepting that we should do an action while being unwilling to undertake the means required. If the necessary means are unacceptable, we cannot consistently will the end. Conscientiousness involves keeping our actions, resolutions, and desires in harmony with our ethical beliefs.

The next kind of consistency is impartiality, the requirement that we make similar evaluations about similar cases, regardless of the individuals involved. To derive his impartiality theorem, Gensler uses a universaliza-bility axiom, which, intuitively formulated, is this: "If act A ought to be done (would be all right), then any act exactly or relevantly similar to act A in its universal properties in any actual or hypothetical case also ought to be done (would be all right)."[39] In cases where it is hard to specify relevant similarity, one can revert to exact similarity. According to univer-salizability, if it would be all right for you to do A to X, then in an exactly similar situation it would be all right for A to be done to you. The impar-tiality theorem, which leads to the golden rule, is this: "Don't combine (1) believing that it would be all right for you to do A to X, and (2) not believing that in an exactly reversed situation it would be all right for X to do A to you."

On the basis of the axioms and theorems just summarized, Gensler is in a position to give a strict proof of his formulation of the golden rule. In addition, he shows that an impartial and conscientious agent would necessarily accept the golden rule, and that there are many (at least 4,320) variations of the golden rule that are also theorems, and more (at least 30,240) misformulations which, combined with factual premises, can be used to derive absurdities. The correct formulations usually have a don't-combine form, a similar-situation qualifier, and a phrase expressing one's present attitude to a hypothetical situation.

Gensler then explores a *generalization* of the golden rule, the formula of universal law, which requires that we act only as we're willing for anyone to act in similar circumstances. This formula covers cases where we are (primarily) simply treating *ourselves* in a certain way (such as neglecting our health) that we are unwilling for others to do in a similar case, or in a way we would later regret.

Consistency, as Gensler recognizes, is not everything in ethics. We may be consistent and still be wrong. Discussing the problem of racism and rationality, Gensler relates a report of a Nazi who, upon discovering that he had Jewish ancestry, arranged for himself and his family to be put in concentration camps and killed. "This Nazi," Gensler comments, "was consistent." Formal ethics cannot, by itself, declare his action wrong, but there is one more thing that it can do to further minimize the possibility that people willing to engage in ethical reasoning will be able to retain such terrible prescriptions. This final contribution is to assist in con-structing ideals of moral rationality in addition to the formal consistency requirements already mentioned. These conditions are semiformal; they cannot be usefully systematized using variables and constants, yet they are theory-neutral and depend upon the formal conditions. These added conditions are ideals that we are to approach as much as is reasonably practical. First, we should have all the helpful factual data about circum-stances, alternatives, consequences, pros and cons, and so on. Next, it is important vividly to imagine ourselves being in the exact situation of the other person. Then, there are various personal qualities, such as being motivated to find out what one ought to do, being creative in exploring alternate means, being receptive to advice from others who better satisfy the conditions of moral rationality. Such a list is admittedly incomplete, but it can be recursively revised: do your best with your initial list, then revise the list; do your best with the revised list, then make further adjustments, and so on. At each stage of growth, you are to deliberate by satisfying, as well as possible, the conditions that you want others, ideally, to satisfy.

Gensler's ethics is formal in a complex sense. He explains that formal ethics, like formal logic, has principles that are largely uncontroversial, however much disagreement there may be about their meaning and justification and about how useful they are. Formal ethics is theory-neutral since it does not make substantive foundational commitments (e.g., about the inherent dignity of each person). Gensler aims to provide some formal tools of moral reasoning that can be incorporated into practically any approach to ethics. He believes that Hare's insights into golden rule reasoning are so valuable that they should be articulated to make them available for use by people no matter what theory they subscribe to—egoism, naturalism, emotivism, non-naturalism, or Gensler's briefly sketched Kantian moral realism. He illustrates how each theory has reasons to accept the conditions of moral rationality that he proposes.

Though neither formal logic or formal ethics is a realm of absolute clarity and order, both deserve the same broad acceptance, according to Gensler. Principles in both areas are tested by looking for absurd instances. Both articulate certain rational patterns in our thinking into an axiomatic system; Gensler states, however, that his informal analysis has been adjusted to fit formal requirements rather than the other way around. Both formal logic and formal ethics require predicates with no vagueness, and each term must have a constant meaning and reference. No formal system can prove everything. Thus, intuition is needed to grasp first principles. Where we disagree on intuitions, however, we appeal to logic and consistency. Formal ethics uses expressions containing variables, logical terms, and a few other fairly abstract notions like *ought*, *ends–means*, *believe*, *desire*, and *act*. Formal ethics does not, by itself, tell anyone what to do. Rather, it provides tools of reasoning that will sharpen anyone's moral thinking.

CONCLUSION

The golden rule might be dubbed "mother of theories." The variety of productive analyses of the golden rule examined here suggests that the rule's capacity to stimulate formal ethical thinking is far from exhausted. Contemporary studies of generalization, the implications of moral language, and universalizability demonstrate connections between rationality and morality and form an essential chapter in the comprehension of the golden rule. These studies show that there is much more of interest in the rule than facile refutations would suggest. Counterexamples will only harrass the rule if it is abstracted from every context, taken literally, and made to function as a necessary or sufficient condition for sound moral judgment or as the sole normative axiom in a system of ethics. One always has more to learn from the tradition of Singer, Hare, Alton, Hoche, Kese, Gensler, and others. Nevertheless, although they do not contradict most of what I am about to say, several comments are in order about the limits of formal interpretations of the golden rule.

Each formal reconstruction of the rule incorporates some discovery of meaning in the rule, but does it include every insight that other inter-preters have gained? Formal interpretations remain partial, however illu-minating they may be. In Alton's system, the rule is an axiom, in Gensler's, a derived theorem. The fact that the rule can function variously in differ-ent systems is a clue that morality transcends any one axiomatic system. The point is not that systematic thinking is unhelpful, only that no such system can capture and organize everything in a manner ideally suited to every concern.

If the golden rule is reduced to a principle of consistency or univer-salizability, then an intuition implicit in the rule is sacrificed. The rule implies respect for persons, as Kant expressed in his second formulation of the categorical imperative, giving his philosophy a balance that we intu-itively sense in the golden rule but which the universalizability principle taken in isolation lacks. The formal approaches leave open the question about what the relevant similarities are between persons that help us un-derstand our duty. Alton writes of persons and Gensler's system uses vari-ables that refer to persons, but it is just this notion of person that chal-lenges philosophy. To use the term "person" to classify myself and others presupposes that we have something important in common, though a logical system cannot determine what that is; rather, talk of rationality and consistency defers the issue. What is it to be a person? Progress in metae-thics or deontic logic may give the misleading impression that ethics can be worked out without having to trouble with such basic philosophic in-quiry.

Formalism talks of "the facts" as though the notion were philosophi-cally unproblematic, and in many practical cases this is so. In some cases, however, the facts need to be scientifically established, and social science is often problematic since philosophic and religious issues regarding the concept of what it means to be a human being are in dispute.

Sometimes it seems as though the goal of formalism is not to sharpen moral intuition but to replace it as completely as possible by carefully stated propositions. Moral intuition, however, is better conceived as the capacity for insight into duty; consequently, the task of ethics is to sharpen, not replace, intuition on the path toward insight. We need intu-ition not only for daily living when there may be no time to compose a reflective response to a situation; we also need intuition to suspect that we need to reflect on a course of action, to suspect that something has gone wrong in a given moral theory, to choose first principles, to help validate rules of inference, to formulate appropriate action descriptions, and to see the point of arguments. Most theorists acknowledge that we cannot demonstrate the validity of our basic, intuitive concern for duty. Intuitions are corrigible, and they are corrected through argument; but argument depends upon the marshalling of evidence based on other intuitions. Theory does not descend from the intellectual heights to instruct poor intuition; rather, theory sharpens, extends, builds on, clarifies intuition. There is an unending mutual correction of intuition by reflection, and of reflection by intuition.

For all its advantages, formalism misses the beauty in goodness. To some extent, we cannot define—and thereby express as a rule—the flavor of how we want to be treated. Perhaps we can devise a label for it (e.g., "with love," "with spontaneous good cheer," "graciously"). People manifest graciousness very differently. No behavioral description can capture it. Heartening, enjoyable, luminous, it is partly an aesthetic quality that defies formal ethical treatment. Acknowledging the importance of how we act (as well as what we do) opens a door for an aesthetics of ethics.

The golden rule of rational consistency is thus an essential part of the story, but not the whole story. If there are not just two levels of ethics—rough intuition and rational clarity—then it cannot be assumed that scientifically philosophical discourse is the arbiter of its own place within the whole.

This critique of the limits of formal ethics can be put positively by saying that the golden rule functions properly within the context of a wider philosophy of living.

eleven

A Principle of Sensitivity and Respect

Contemporary philosophies of self and other are providing a new context for interpreting the golden rule, especially for thinkers developing the continental European traditions of philosophy. One cannot help remarking that world war has marked the lives of surprisingly many of the authors treated in these chapters, including three discussed here, heightening sensitivities, strengthening moral conviction, and showing the reciprocal influence of philosophical reflection and committed human living.

THE EXPERIENCE OF EMPATHY: EDITH STEIN

The careful study of empathy has been undertaken in the philosophical tradition of phenomenology. This discipline, as developed by Edmund Husserl (1859–1938) and others, originally aimed to describe rigorously the most general features of experience, and it may be regarded as a philosophic approach to psychology. Describing the experience of other persons, Husserl focused on the phase of relating in which the self, the conscious subject, forms its sense of the other. According to Husserl (philosophizing in the first person singular, inviting the reader to see for himself or herself and speak forth his or her own insight), I, as an embodied ego, in the presence of another person before me, recognize that person as analogous to myself. The other person's stream of experience is never intuitively presented to me as though it were part of my own stream of experience. For this reason, in talking about intersubjective understanding, Husserl speaks of *apperception* rather than intuition, to indicate that I do not perceive the other's experience, even though I do have a sense of it: I apperceive it. Nor do I go through a process of inference, reasoning that the other person's body is similar to what mine would look like if I were experiencing X, so the other person must be experiencing X (or something similar), too.[1] There is no reasoning that goes on in the miracle of the recognition of one embodied ego by another. I do not first view the other's body as a material thing and then imagine that there must be some subject inside this thing; rather, I see the body of the other as already animated by consciousness, as a living body.[2]

Husserl never published an extended discussion of empathy, but that was done by his assistant Edith Stein (1891–1942), whose life illustrates the mutual reinforcement of academic and practical commitments. While an assistant to Husserl, she interrupted her studies in 1915 to serve in the Red Cross. In 1916, back from the war, she completed a dissertation under Husserl on the phenomenology of empathy. Raised an Orthodox Jew, she had lost her faith early, but became interested in religion through the influence of Max Scheler and others whom she met in Gottingen where she had gone to study. She was baptized a Roman Catholic in 1922, and taught in a convent school run by Dominican nuns; then, in 1933, no longer permitted to teach, she entered a Carmelite convent, where she continued writing on philosophy, women, and spiritual living.[3] In 1938 she was transferred for her safety to the Netherlands, but she was apprehended by the Gestapo on August 2, 1942, and sent to a concentration camp in Westerbork. There are accounts of her in Westerbork before her transfer to Auschwitz on August 7 and her execution on August 9. Hilda Graef has pieced together the story of Stein's last days.

> Some prisoners who were fortunate enough to be released have preserved accounts of their impression of Sister Benedicta. They stress her extraordinary calm and the great charity with which she devoted herself to the care of the children in the camp, whom she washed and dressed as best she could, since their own mothers, beside themselves with fear, were too distressed to do so.[4]

In her book on empathy, Stein observed that controversies over empathy are "based on the implied assumption that foreign [fremd] subjects and their experience are given to us."[5] She uses the term "empathy" as the title for our basic recognition of other consciousness; her book examines every phase of human recognition, though only a portion is summarized here. Empathy as awareness of another is distinguished from sympathy, which in Stein's strict usage, means feeling the same thing together with someone, for example in rejoicing over the same good news.[6]

Stein's contribution most immediately relevant to the golden rule is her explication of an empathic comprehension prior to the imaginative role reversal, showing, by contrast, how the latter can be regarded as derivative.

Like Husserl, Stein emphasizes that the experience of empathy is an experiencing of another's experience, although the other's experiences do not become one's own. One's own experiences are "primordial"—they belong to one's own stream of experience—whereas another's experiences are not primordial. "While I am living in the other's joy, I do not feel primordial joy. It does not issue live from my 'I.' "

Stein portrays a process of empathy moving through a cycle of three phases. The first phase is empathy in the simplest sense:

> Let us take an example to illustrate the nature of the act of empathy. A friend tells me that he has lost his brother and I become aware of his pain. What kind of an awareness is this? I am not concerned here with going into the basis on which I infer the pain. Perhaps his face is pale and disturbed, his voice toneless and strained. Perhaps he also expresses his pain in words. Naturally these things can all be investigated, but they are not my concern here. I would like to know, not how I arrive at this awareness, but what it itself is. . . . I perceive this countenance outwardly and the pain is given "at one" with it.[7]

Starting from phase 1, initial empathy, one may be spontaneously drawn into phase 2, experiencing the situation from the other's position, and then one returns, in phase 3, to face the other person directly, so to speak, once again, having deepened one's sense of the other's experience. Initially, the other's experience

> arises before me all at once, it faces me as an object (such as the sadness I "read" in another's face). But when I inquire into its implied tendencies (try to bring another's mood into clear givenness to myself), the content, having pulled me into it, is no longer really an object. I am no longer turned to the content but to the object of it, am at the subject of the content in the original subject's place. And only after successfully executed clarification, does the content again face me as an object.[8]

Moving into the second phase is not an imagining, not a deliberate act to approximate an impossible cognition, but something more like following out the threads of one's present involvement, being engaged in attending to the other's experience. Immersing oneself in the other's experience more thoroughly brings it into fuller view. "To project oneself into another [hineinversetzen] means to carry out his experience with him."[9] Indeed, there is a phase of empathy which involves sustained, self-forgetting involvement in the other as the drama of the other unfolds before one's "eyes" (in text or conversation or conduct). For example, watching an acrobat: "I am not one with the acrobat but only "at" him. I do not actually go through his motions but only quasi."[10] Rather, at the "highest grade of the consummation of empathy—we are 'at' the foreign subject and turned with it to its object."[11] Phase 2 involves self-forgetting, but not (normally) a feeling of oneness, an emotional fusion of self and other, a regress to a level prior to interpersonal differentiation.[12] In particular, empathy does not imply living in feelings that are spontaneously transmitted from one person to another. Stein emphasizes the difference between empathy and emotional invasion:

> When I want to stop worrying, I seek out gay company. . . . It is certain that as we are saturated by such "transferred" feelings, we live in them and thus in ourselves. This prevents our turning toward or submerging

ourselves in the foreign experience, which is the attitude characteristic of empathy.[13]

Stein insists that "empathy" is the fundamental experience, and that the imaginative moves of putting oneself in the other's situation and bringing to mind the other's situation are derivative and secondary phenomenona.[14] The point is not that there is something wrong about the imaginative role reversal. "Should empathy fail, this procedure can make up the deficiency . . . . We could call this surrogate for empathy an 'assumption' but not empathy itself."[15]

BEYOND EMPATHY: HANS REINER

From the natural law tradition of ethics, relatively marginalized in contemporary ethics, has come, in the writings of Hans Reiner, a major boost to research and thinking about the golden rule. Twentieth-century Western scholarship on the golden rule has been marked by enhanced historical understanding, careful reasoning, and creative encounter with a diverse philosophic and religious traditions.[16] All these features are represented by Reiner, who drew especially on Aquinas and Kant to offer an updated statement of several central strands of Western ethics.[17]

Reiner's 1948 article "Die 'goldene Regel,'" influential for German discussions of the rule in philosophy and theology, merits a detailed review, since it uses fresh philosophical reflection on new historical research to develop a sequence of interpretations of the rule.[18] Mindful of objections to the rule raised by Leibniz (that the rule presupposes social norms) and Kant (e.g., that a judge would have to forgo punishing a criminal), Reiner insisted that it is necessary to avoid "the mistake of taking the . . . self-evident character of the golden rule as a sign of something final, incapable of further explication."[19] One must not rely simply on the verbal formulation in order to interpret the rule.

According to Reiner, the golden rule must be distinguished from a number of ethically unsatisfactory principles sometimes associated or confused with it: repaying good with good and evil with evil; conforming to custom; and doing whatever the other person wants. The golden rule has three distinct, essential forms or meanings. What all three have in common, it turns out, is that they use one firm and definite willing (about what one wants to experience or does not want to suffer, or about what one judges to be right or wrong) as a standard for deciding about some action of one's own that is in question.

In its first essential form, the golden rule enjoins action based on empathy (Einfühlung). Most formulations of the golden rule do not explicitly exclude this interpretation. What concept of the will is implicit in the antecedent clause, "Whatsoever you will that people should do to you"? The will envisaged in this interpretation is naturally and egoistically striving for what is pleasant and useful and avoiding what is unpleasant and frustrating. Both positive and negative formulations of the rule are thus relevant, corresponding to what one does or does not want to experience or suffer. The practice of the rule of empathy is an exercise of practical love—being considerate of others, not acting unpleasantly or harmfully, bringing aid and comfort.

The rule of empathy calls for the crucial transition from self-centeredness to ethical willing. Although the will that here serves as the standard for how to treat others is the egoistic will, the rule of empathy precisely calls for transcending the egoistic standpoint.[20] The rule of empathy is attuned to "relative" values that not everyone enjoys or possesses, values that are relative to oneself or to others (e.g., the value of having enough to eat). Though we originally experience ("feel") these values in our own case, the values are to be actualized for others, too, and so we must promote others' realization of them. Additional principles are required to decide what to do in cases where an action can avoid harm to another person only at the cost of injuring oneself or a third person, and in cases where higher and lower values conflict.

Since he saw the golden rule as a principle of natural law transcending any particular human social order, and since he had studied how medieval Christian ethics became a static ethics of order, Reiner paid keen attention to the worry that the golden rule presupposes existing social norms. He argued later that this dependence of the rule on existing social norms does not pertain to the second or third essential forms of the rule and can therefore be regarded as a defect merely of the rule of empathy, not a fatal objection to the golden rule in its full development. How, then, from the limited perspective of the rule of empathy, could one respond to the counterexample of the criminal appealing to the golden rule in order to get released by the judge? The counterexample provokes the realization that the rule is tacitly understood to operate only within certain limits. The rule of empathy is obviously not intended to preempt valid values of social order, such as law, ownership, and punishment. Such values are tacitly accorded precedence over the values evoked by the rule, so the rule has no fundamental importance; it supplements the principles governing daily life and the social order. Despite the value of such a golden rule in sustaining legitimate institutions, the rule would presumably be deprived of any power to criticize institutional norms.[21]

The second essential form of the golden rule Reiner calls the "rule of autonomy." "Autonomy" refers to the standard or law (nomos) that one takes for oneself (autos). The central idea of the rule of autonomy is that one's praise or blame for others' conduct is to be taken as the standard for one's own conduct. This rule covers not only interactions with others, but all conduct.

Much more is involved in the rule of autonomy than the idea that our estimate of the ethical quality of others' actions is likely to be less distorted than our judgment of our own actions. Unlike the rule of empathy (pertaining to what we do or do not *want*), the rule of autonomy starts out from an *ethical* judgment. This does not involve *presupposing* existing social norms. Now we come to the core of Reiner's philosophy of ethical judgment as presented here (setting aside the theological dimension of natural law theory) affirming that values, real values, are felt, and that laws of ethics are based on values. We spontaneously feel the values (or disvalues) in another's conduct, and then acknowledge the necessary connection between our ethical valuations and ethical requirements that we ourselves must accept.[22] Expressing valuations of another's conduct implies our will that actions, including our own, accord with them. Autonomy implies that the will freely recognizes and adopts the demands arising from the most basic value judgments. This rule of autonomy differs from Kant's categorical imperative: whereas moral reasoning for Kant begins with the principle that only universalizable maxims are acceptable, moral reasoning with the rule of autonomy proceeds from particular valuations.

In all the literature of the golden rule, there is no more compelling account of the import of golden rule consistency than the one Reiner gives. Writing just after World War II, he describes the consequences of betraying the rule of autonomy, violating one's conscience, failing to act according to the standards set by one's judgments of others' conduct. To set a high standard for others but not for oneself brings both experiential and objective consequences, shame and loss of credibility, as one's show of being ultimately serious about high standards is exposed to oneself and others. Thus one is centrally untrue to oneself. Crucial to being human is the ability to determine oneself according to principles that express absolute and relative values. To appear to commit oneself and then to give up when it becomes burdensome corrupts one's value as a person of enduring unity and wholeness. To fail the decisive test is not a matter of logical consistency but an issue of character. Moreover, there is a social expectation that all will do their part in promoting values; thus it is unjust to seek a special advantage for oneself by not doing one's part. Any citizen who wants to live in a civilized condition with a degree of trustworthiness cannot exempt himself or herself from being trustworthy, too. It is not enough to defer responsibility to the police or other authorities, for the state depends on *people* of a certain character. One loses the right and the ability (insofar as one's betrayal is known) to communicate moral expectations to others; this is especially true for parents, teachers, and those in positions of political power. To want others to act morally expresses one's wish to live in an ethical world. Part of one's interest in such a world is egoistic, but part can be love for objective values in themselves; to betray them is to be unworthy to live in the ethical community. The rule of autonomy directs us, in a certain way, to these discoveries.

The golden rule in Reiner's third form, the rule of reciprocity (*Gegenseitigkeit*), is the same as the rule of autonomy, with the restriction that it envisages only conduct affecting others. Whereas the rule of empathy had focused on what one wants to experience or does not want to suffer, attention shifts to what the other person *does* and to one's *ethical judgment* of the other's conduct. In the rule of reciprocity, the standard for one's own conduct is the treatment of oneself by others that one recognizes to be right. In the rule of reciprocity we have, at last, a golden rule that can be put into practice. It also can serve as a foundation for social order, though an additional principle is needed to instruct the judge what to do to "restore the rule in cases where it is violated."[23] The golden rule can thus be "completely understood and justified as a principle of 'natural law.' "[24]

In systematic ethical writings drawing on Aquinas and Kant, Reiner placed the golden rule in a wider context, emphasizing the function of conscience in free human personality. Our obligations to *act* in certain ways are grounded in objective obligations about how we are to *be*, and feelings of responsibility and respect point to these objective obligations.[25] The golden rule plays a key role alongside many other principles, including principles of justice, love, reverence for life, and recognition of higher and lower values.[26]

In a 1977 article Reiner explored the relation between the golden rule and natural law, presenting new historical research and arguing that the golden rule plays a key role in demonstrating certain basic rights, evident to reason. Here, in a nutshell, is the argument. The initial thought is that a just social order is prefigured by our response to an attack on our body or life.[27] Then, according to the golden rule as Reiner had previously interpreted it, insofar as our judgment on others' behavior presupposes a norm, we already grasp an ethical reason for our own action. (In other words, we do not merely dislike it when others interfere with our possessions or capacities; we feel that wrong has been done.) Putting oneself in the place of others, then, leads to recognizing the demand for equity, since one can only expect one's own claims to be recognized as objective if one recognizes others' comparable claims (regarding security from attack). The same reasoning can be extended to other rights than the basic rights regarding one's body or life. Those who apply the golden rule are thus led toward a social order in which fundamental rights are recognized.

THE INFINITE DIGNITY AND NEED OF THE OTHER: EMMANUEL LEVINAS

The philosophy of Emmanuel Levinas, a French Jew imprisoned by the Nazis, developed in response to totalitarianism, which accords ethical recognition to people only insofar as they are the *same*. Levinas portrays each other person as radically different from the self-absorbed, separate ego, whose private enjoyments conceal hatred of the other. The other breaks into the separate ego on a level prior to the ego's opportunity for a self-collected act of conscious commitment. The very face of the other carries the absolute command "You shall not kill," and the abyss of the other's need calls the self into radical responsibility.

Levinas explored how the categories of Western philosophy, in contrast with Jewish religion, cooperate with the domination of the same over the other. Inasmuch as the ego lives in the project of assimilating everything to itself (e.g., by scientific and philosophical understanding and technical control), relation becomes impossible. His claim is that each of us is wrapped up in the ideology and the totalitarian practice of "the same" until we acknowledge our own abjection before the other, recognize the other as the master of justice, give ourselves over sacrificially to the service of the other. Levinas exhausts the resources of language in his extreme insistence on recognizing the otherness of the other. To look into the face of the other is to confront the infinite, and the dignity of the other calls for a degree of respect that borders on self-abasement. The claim of each other upon the self is so thoroughgoing that it is difficult to think how to respond to multiple others in a group.

The response to the other that is required is to put oneself in the place of the other; but this, for Levinas, is not a cognitive adventure to guide one in applying an abstract moral principle. No sympathetic appropriation of the other's "interests" is authentically possible; no technology of social welfare judgments does justice to the other who faces you. The mind's effort at comprehension obscures the infinity of the other. To put oneself in the place of the other means bearing responsibility for everything that every other is and does, for example, by taking the other's punishment. An example may be found in a story told by Edith Wyschogrod of the Polish Franciscan Maksymilian Kolbe, who was sent to Auschwitz and who persuaded a camp official to substitute for a fellow prisoner sentenced to death.[28] Insofar as the rule "Do to others as you want others to do to you" participates in simplistic assumptions that ignore the otherness of the other, it, too, is caught in totalitarian thinking.

According to David Goicoechea, Levinas provides "a profound alteration and yet renewal of the golden rule."[29] A key issue is whether the relation to the other be interpreted as symmetrical (as in the equalitarian interpretation of the rule in modern Western philosophy) or asymmetrical, as in various stories of the Old Testament (e.g., Abraham obeying Sara's command to send away Hagar and Ishmael), and in various images (e.g., the suffering servant). According to Goicoechea, "The suffering face of the other obligates me to do unto her or him as she or he would have me do unto her or him." The question arises, "How does the suffering servant who submits and is committed to the suffering other respond to the right other and the right command?" Prior to any knowledge, prior to any decision, comes the appeal of the other. The abused other cannot relate reciprocally; but the guilty me can give and serve sacrificially, can suffer as a substitute for the other, can be a hostage for the other, in the hope of reconciliation, in the hope, never guaranteed, of reciprocal relation.

A MIDDLE WAY: PAUL RICOEUR

Paul Ricoeur, a French philosopher who also knew the inside of a Nazi prison, spent much of his career at the University of Chicago and shows close contact with many currents of philosophy. In his earliest book, *Freedom and the Will*, he investigated how active, voluntary phases of willing are always correlated with involuntary, passive phases, in which the self is involved in responding to conditions not of its own volition. That same theme is developed in terms of interpersonal relationships in his most recent book, *Oneself as Another*, where he explores the moral relation with the other to elucidate the nature of the self. His thesis is that action is interaction that always comports a passive aspect. Ricoeur assigns the golden rule a significant place in a morality in the context of a philosophy of the relation between self and other. The key to Ricoeur's use of the golden rule is the recognition that in action there is experienced an unbalanced relation between the agent and the recipient of the action. The agent exercises a certain power over the recipient. What the agent does (or what the speaker says) affects the other, who has an unavoidable degree of passivity as the recipient of the action. Insofar as violence (in a gross or subtle way) infects action, or when "disesteem of self and hatred of others" come into play, the passivity of the recipient is turned into real suffering.[30] "Do to others as you want others to do to you" is a call for reciprocity in light of the fact that in the exchange of roles the agent becomes the sufferer. In dialogue, moreover, the exchange of roles is not merely imagined, but actual, since each person, in turn, adopts the role of self, by saying "I" and addressing the other as "you." Each in turn poses a question calling for an answer.

In order to comprehend Ricoeur's interpretation of the golden rule, it is first necessary to grasp his relational concept of the self. He positions his philosophy between what he presents as two extremes, the philosophy of Husserl, which tends to regard the other as analogous to the self, a variation on the theme of the self, and the philosophy of Emmanuel Levinas, which posits an other so absolutely commanding and suffering, so radically other than the self-absorbed ego, that a relationship of equals is hardly envisioned. Ricoeur interprets these philosophies as bearing complementary insights that can be clarified and synthesized. Ricoeur responds to Husserl and Levinas by drawing on Aristotle, Kant, and diverse contemporary analytic and phenomenological philosophers to develop a new concept of the self. What does it mean to be a self, and how do I know? One possible answer is that each person knows himself or herself intuitively, introspectively. What could be more obvious? And yet we often conceal ourselves from ourselves. Therefore, it is only by way of an extended detour that we approach self-knowledge.

Ricoeur presents the self as an agent in the objective world, as understood through narrative, and as ethically and morally related to others.

When we ask *what* the agent is, we think of a character, a (relatively) continuous sameness, a set of predicates in terms of which it is possible to
objectively identify someone as the same person from one year to the
next.[31] These stabilities, however, never make up the whole story. When
we ask *who* the agent is, we turn to the dramatic dynamics of the self as
an embodied subject whose initiative produces effects in the objective
world, even though it transcends the predicates of the objective world.
Ricoeur uses the term "flesh" to name the body as subjectively lived. The
self is not like a log, waiting to be described with the fixed predicates of
things. The self, rather, is a process, never complete, never all wrapped
up in a package tied with a nice bow. Given the possibility of lies, deceit,
misunderstanding, and illusion, the question of veracity haunts the agent's
self-descriptions.[32] The question of how trustworthy the agent will prove
to be is at issue in every promise.

Narrative highlights the self as agent and sufferer. It is in narrative (including stories not intended as imaginative fiction but as history), that the
self acquires a relatively unified, coherent sense. Narrative synthesizes the
stable predicates of character together with departures, reversals of for-
tune, and contingent events. The self resulting from this synthesis involves
"a dialectic of ownership and of dispossession, of care and of carefreeness,
of self-affirmation and of self-effacement."[33] Since our lives are interwoven
with one another, we do not absolutely determine our own lives, but are
rather coauthors.[34] Therefore, the golden rule does not impose itself as a
merely external or arbitrary demand, since the self is not, to begin with, a
self-constituted, self-understood, self-sufficient entity. "Action is interaction."[35] While sometimes the projects of different individuals dovetail
nicely, sometimes they diverge and conflict: one person's action is another's suffering. In Ricoeur's broad sense, sufferers are "those affected by
processes of modification or conservation"; agents are those who initiate
those processes.[36]

The speaker or agent "imposes" something on the listener or recipient; hence their relation may be said to be asymmetrical, with "suffering"
imposed upon the recipient. In caring ("solicitude"), however, the asymmetrical relation between agent and sufferer can become a relation of giving and receiving. Despite the obvious difference between giving and receiving, Ricoeur discerns a "sort of equalizing" that keeps sympathy, "the
wish to share someone else's pain," from becoming "simple pity, in which
the self is secretly pleased to know it has been spared."

> In true sympathy, the self, whose power of acting is at the start greater
> than that of its other, finds itself affected by all that the suffering other
> offers to it in return. For from the suffering other there comes a giving
> that is no longer drawn from the power of acting and existing but pre-
> cisely from weakness itself. This is perhaps the supreme test of solicitude,
> when unequal power finds compensation in an authentic reciprocity in
> exchange, which, in the hour of agony, finds refuge in the shared whisper

of voices or the feeble embrace of clasped hands. . . . A self reminded of the condition of mortality can receive from the friend's weakness more than he or she can give in return by drawing from his or her own reserves of strength.[37]

Aware of its lack, its need of friends, the self perceives itself, not as self-sufficient, but as "another among others"; thus friendship can be mutual. This involves the element of reversibility—that self and other can exchange roles, for example the roles of speaker and the one spoken to, saying "I" and "you" to each other, or in putting oneself in the other's place in imagination and sympathy. Nevertheless it remains true that persons are not substitutable for one another; each is irreplaceable, as one discovers in losing a loved one.

What role does the golden rule play in the larger drama of ethical and moral living? Ricoeur defines ethical fulfillment as the good life with and for others, in just institutions. He bases self-esteem primarily on a common human capacity: "I am that being who can evaluate his actions and, in assessing the goals of some of them to be good, is capable of evaluating himself and of judging himself to be good."[38] Ricoeur, like Kant and Mill before him, offers an argument for other-regarding action. Since the other, too, is a oneself capable of the achievements that encourage self-esteem, "I cannot myself have self-esteem unless I esteem others *as* myself."[39] At times the capacity is actualized, the "resources of goodness . . . spring forth"; one has "the conviction of judging well and acting well in a momentary and provisional approximation of living well."[40] It is not enough, however, merely to aim for the good life and to enjoy self-esteem. Radical evil, for which the individual is responsible, corrupts human motives to such an extent that the individual alone cannot put things straight, and domination tends to corrupt the relation between agent and recipient. Self-esteem tends toward conceit and toward taking excessive advantages for oneself. The remedy that Ricoeur proposes is a moral filter to purify self-esteem into self-respect.

Morality requires the agent to act only in ways that are universalizable, fair for everyone. But morality involves more than the principle of universalizability and a respect for humanity as a unitary concept. Morality also requires respect for persons, for a plurality that cannot be reduced to the set of predicates that are shared by humanity.[41] Kant's imperative of respect for persons expresses clearly and formally the gist of the popularly phrased golden rule.[42] Where Kant had elevated respect for the moral law above respect for persons, Ricoeur holds to the golden rule as getting the priorities right.

Ricoeur presents both positive and negative formulations of the golden rule as expressing legitimate principles. The negative form cannot be eliminated because there is an enduring need to say no to violence. The rule implicitly prohibits all types of evil, from manipulation to violence concealed in language, torture that destroys self-respect and the power to act, violation of property rights, sexual violence, and murder.[43] Ricoeur finds that the negative form facilitates moral creativity: it "leaves open the range of things that are not forbidden and in this way makes room for moral invention in the order of what is permitted."[44] It is clearer in the positive formulation that morality requires actually engaging in benevolent action. Finally, the positive formulation is implied in and hence is more basic than the negative formulation, because prohibition presupposes something that is affirmed. In the mutual exchange of self-esteems, original affirmation arises.

For Ricoeur, the special merit of the golden rule is that it calls for the norm of reciprocity over against the power asymmetry implicit in the difference between agent and recipient. A morality that only emphasizes regard for the common humanity of persons eliminates difference, but the golden rule keeps alive the sense of the difference of agent and recipient. On this analysis, even solicitude, it would seem, cannot avoid domination. Thus the golden rule is a norm that enjoins respect for persons "in their plurality and in their otherness."[45] Ricoeur refuses, however, to embrace "difference for the sake of difference, which, finally, makes all differences indifferent, to the extent that it makes all discussion useless."[46]

Ricoeur's concept of the golden rule is summarized in the following passage:

> The passage from ethics to morality—from the optative mode of living well to the imperative mode of obligation—occurred . . . under the protection of the Golden Rule, to which we thought we gave full credit by assigning to it the merit of interposing the commandment at the very intersection of the asymmetrical relation between doing and undergoing (the good you would want to be done to you, the evil you would hate to be done to you). Acting and suffering then seem to be distributed between two different protagonists: the agent and the patient, the latter appearing as the potential victim of the former. But because of the reversibility of the roles, each agent is the patient of the other. Inasmuch as one is affected by the power over one exerted by the other, the agent is invested with the responsibility of an action that is placed from the very outset under the rule of reciprocity, which the rule of justice will transform into a rule of equality. Since each protagonist holds two roles, being both agent and patient, the formalism of the categorical imperative requires . . . a *plurality* of acting beings each affected by forces exerted reciprocally.[47]

Responsible life with others is of course not merely an affair of conformity to rules. This is true, for Ricoeur, for many reasons: because rules may come into conflict, and communities cherish an irreducible multiplicity of goods; because discernment is needed for the concrete historical and communitarian aspects of situations; and also because (e.g., in medical ethics problems such as abortion) there is no sharp distinction between persons and nonpersons.[48] Moreover, the tendency toward finding equality in relationships of solicitude leads to the quest for equality in just institutions.

Thus, for Ricoeur, the golden rule has a crucial function within a life aiming for happiness with and for others in just institutions. The rule does not simply call for agents to imagine themselves in the other's position. Rather, the rule reflects the actual reciprocity between speakers and interacting persons, between agents and sufferers.

CONCLUSION

In this chapter and the two previous ones, there is a pervading theme: the golden rule illumines the transition from egoism to sympathy, and from sympathy as a merely immediate response to reasonable, thoughtful, rational, morally active living.

If the world were to act on a golden rule of sympathetic regard for others, violent crime would cease, and altruism would multiply. The greatness of sympathy is that when we reach out spontaneously in heartfelt sympathy, we can incorporate the highest wisdom and love in response to human suffering. Sympathy is human warmth, especially attuned to emotional and physical needs.

I believe, however, that any psychologist or philosopher would agree with a balancing point. If sympathy can rise to the level of wise compassion, it can also be naive, shortsighted, impulsive, egocentric, and harmful. Someone who feels pity at the sight of a handicapped person may react in a condescending and patronizing manner. Problems with extreme sympathy show up in cases where parents overindulge their children's desires, or where a weak person plays along with a spouse's addiction, or where the politics of pity violate wisdom. Overemphasis on consideration for others' feelings, moreover, leads to a morality of merely being nice, and it is never nice to respond decisively to evil. Excessive sympathy, moreover, disrupts mental poise. In other words, sympathetic intentions often require more than sympathy to be effective. Insofar as sympathy operates as a merely emotional reaction, it stands in need of being infused with a higher perspective; the critique of sympathy is simply that it may be exercised in isolation from intellectual and spiritual qualities.

Upon reflection, most people do not simply want their immediate desires to be gratified. We know that sympathetic indulgence is not how we want to be treated and not how we should treat others. We consider long-term welfare in addition to the pleasure of the moment, and we care about whether the means are likely to achieve the end. Reason is thus required in order to interpret the golden rule appropriately.

Stein shows how genuine identification with others allows one to approximate their perspective in a way that does not require an act of imagination, though in the adventure of comprehending another person, all useful means should be welcomed. Reiner has shown a way to trace a logical path beyond the golden rule as a principle of sympathy to the rule as involving ethical judgment. He lucidly recognizes the intuition of higher and lower values and the fact that the golden rule presupposes some ethical judgments. In the dialectic between sympathy and moral reason, Ricoeur moves from sympathetic responsiveness to respect for unique persons, and gives respect for persons priority over the notion of universal moral law. Ricoeur's notion of moral reason thus goes beyond self-consistency to responsibility. Ricoeur finds in the golden rule a principle of movement and transition between sympathy and moral reason.

Adding ideas of Reiner, Levinas, and Ricoeur to Stoic and Kantian ideas deepens the concept of golden rule respect. Respect for persons involves recognition that each individual has, to a significant degree, the power thoughtfully to determine his or her commitment and conduct. Respect refuses to manipulate or distort the mind's adventure in coming to grasp truth and walk in the light of truth. Respect involves an emotion bordering on awe for the sublimity of the beauty of each unique, indefinable, uncountable, and irreplaceable personality. Respect for the other is coordinate with respect for oneself. Profound self-respect requires living in loyalty to values, including ideals that one cherishes for the other as well as for oneself.

The risk in an ethics of sensitivity and respect lies in placing disproportionate emphasis on the problems of imposition and appropriation. It is also important to describe and reflect upon experiences of interaction when what one person does is welcomed by the other as expressing love. When we interact in the momentum of shared understanding and positive inspiration, we do not feel imposed upon or made passive by the other's speaking and doing, nor are we prey to self-concern about offending the other. We do not in fact experience the other person as other; the experience is one of kinship. Otherness is not annihilated in a mystical oblivion, but neither does it confront us as a challenge. We do not pause to imagine ourselves in the other's shoes because we are not worried about stepping on the other's toes. We engage not in deliberation but in action, and we spontaneously make course corrections as we apprehend the other's changing needs and adjust our own grasp of things. When we live in faith as brothers and sisters, we are not staggered by the otherness of the other, and faith learns to embrace situations when otherness is stark and difference looms large: those, too, are situations that arise within the family.

twelve

Twentieth-Century Religious Interpretations

The very impulse to philosophy, metaphysics, and religious thought seems often to be motivated by a desire to explicate the common ground among human beings. The Hindu identification of the spiritual self of the agent with the spiritual self of the recipient of the agent's action provides a basis for golden rule thinking. Buddhism analogously emphasizes the equal emptiness of agent and recipient, each one arising as codependent phenomena of body and mind, each one lacking independent, substantial reality; after such a deconstruction of self-love, a new quality of compassion is to emerge, expressing the Buddha nature within.

The last of the histories presented in this book reviews efforts in religious philosophy and theology to articulate a spiritual interpretation of the golden rule. Marginalized in contemporary secular discourse, religious writing on the golden rule is scanty; in addition, the authors build so little on one another's work that this history is more a narrative of the absence of a tradition. Christian scholarship has focused less on the golden rule and more on scriptural interpretation, theologies of love, and specific ethical issues. Since the "humanism" of the golden rule has seemed disconnected from the high moral standards of the Sermon on the Mount and from the teachings that have made Christianity unique among religions, the evangelical Christian revival following World War I has given little emphasis to the golden rule and has scarcely viewed the rule as a principle of harmony among religions. This remains the case, despite the fact that Karl Barth, the period's leading evangelical theologian, who had argued against Harnack that world war demonstrated the abyss of human sinfulness and the naïveté of theological optimism, finally turned to embrace the concept of the brotherhood of man.

THE SPIRITUAL LEVEL AS THE CULMINATION
OF PERSONAL GROWTH

In a 1911 article, English philosopher Arthur T. Cadoux proposed that the rule implies that one should begin, not by imagining oneself in the recipient's position, but by bringing to mind how one likes to be treated. He goes on to present a sustained argument setting forth the golden rule as a stimulus to personal growth:

> [The rule] starts from desire actually existing in me, "whatsoever ye would," but it does not contemplate the satisfaction of that desire. My action is to be aimed at the concerns of another, but not at the satisfaction of his desire: it is not a doctrine of complaisance, it does not say, "Do unto others as ye imagine they would have you do." The guide of my action is not to be my supposition of what my fellow's desire may be, but my own desire transferred in imagination to him, "Whatsoever ye would that men should do unto you, even so do ye also unto them." The result is that the desire at the satisfaction of which my action aims is neither my desire nor his, as it existed prior to the application of the Rule, but my desire as seen through, and modified by, something that unites us, directing my action towards him and projecting my desires into him. Without the modification so effected the Rule would be meaningless, for if the satisfaction of any given desire is good, why not as good in me as in another? Unless, therefore, the Golden Rule, when we are willing to act on it, modifies our own desires and therefore the standard by which we act, it affords no guidance. And since its guidance lies in this modification, it is here that the good sought by the Rule will be manifest.[1]

Cadoux discusses several examples showing how the practice of the golden rule conduces to growth. "I am fond of the praise of others, therefore I must set myself to praise them." That praise, however, is not to be ridiculous, so I am led to seek out the genuinely praiseworthy features of those around me. "I love to behold or to hear or to read what is beautiful, and therefore I must create the beautiful for others to enjoy." "I desire health and healthy conditions of life, therefore I must do all in my power to make them possible for others." In general, "I wish to be happy," and so must promote others' happiness. "The one result, common to every application of the Golden Rule, is that the desires which form its raw material are so modified as to increase, both in the agent and in his fellows, the amount of satisfaction of desire or of unthwarted activity."[2]

Cadoux makes his transition to an explicitly spiritual culmination as follows:

> Implicit in [the rule] lies the assurance, that when human nature attains its maximum of activity or of satisfaction, it will be found also to have reached what we have been accustomed to recognize as the highest quality of life, for in Him who gave the Rule we see to what height of charac-

ter it leads. The total amount of fulfilled longing, of successful activity, of active, happy life in the world, is thus seen to be in proportion to its obedience to His Rule. "I am come," said He, "that they may have life, and may have it abundantly."

Like Kant, Cadoux emphasized conformity with a right rule, but unlike Kant he regarded religious obedience as consistent with personal authenticity. The golden rule pursuit of happiness, for Cadoux, leads persons to acquire a character like that of Jesus.

The golden rule, as we have repeatedly seen, can be interpreted as promoting growth through a sequence of increasingly mature stages. Another sequence, combining historical and personal perspectives, is found in *La Réciprocité* by Olivier du Roy. Reciprocity is an infinite adventure that presupposes obedience to law (cf. Moses) and imitation of virtue (cf. Aristotle).[3] Someone awakened to the universal humanity of reciprocity does not stop obeying laws or cultivating virtue, but the motivating ideal becomes the interpersonal communion of love. The lower activities are put right by the highest one: reciprocity removes the taint of servility from obedience and admiration.

Appropriating and modifying Reiner's three-level scheme, du Roy distinguishes three levels of the golden rule, each of which may be expressed positively or negatively, and each of which expresses a stage of moral education. First, there is a golden rule of *sympathy*. The golden rule engages the agent in a movement from egoistic desire to sympathy or "affective fusion." On account of its reference to what we desire, the verbal formulation of the golden rule gains a compelling force, even though this very appeal implies a limitation at the same time, and points beyond itself.

The second level of the golden rule involves a certain consistency of thought, word, and deed; du Roy calls it a golden rule of *authenticity* (conducting oneself by the standards one uses to judge others' conduct). Authorities and those who teach morality must pay special attention to this principle. The corresponding stage of moral education is the recognition of objective, impersonal law, which we need to learn in order to recognize others as genuinely different from ourselves. In order to interiorize law in a fully human way, we need an original, personal grasp of the values that the law encodes; otherwise order is cherished for its own sake, and morality becomes an end in itself. To fulfill the law we must transcend the standpoint of law.

The highest level of the golden rule is the principle of *reciprocity*. For du Roy, the profound meaning of reciprocity is decentering—that one should judge from the *other's* viewpoint. This stage is characterized by a special quality of will (distinct from desire) for the other's good. This benevolence, however, needs some qualification in terms of an objective norm, say, about what is truly good for the other person. Often specification is gained by appeal to the phrase "Love your neighbor as yourself,"

though further qualification remains necessary: the love should be appropriately directed, and so on. The level of reciprocity is thus difficult to
express. For du Roy,

> It is necessary that happiness consist in happiness willed for the other as
> for oneself, in reciprocity itself. It is the joy of loving that one wills for
> the other, as one wills for oneself. One cannot will it for oneself without
> willing it for the other; this would be contradictory. This reciprocity of
> love, which is the ultimate requirement and the highest human aspira-
> tion, includes infinite requirements of truth, self-giving, welcome and
> openness to others.[4]

Golden rule benevolence, then, is fulfilled not simply by satisfying
some material need that another person may have, but necessarily also by
facilitating in the other the same enjoyable and benevolent activity that
the agent performs.

Using the golden rule on the way to a communion of persons is how
decentering evolves. Although decentering can succeed in going all the
way to "infinity," du Roy notes the danger that one may become more
concerned with the quality of one's own love than with the other person.
It is possible to use the other merely as an occasion for loving, projecting,
and enjoying oneself. Reciprocity, interpersonal interaction, remains necessary. We may try to escape from our desires by self-sacrifice, but deeds
of generosity do not resolve the problem.

For du Roy, generosity comes from self, but charity comes from the
other and from God. Decentering is not something we can accomplish on
our own; rather, someone—God—must have loved us first. The standard
for this level of the golden rule is not to love as we love ourselves but as he
loved us. To love an enemy with whom one cannot identify, who refuses
reciprocity, and from whom no reciprocity can be expected—this is really
to experience love. This ideal could be proposed only if it has already
been actualized, and the power to realize it comes from a grace beyond
what we could have imagined.[5]

INTEGRATING SPIRITUAL EXPERIENCE WITH
ETHICAL DEMANDS

Once a person has been blessed with the realization of spiritual love,
problems arise of how to express that love appropriately. One may be
prepared for sacrificial giving, but the situation may call for justice. Paul
Ricoeur has brought philosophy together with biblical interpretation in
order to address this problem. His 1991 article, "Love and Justice," begins
with three biblical points about love: love praises, rejoices, cherishes
greatly; the commandment to love is prelegal and premoral; love mobi-
lizes a wide spectrum of affects (such that *eros* can symbolize *agape*). Justice

is characterized as a social institution, as involving communication, listening to arguments, and arriving at a decision backed up by force; justice also is an idea or ideal of equitable distribution. Action, for Ricoeur, lives in the tension between love and justice. The command to love one's enemies is part of the "economy of gift"—since it has been given to you in abundance, you should bestow on others. The economy of gift transcends the legal logic of equivalence, reciprocity. The golden rule can be interpreted either as an expression of reciprocity or, as reinterpreted by love, in terms of generosity. Both love and justice are necessary to each other, partly since love without justice does not know how to translate its supreme commitment into reasonable action.

ACTING AS JESUS WOULD ACT

S. B. Thomas is more optimistic than Ricoeur. Since Jesus of Nazareth is not only a past historical figure but an abiding and accessible spiritual reality, we can, according to Thomas, adopt the perspective of the mind of Jesus as a way to fulfill the rational requirements of morality. The golden rule is the spiritual teaching whose external and formal counterpart is the categorical imperative; they are "two sides of the same coin." Kant's categorical imperative clarifies the "rational scope" of the golden rule, and Jesus' golden rule provides the spiritual basis for applying the categorical imperative correctly.[6] Conflict arises between the rational and spiritual standpoints only if one refuses to acknowledge the primacy of the spiritual.

According to Thomas, it is possible to adopt the standpoint of Jesus, indeed, to partake of Jesus' being. In so doing, one adopts the standpoint not just of a man but of Universal Man. From this standpoint, the morally relevant features of a situation stand out most clearly. "Relieved of the necessity of assessing actions from an external and formal point of view," we are "released to act spontaneously."[7] After the fact, investigation by means of the categorical imperative would show that rational moral standards had been satisfied. The experience of empathy that Thomas describes is "a sensed in-dwelling in the person of the other."

THE GOLDEN RULE WITHIN A COMMUNITY OF FAITH

The golden rule in its spiritual interpretation has a unique flourishing within a community disposed to interact on this level. The experience of love in an actual community is highlighted in the treatment of the golden rule by Roman Catholic theologian Hans Urs von Balthasar. For him, Christ is the fulfillment of ethics. Von Balthasar calls Christ the "concrete categorical imperative," not to imply that Christ shows the fulfillment of what Kant had formally delineated, but to imply that the moral import of

Christ is unconditional. Christ's fulfillment of the Father's will cannot be improved upon, and is thus universally normative. The will of the Father is that, in him and with him, we love his children, and that we worship in spirit and in truth. Christian conduct is not an affair of what one must do so much as an affair of what one *may* do, in freedom. In the church and through its sacraments God's offer of salvation is extended to all the world. Although von Balthasar insists that fulfillment is available only in Christ, he also warns Christians not to judge those who adhere to other religions and ethical philosophies, since what someone may not explicitly believe may nevertheless be existentially effective in the person's life.

Von Balthasar's essay affirms that the high standards implied in the contexts of the golden rule in Matthew and Luke (the Beatitudes, the renunciation of justice to get even, and the call to be perfect and merciful as is the Father in heaven) indicate what one member of Christ may expect from another and what one member must provide for another. "The mutual expectations of the gift of God (which Christ is) and assurances among the members of Christ ground [the golden rule], thus transcending mere co-humanity and embracing the interpersonal emergence of the divine life."[8] In other words, the golden rule does not draw its meaning and power from association with one's fellow human beings. Christians expect Christ in their interactions with one another, and, since God's gift of absolute love has become real in Christ, the life that emerges in the community is not a merely human life; children of God already taste the divine life.

A vision of humanity divinely united in the practice of the golden rule in a universal community is advanced by Baha'i author H. T. D. Rost.[9] According to this view, the golden rule comes from God and the manifestations of God, including Krishna, Abraham, Zarathustra, Moses, Buddha, Jesus, Muhammad, and, most recently, Baha'u'llah (1817–1892). Since all the great religious leaders have taught divine truth, and since all their followers are destined to be united, the proper approach to comparative religion is to display harmony among religions. Revelation is progressive and continuous, and no revelation can be regarded as final. The practice of the golden rule breaks down barriers such as race, religion, nationality, and class that divide humankind into "us" and "them." In a universe teeming with worlds, where the potentials of reciprocity stagger the imagination, the purpose of this life is to acquire the qualities of divinity that will be needed in the life to come—spirituality, faith, assurance, the knowledge and love of God. Baha'u'llah set aside his divine station and related as a man with a message for other humans when he wrote, "I have desired for them that which I have desired for myself."[10] The message of equality, however, is not the ultimate message of the golden rule, since the unity of humankind is brought about by a preference for altruism, seeking the other's good before one's own, and willingness to sacrifice for the other.

CONCLUSION

In reviewing these authors, the complementarity of their topics and treatments seems most noteworthy. They have overlapping and supporting advantages, while none is free of problems. A discourse on the growth stimulated by the golden rule has the advantage of showing what can happen once the golden rule is sincerely embraced, though by leaving talk of the spiritual to the end, Cadoux leaves questions open about why someone might embrace the rule so progressively in the first place (an issue addressed by von Balthasar and Rost). Growth discourse, as exemplified by du Roy, articulates a series of levels whose advantage is to make clear that there is a sublime goal of attainment and to say enough about the signposts along the way to be helpful to the reader (despite the fact that tastes of sublimity, genuine and spurious, make it hazardous to judge one's own location on the map). The counterpoint to the notion of levels of achievement is a warning about the dangers of exaltation plus the recognition that the summit in question involves self-forgetting identification with the neighbor; du Roy, to be sure, is helpfully lucid about these concerns.[11]

I can never forget a comment made by a Buddhist speaker on an interfaith panel. He remarked on "the stink of religious experience." I take his point to be not that religious experience must be deceptive, but that it tends to bring, in its wake, an offensively self-conscious display. If these topics were not worth the effort, silence would surely be safer.

One who has experienced divine love as a new quality of engagement in life encounters problems addressed in the type of discourse represented by Ricoeur. Despite his nuanced understanding of love and justice, Ricoeur finds that neither reasonable justice nor spiritual love can stand on its own; each has inadequacies that must be compensated by the other; but there is no stable synthesis in sight, only the ongoing need for mutual adjustment. Since Ricoeur does not define the spiritual so as to include the wisdom of reasonableness and fails to redefine justice as the administration of love, both poles of his tension remain incomplete. Nor does he distinguish justice as a historical, evolving social institution from justice as a standard for personal living. Ricoeur's interpretation succeeds in avoiding a complacent and static result, and he remains true to the finitude of human experience. True, love does not, by itself, solve complex ethical problems; but Ricoeur seems reluctant to encourage the reader to be faith-confident about progressing, however imperfectly, toward a divine destiny.

Thomas offers a solution to Ricoeur's problem by testifying to the human capacity to participate in the spiritual presence of Jesus, to gain, beyond the instruction available in rational principles, spiritual strength and divine wisdom for the practice of the golden rule. Thomas acknowledges that we are fallible in our efforts to identify with that mind, to intuit on that basis, and to abide in it, but he does not discuss the philosophic and religious activities needed to deal with that problem. Nevertheless, he does speak of two kinds of verification for his thesis: using Kantian standards to interpret the life of Jesus, it is possible to show, first, that Jesus' actions are in accord with the categorical imperative; reflection on Jesus' life is thus the way to whatever can be demonstrated here. If Thomas's boldness in faith is a corrective to Ricoeur's chronic tensions, Thomas could use a more explicit acknowledgment that sometimes hard moral thinking is precisely what spiritual living requires. Why should assuming the mind of Jesus exempt one from the labors of moral reason? Shall we assume that Jesus never wrestled with a decision? What image of spontaneity is being assumed? Integrating the perspectives of moral reason and faith need not be so much an experience of an additional tension as of an extension of the same faith to which both Thomas and Ricoeur testify.

Another type of discourse, illustrated by von Balthasar, speaks for the quality of community resulting from positive religious decisions. As von Balthasar implies and Rost demonstrates, however, no religion has a monopoly on spiritual experience with the golden rule. One value of including the Baha'i message is to observe its structural similarities with Christian messages. Each writer proposes to offer universal truths that each person can come to accept, each has some link to a particular set of scriptures. A religionist inevitably conveys a particular religious commitment when promulgating universal truth, and the happy fact is that each religion may contribute to peace among all humankind without compromising itself. The authors' texts may be regarded as tacitly autobiographical, since they disclose individuals with various vocations and intellectual backgrounds following an adventure of personal discovery.

New conceptions of the relation of religion and ethics are at work here. Kantian ethics (referred to rather than advocated by these writers) acknowledges a difference between moral reason and religion, but assigns to moral reason the unique responsibility for critically determining what is right, while religion provides enhanced perspective, supporting motivation, hope for grace to act in genuine benevolence, and hope for a heavenly reward. On a variation of Kantian thought, God has blazed the trail which reason often cannot discover by itself; once the trail has been discerned, reason can pave it with a universally accessible rationale. For the authors summarized here, however, morality based on sympathy and duty is incomplete in ways that are only healed on the spiritual level. For von Balthasar, the divine is the content of spiritual interaction; it is given by grace, commanded, and enjoyed. For Rost, the moral life simply is the expression of divine love to others; the alternative is for the person to be directed by material interests.

II.

AN ETHICS
OF THE
GOLDEN RULE

thirteen

The Golden Rule in a Philosophy of Morality

Working with a single fragment, such as a fossilized jaw bone, a paleobiologist may be struck by how sharp the teeth still are, quite apart from the rest of the animal. It nevertheless remains interesting to envision the whole skeleton. Similarly, the golden rule hints at a fuller philosophy of moral living and requires one for its full functioning. Previous chapters have made much use of the notions of growth, evolution, development, and progress, all of which presuppose value commitments. It is time now to render a fuller account of the religious philosophy operative in these histories and to return to some of the objections raised in chapter 1.

It cannot be a question of proving the reality of God: the primal decision to acknowledge the validity of spiritual experience cannot be extorted by logic, any more than the decision to honor the validity of moral consciousness, or to affirm the validity of our perception that we live in a realm of causally interconnected things of nature. Attemped proofs of such basic affirmations or axioms assume too much or prove too little. Reason and wisdom can only operate once these windows to experience are open.

BEYOND A FORMAL MODEL OF ETHICS

The golden rule is a searchlight, not a map. A moral principle is not a system of ethics, nor is a system of ethics produced by the extension of an abstract principle. A moral principle is an expression of life; to understand a moral principle and to develop a wider ethics requires vastly more than deduction. It still remains interesting to interpret and try to represent our moral thinking formally, however much may be lost in translation.

Golden rule reasoning is represented in the following model with a major premise, a minor premise, and a conclusion:

1. Treat others as you want others to treat you.
2. You want others to treat you with appropriate sympathy, respect, and so on.
3. Therefore, treat others with appropriate sympathy, respect, and so on.

Notice that our sense of what is *appropriate* represents an estimate of *value*, an estimate that is adjusted in the process of thinking over the parity of self and other that is the primal assumption of the rule. The golden rule cannot be the supreme principle of morality in the sense of functioning as the sole normative axiom in a deductive system of ethics, because it cannot operate in a value vacuum. Nevertheless, the model serves to make clear that the golden rule does presuppose a certain maturity in the agent. To retain the rule requires supplementing its formal character as a major premise in reasoning about how one wants to be treated with a conception of character growth. As the person grows, the values expressed in the minor premise expand, and the ethically-logically resulting conduct improves. Moreover, continued practice with the rule plausibly conduces to such growth. The rule can function reasonably well as an axiom in the derivation of moral judgments because as we mature by genuine moral inquiry (and as our desire becomes more refined), so does our interpretation of the rule.

To block counterexamples by assuming a certain level of moral maturity on the part of the agent seems to render the appeal to the golden rule circular. On the one hand, the rule is used to make clear why certain actions are wrong—is that the way you would want to be treated? On the other hand, it is assumed that the individual working with the golden rule is not the sort who wants to torture, commit adultery, and so on. If we abandon a simplistic notion of a deductive system of ethics and acknowledge the need for a reasonable interpretation of the rule, we can avoid vicious circularity. The main point is that "maturity" must not be defined in such a way as to include insight into what one ought rightly to desire for oneself. Maturity enables one to play the game of moral thinking; it does not guarantee that one will win. The complementary side (of a "virtuous circle") is also true: maturity is gained, in part, by efforts in moral thinking and acting. It is more helpful to elaborate a different model of moral thinking.

FROM MORAL INTUITION TO MORAL INSIGHT

We do not walk around with a set of definite desires about how we want to be treated in various types of situation. We do not even experience life in terms of "situations" at all unless we become aware of some particular challenge. Often our life of desire is inchoate, vague, ill-defined. We may feel ambivalent, conflicted, or simply confused at times about our response to certain interactions. We received a criticism that felt abusive, and yet acknowledge that a very needed point was delivered. We are gratified by another's kind words, yet wonder about basking in flattery. Some-times, however, we are resolutely clear. A particular interaction does not merely frustrate and irritate us; we are indignant over the unfairness of treat-ment that denigrates our humanity. And sometimes we are treated su-perbly and feel ennobled as a result. Such recognitions illustrate the oper-ation of moral intuition.

We intuitively know the difference between times when interactions with family and friends are characterized by what feels like love and times when strains eclipse love. We prefer the first sort of interaction, and hence we know what the golden rule requires of us. As travelers, or in a store or company or government office, we know the difference between times when the other person manifests a personal touch and a spirit of service and times when treatment is cold. In the preferable interactions, we do not feel that we are being "treated" at all. A more suitable formulation of the golden rule would therefore be "Relate with others as you want others to relate with you."

Sometimes we know intuitively what is to be done in a given situa-tion. At other times we approach a problem confidently, further experi-ence leads us to change our mind, and we look back on former certainties with a smile. The fact that intuition may stand in need of sharpening shows that it is not an infallible grasp of truth or duty. Neither is intuition a mere hunch, waiting to be instructed by argument. Intuition frees the less-educated person from intellectual subservience to scientific, philo-sophic, and religious elites. Thanks to intuition, the mind of each person can participate in a given realm of experience, without having to submit to whatever dogma may be backed up by impressive argument. Intuition—whether of fact, duty, or spiritual reality—is the precondition of reasoning. All arguments must ultimately rest on unproved assumptions, and these assumptions are formulated as a result of meaningful particular experi-ences. As previously remarked, we need intuition to sense the need for moral reflection, to choose first principles, to describe actions appropri-ately, to validate rules of inference, and to see the point of arguments. Stories of personal experience are especially valuable for getting intuitions out on the table for discussion.

A principal advantage of the golden rule is that it implies a high regard for an individual's intuition about how he or she ought to be treated. Some writers mention the effect of one's personal history on one's moral intuition as though it were a pollutant or an obstacle to reason, or merely an occasion for a remark about the cultural relativity of intuition. Pedagog-ically, it is wiser to encourage people that moral intuition qualifies as a genuine participation in the moral realm, a participation that continued experience and thought will sharpen, rather than to derogate people's ex-perience or to suggest that matters are "relative" in a sense that under-mines the point of serious moral inquiry.

Moral intuition grows by reflection on experience with particular actions, persons, relationships (between two persons), and social systems (of three or more persons). Moral thinking, ideally, involves mature identification with the recipient(s) of actions, based on the most accurate and complete understanding of the recipient(s) and the situation that it is reasonable to seek. The process of moral thinking sharpens (not supplants) moral intuition, so that the conclusions from today's philosophical-ethical reflection inform tomorrow's moral intuition.

Moral reflection, ideally, culminates in insight. Indeed, in the happy case, there is no need for new reflection, no difference between intuition and insight, and a spontaneous response is fully adequate. The process of moral thinking—if it seems called for—begins with an intuitive grasp of some of the morally relevant features of a situation; moves through philosophical-ethical reflection with clarified concepts, propositions, and lines of reasoning, wisely integrated with a sense of proportion; and culminates, possibly, in insight, which cannot be shaken by opposing voices, nor overturned by the refinements of hindsight.[1]

Some morally correct judgments (e.g., about the immorality of murder and slavery and the wickedness of Adolf Hitler) are easy to make today, and do not necessarily convey insight into the value of a human life, the significance of human freedom, and the importance of acquiring a good character. Not that insight is stipulated to require intellectual uniformity in lockstep with any given system of philosophy, but the insightful mind must attain a quality of thinking marked by philosophic depth and clear reasoning. Insight requires not only doing one's best, but also grasping what the situation requires. Insight is easier to experience in simple cases; in complex issues, the quest for insight may get no farther than to grasp just a single relevant value without being able to gain an adequate perspective on the situation.

Some skeptics reject the notion of insight, hoping thereby to avoid presumption. A more tentative way of thinking avoids some errors, though it is dangerous when the time calls for boldness. It takes insight, moreover, to raise telling objections and criticize presumption judiciously, and the skeptic and the seeker after insight would do better to combine their strengths. The simplicity of the golden rule as an imperative communicates confidence that the agent can find the right course.

There is a certain ineliminable realism in moral judgment; in other words, it is not enough simply to content ourselves with regarding all moral judgments as merely subjective, relative to the individual's culture, and reflecting no grasp of genuine meanings and values. Even if we recognize that expectations that are morally appropriate for one person often differ from expectations that are morally appropriate for another person because of morally relevant differences between the individuals (degree of maturity, cultural background, interests, vocation, education and training, condition of health, socially comfortable or uncomfortable situation, etc.), most of us nevertheless hold that *some* moral expectations are (objectively) appropriate, and that people ought to have appropriate expectations of themselves and others, not inappropriate ones. Whoever can recall an experience of making an excellent decision in a morally challenging situation or of seeing a difficult situation handled well has the requisite intuition. This is the minimal conception of realism needed to make sense of talk of moral insight.

In working with the golden rule intellectually one moves not only beyond simple identification with one's own present feelings but also beyond simple identification with the recipient's feelings. There is an attempt to take an impartial, third-person perspective. This does not involve abandoning sympathy, but adds a long-range perspective of consistency and fairness to the best of one's ability. In addition, the golden rule, functioning within the context of an adequate philosophy of living, is linked to a hearty affirmation of human dignity. Whatever deficiencies of respect may be suffered by an agent do not constitute the standard for consistency in moral judgment. A consistent Nazi, who would be willing to be exterminated if it were proved that he was Jewish, might satisfy a rule of consistency, but he would not satisfy the golden rule. Theorists point out how improbable it would be that a Nazi would actually satisfy the requirement of consistency after performing the required acts of vivid imagination on the basis of an excellent knowledge of facts combined with correct reasoning. This point is well taken. Nevertheless, I repeat, a consistent Nazi, real or imagined, does not fulfill the golden rule.

If a philosophy of morality begins with sympathy, consistency, fairness, and a regard for human dignity, it need not end there. Is it possible to discover higher patterns of individual character and relationships and systems that illuminate what is truly appropriate in a given situation? If this approach to moral questions is uncommon today, it is not unprecedented. Confucianism developed a notion of heavenly patterns. Jesus prayed, "Your will be done on earth as it is in heaven." In the tradition of Plato, Philo, and Augustine the concept emerged of eternal ideas "in the mind of God" that are discoverable by the human mind. Hegel disputed the notion of preexistent, heavenly patterns, yet argued that social evolution can be rationally understood as having actualized logical possibilities, thereby producing structures of enduring validity, such as the family, economic organizations, and the state. According to Alfred North Whitehead, each choice we make is illumined by a timely synthesis of the relevant eternal ideas; this synthesis is divinely presented and felt as a lure, to be actualized by our choice. If we have discovered so little of higher patterns, this fact does not discredit the quest; we have the wider field for creativity and intellectual striving in the pursuit of patterns and their actualization.

The advantage of a contemporary religious approach is that it may encompass the best of diverse traditions of thought while remaining oriented to the future, to creativity, to growth in the adventure of the actualization of truth, beauty, and goodness. This approach adds special import to the talk about exploring meanings of a particular situation. Implicit in such particulars are meanings with a certain generality, and a grasp of those meanings amounts to an intuition of a cosmic structure or pattern or truth.

What is the place of the golden rule in a philosophical process leading to insight? Despite its intuitive simplicity, the rule tends to engage the agent in a process of moral thinking. The most elementary leverage that the golden rule exerts is to encourage a self-centered individual toward a sympathetic regard for others. The rule is, first of all, an antidote to self-centeredness, conscious and unconscious. For example, the rule instructs hedonists to place the other's desires on a par with their own—which brings (egoistic) hedonism to an end. The rule puts wants through a socializing test, and selfish wants (not merely for food and affection, say, but for a surfeit of food and a monopoly of affection) do not pass the test. Since the golden rule calls for a balanced valuation of self and other, it should serve as well as an antidote to the imploded self, the self deficient in self-respect.

As the individual grows in self-realization, the golden rule equation of self and other remains a valuable antidote to subtler forms of egoism.[2] The other person is not only a bundle of material needs and emotions, but also someone with moral awareness, philosophic convictions, and so on. The interior complexity of the golden rule, suggesting a comparison of self and other, orients and points out the possible need for moral thinking.

The golden rule engages the agent in a transition from the intuitive to the reflective stages of the process leading to insight. In its searchlight function, the rule's question, "How would I want to be treated in this situation, where I must decide how to treat others?" does aid in finding the best and right way (a discovery that may then be generalized and tested). Moreover, using the rule can generate a sense of dissatisfaction with a given procedure, prompt an individual to inquire for a better one, and validate the better one once it has appeared.

The intuitive recognition of another personality indicates the other as someone of dignity, indeed (and this is where the move of moral reason from a concept to a proposition begins) as someone of dignity comparable to one's own dignity. The recognition of comparable worth is what gets variously articulated in ethics through the formulation of principles such as the categorical imperative, the principle of utility, and other versions of the idea of moral consistency. The golden rule is the mother of such specific principles. True, the rule cannot substitute for them, but neither can they substitute for it. In rigorous reasoning it is normal for the golden rule to be reformulated, and it would be foolish for a defender of the rule to resist such attempts in the name of a static, traditional wording. If the rule as traditionally worded leaves open the possibility that corrupt desires, say, could be interpreted as a criterion of morality, that possibility can be explicitly excluded: "Do unto others as you rationally desire that they do unto you." The problem with replacing the golden rule in every context with such a reformulation is that it tends to rivet attention on a single level of meaning and thus constricts the progressive dynamism of the rule.

A religious account of moral thinking could go further, setting forth the mind's quest for insight as the exercise of a God-given capacity to realize truth, whose standard is divine, not human. The "guarantee" of the possibility of insight is the fact (for faith) that revelation has occured, that the divine mind has expressed truth in human categories. Ultimately, the most basic truths of human thinking derive from the universal mind, operating on a humble level.

AN ETHICS OF RELATIONSHIP

Different approaches to moral thinking are characterized by how they apportion emphasis on the individual, on relationships (between two persons), and on social systems. To overemphasize the individual impedes relationships and obstructs community; extreme individualism remains atomistic and egoistic, no matter how refined its calculations may be about how to procure individual satisfaction. If ethics overemphasizes relationships between human beings, it offers no stability to the individual and cannot cope with the potentially conflicting demands of multiple relationships and social systems. If ethics overemphasizes social systems, it undermines individuality and subordinates relationships to the goals of a rootless solidarity.

The golden rule accords with the preeminence of the individual recognized in traditions of prophetic religion and Stoic ethics, since the rule takes the individual's conduct and decision making and character seriously, and since it governs the individual's interactions with any and all other individuals, who are regarded as comparable with oneself. The golden rule also encourages the individual, by tacitly affirming the agent's moral intuition about what it means to be well treated.

Most of all, the rule takes its place in an ethics of relationship. It construes action, first and foremost, not as a quest for self-actualization, nor as a theme for reasoning, nor as determined by social structures, but as interaction. Even though the rule does not cease to apply when interaction is impossible between the agent and the recipient of the action (e.g., in criticizing someone who is remote in space or time), the rule is primarily designed for relationships. The agent identifies with the recipient and acts in the light of that identification. The plot thickens when the relationship with God becomes primary. It is in relation with God that the individual gains a stability which makes full interhuman relationships possible, and which places such relationships in the framework of an ultimate social network.

The golden rule is sometimes regarded as incomplete, since it only indirectly implies duties to exercise self-mastery, to exhibit courage, and generally to acquire a strong character. If it makes sense to speak of duties to oneself (as independent of duties to others), then the golden rule is incomplete in not prescribing anything in this regard. The rule, however, suggests a social conception of the self; and an ethics of relation calls into question the notion that there is a separate and autonomous category of duties to oneself.

In addition, an ethics centered on relationships leads to rethinking character and virtues in relational terms and rethinking character growth. Some virtues are obviously relational—consideration, respect, fairness, love. A relational approach could be extended to self-mastery and courage, pointing out, say, how the fulfillment of one's opportunities and obligations may be hindered by desires and fears, and it would focus on how living as a responsible person in relationships and systems helps one grow in these virtues.

SOCIAL, ECONOMIC, AND POLITICAL IMPLICATIONS

The golden rule is, first and foremost, a principle in the philosophy of living, expressing a personal standard for the conduct of one-to-one relationships. A Chinese teaching illustrates priority of the personal dimension: "If there is righteousness in the heart, there will be harmony in the home. If there is harmony in the home, the nation will be well governed. If the nation is well governed, there will be peace in the world."[3] This approach does not imply that political reforms must necessarily be delayed until there is a regeneration of righteousness in the hearts of individuals, nor does it conflict with the fact that well-designed and well-led organizational structures facilitate individual progress. It does imply that primary leverage occurs at the level of the individual, and it emphasizes that unless individuals cooperate ideas for reform will never be implemented. If the limitation of a radical ethics of relationship lies in its inability to cope with systems, its strength is in honoring the way relationships transcend social systems.

The implications of the golden rule are not confined to personal relationships, since a sensitive application of the rule takes into account those *indirectly affected* by one's actions. Moreover, modern ethics has stressed the equal, basic value of *each* individual, and, hence, the obligation to consider remote as well as proximate others in thinking about what to do. Furthermore, some interactions occur specifically within the context of social systems. The rule has implications for such systems; indeed, the nonspecificity of the plural object, "Do to *others*," opens the door for philosophical ethics to explore such applications of the rule. The aspiration to organize systems in harmony with the golden rule expresses the belief that moral standards for individuals in the conduct of their relationships with others should come to prevail in these realms as well. If the golden rule is to be a truly universal principle, then there must be threads of consistency linking moral judgments about personal problems with ethical judgments about social, economic, and political affairs.

There are different norms for different types of relationship; we relate differently to a parent, a spouse, a child, a coworker, and so forth. The golden rule, if it is to serve within systemically structured relationships, must have the flexibility to take on secondary meanings within a system context. Put another way, golden rule reasoning makes room for additional minor premises, as in the following model.

1. Treat others the way you want others to treat you.
2. You have been a leader, and you know the quality of cooperation you desire to receive.
3. When you are a team member, give the leader that same quality of co-operation.

The equality of agent and recipient implied by the rule requires that a relationship be understood as basically a relationship between equals. Within the framework of human equality, the golden rule is fully compatible with leadership and teamwork, so long as teamwork is voluntary and leadership is understood as a functional matter, not a matter of being superior.[4] The golden rule invites leaders to lead as they would be led, and it invites team members to give the quality of teamwork they would want if they were leading. A good team member, let it be noted, is prepared to seize the leadership if leaders radically betray the values which legitimate their function. Ideally, any conflict that might arise between equality and complementarity should be able to be resolved; and it must not be assumed that one must choose between either an equality model or a complementarity model of relationships within social systems. Leadership is often best shared with a coleader, for example, and there may be a division of labor in leadership as well as in teamwork. The openness of the golden rule should stimulate moral creativity.

In a personal philosophy of living, the golden rule promotes social service, and its most basic systems application is a commitment to social equity. Applications to economic and political affairs extend that underlying commitment. The philosophy of living, in general, and the golden rule in particular, do not offer detailed patterns for social systems, or specific steps for a particular generation to follow toward actualizing ideals. The rule inclines toward peace, but cannot construct proposals for defense and disarmament. When it is clear what military policy is best for political evolution toward enduring world peace, then the golden rule will clearly authorize that as the policy it requires. Those whose perspective on economics are clearest can see how to apply the golden rule in that realm. There is just one caveat: the way to apply a moral principle to complex systems is not always immediately obvious. Without the wisdom of evolution, moral idealism and fanaticism take bold steps backward. The weakness of much modern political philosophy is its failure to keep pace with Kant's appreciation, expressed in his essays on history and politics, of the importance of a gradual and proper evolutionary approach to the ideals of an advanced civilization.[5] Complacent conservatism and attempts at revolutionary social transformation prove equally self-destructive.

What the rule does for systems is to prompt questions that imply norms for systems. In the family, does parental authority degenerate into patriarchy, violating the equality of men and women and making fear predominate in the child's relation to the parent? In society, are extremes of inequality of wealth and power tolerated? Does talk of "community" along ethnic lines betray human kinship? In business, does the profit motive eclipse the service motive? In politics, does a nation go beyond intelligent patriotism to assert its sovereignty without regard for planetary responsibilities? Does an organization benefit those within and those without? By virtue of its implied respect for human dignity, the golden rule is inconsistent with sexism, nationalism, racism, and mistreatment of others based on distinctions of class, age, condition of health, religious belief or disbelief, level of education, linguistic preferences, and so on. The rule illumines the ethics of social systems, but its primary benefit is to individuals. The golden rule raises the question; a successful inquiry enables a golden rule explication of the result. That much, but no more, can be expected of a moral principle.

THE GOLDEN RULE AND PRESUMPTION

Important current criticisms of the rule prompt a further unfolding of a golden-rule ethics. The rule, it has been charged, cultivates blindness to the otherness of the other, since it assumes a basic commonality between agent and recipient.[6] Some challenge the notion of a common humanity, citing (1) the pervasive influence of differences such as gender, race, and class, and (2) the uniqueness of individual personality. However, in saying what humanity has in common it is not necessary to confine oneself, say, to basic needs and to shared facts about the human condition (e.g., the inevitability of death). The dimensions just mentioned—such as gender and uniqueness of personality—are also common: gender is a factor for everyone, and everyone is unique. These universal statements importantly characterize what it means to be human. The golden rule does assume a common humanity in this expanded sense. Each of us wants to be treated with due regard for the features that we have in common with others, *and* with due regard for the features that classify us in one way or another, *and* with due regard for our uniqueness.

To act in accord with the golden rule is to treat others as comparable to oneself. Comparability, however, does not entail homogeneity; it does not involve the assumption that people think alike, feel alike, or are alike.

The concept of comparability includes difference and a respect for difference, even a willingness to listen when the other rebuffs one's empathic and benevolent pretensions with the command to back off. Imaginatively adopting another's perspective helps one gain a sense of the differences between self and other; the rule operates with the assumption that differences need not block understanding.

When deliberation culminates in moral insight, then action can proceed with confidence, and any protests by recipients can be assumed to result from blindness or unwillingness to bear one's fair share of the costs of progress. Nevertheless, insight may be far more rare than false presumption. In the latter case, one's moral judgment remains provincial and one's action arrogant. The human heart can be, as the prophet Jeremiah observed, "deceitful above all things and desperately corrupt."[7] The golden rule has been thought to exacerbate such a possibility, since it may appear to encourage the agent to impose personal standards upon others.

Given the problem of presumption, why has the golden rule such widespread appeal? The answer lies partly in the fact that many human wants are shared—for example, people want food that is not spoiled but fresh—and because what we want (adequate food, decent treatment, and so on) often is good for us. Though sometimes our wants conflict with our good, the progressive practice of the golden rule leads to the discovery of values the pursuit of which transforms our wants.

Of course differences between people occasion misunderstanding and moral missteps. Shaw's sophistic quip, "Don't do to others what you want others to do to you—their tastes may be different," is a clever play against the surface of the rule. The golden rule, if decontextualized, presented as an abstract, eleven-word slogan, and put under an analytic microscope, may seem to encourage a well-intentioned agent to impose unwelcome burdens. Every child learns early, however, that different people have different desires, and it is often automatic to make allowances for such differences. Taking a guest out for ice cream, one does not assume that the guest prefers one's own favorite flavor. Someone who enjoys all sorts of meats and beverages would not serve pork to a Muslim friend, beefsteak to a Hindu, or wine to an alcoholic. Sometimes, of course, we forget to take into account differences that we would recall upon a moment's reflection, and sometimes we do not suspect differences, even deep and important differences, between ourselves and others. The wants of others do at times differ surprisingly from our own, and sometimes well-intentioned acts of benevolence go awry for this reason. This is Shaw's point, taken charitably.

Making assumptions about what is good for others can obviously lead to harm, especially when moralistic dogmatism is reinforced by religion. The golden rule offers two aids to constrain benevolent aggression. First, whoever holds religiously based moral convictions may ask how he or she would like to be treated by those with differing convictions. Second, applying the golden rule puts a subtle pressure on the conception of the ideal (e.g., God): the ideal consistent with the golden rule is one that diffuses itself by appeal, even persuasion, but not coercion.

The protest against benevolent aggression is sometimes associated with a preference for the negative formulation of the golden rule, as being more appropriately humble. One may wonder what humility amounts to if those who claim it regard their views (as indeed everyone must) as *superior* to those of their opponents on the disputed point.[8] Sometimes, though, we are more clear about the harm that is not to be done than about the good that might be envisioned. It seems less pretentious to work at alleviating suffering or to insist on the basics of justice, than to undertake to implement a grand vision. The negative formulation, however, also invites agents to relate with others in the light of the agents' own valuations. The positive formulation aligns with the conviction that the good life is morally active. What if the cultural difference between agents is great? How can one assess vastly different interests without collapsing either into cultural imperialism or into radical relativism? The golden rule, well interpreted, is a bulwark against cultural imperialism, just as the substantive standards—consideration, respect, fairness, consistency, and love—with which the rule is contextually associated are a bulwark against relativism. The rule prompts fair discussion in which the appropriate resolution may ultimately be agreed upon.

THE GOLDEN RULE AND BASE DESIRES

The counterexample of an agent with base desires would not even occur to someone following the spirit of the golden rule. Moral education, moreover, thrives on promoting the good, not on advertising evil. It is regrettable that this sort of objection should require attention, but it has become so common in academic circles that a book of this sort must address it directly. Augustine dealt with the same concern by considering the counterexample of the person who wants to get drunk appealing to the golden rule to get his companion drunk. A generation ago Alan Gewirth used the counterexample of the man who wants his neighbor's wife to climb into bed with him appealing to the rule to justify climbing into her bed. Today, the requisite vividness is obtained from the new standard counterexample, the sadomasochist who treats others as he wants to be treated.

It might seem the most elementary philosophical obstinacy not to abandon the golden rule once such a counterexample has been raised. How many times, in the dialogues of Plato, does Socrates set aside a mediocre, popular thesis with a single counterexample?[9] Surely, the cost of retaining the golden rule in the face of a defensible counterexample is high. There are difficulties, however, with the counterexample. First of all, raising the specter of "the sadomasochist" in a cavalier fashion obscures the bond of common humanity between the person who is making the criticism and the person who is identified simply as "a sadomasochist." The counterexample comes close to evoking the suspicion that if the masses were to act in accord with the golden rule, a reign of gratification and abuse might ensue. This particular counterexample suggests that a sadomasochist, armed with the golden rule, could logically go on a rampage of abuse, although a careful look shows that the rule, taken simply as a principle of consistency, could at most be pressed into service to "justify" a sadomasochist in acting abusively only with others who share the same desires.

Those who would dispose of the rule with this single counterexample do not care to inquire how the rule is meant to be understood. As the previous chapters have illustrated, in the mind of many a sincere practioner, the golden rule benefits from what psychology calls "the halo effect" of its association with a respected teacher.[10] However vague the ideals of a tradition may be in the mind of the practioner, they assuredly are incompatible with such counterexamples. Diverse traditions harbor resources unsuspected by rational analysis, resources which nourish the tradition of rational ethics. Analysis has tended to ask, not what the rule has meant and could mean (in terms of its positive potentials), but rather what the words of its formula can be made to mean in a worst-case scenario. The maxim "First understand; then criticize" is cast aside. The critic assumes that the rule is being proposed as a sufficient criterion of sound moral judgment and as a criterion guaranteed to yield excellent results when applied by anyone at all. However, as Mill noted, "There is no difficulty in proving any ethical standard whatever to work ill, if we suppose universal idiocy to be conjoined with it."[11] The golden rule is not intended as a free-floating guarantee for anyone at any stage of immaturity.

The earlier defense of moral intuition gives additional reason to be careful about taking propositions, moral principles, as isolated entities for analysis as though their meaning were independent of a wider context not all of which is amenable to formal analysis. Sentences occur within paragraphs that are part of discourses, and as speech acts within conversations, interpersonal events participating in traditions of human expression. The concentrated focus of analysis coexists necessarily with the diffuse illumination provided by intuition.

As noted previously, the golden rule can defend itself, since it contains within itself the seed of its own self-correction: any vulnerable interpretation may be challenged: "Would you want to be treated according to a rule construed in this way?" If this reply seems to be merely *ad hominem*, challenging the individual who raises the objection rather than examining the merit of the objection, it should be noted that the golden rule itself is *ad hominem* in the following sense.[12] It is a second-person statement, and in the classic contexts, the hearer is directly addressed by Confucius or Hillel or Jesus, and so on. The rule is given in the first instance to a *you*, not to a him or her. For someone addressed by the rule, the challenge becomes this: Find your answer in the directness of the encounter—how do *you* want to be treated?

If someone of low standards acts in accord with his or her best understanding of the golden rule, that individual will be true to the best he or she knows, and such an effort deserves respect, even if the resulting conduct is so intolerable that others, acting in accord with the best *they* know, are obliged to restrain that individual.

Despite the difficulties with the counterexample, it is worth taking time to consider such objections to the rule. A facile defense of the rule may be worth little more than a facile rejection. Counterexamples often point to genuine human problems, and they help clarify the presuppositions that must be supplied in order to have a reliable moral rule. The present counterexample leads to the recognition of three problems that the rule, taken in its fullness, alleviates. First, people sometimes do project their own selfish urges and physical impulses onto others. A clinical study reported that rapists motivated by the desire for power (a more common motive for rape than anger or sadism) often attribute their own wishes to their victims. One client said, "She wanted it, she was asking for it. She just said 'no' so I wouldn't think she was easy."[13] There is no suggestion, however, that any rapist ever set forth with the goal of practicing the golden rule. Nor does the rapist use the claim that "she was asking for it" in order to claim after the fact that his action was in accord with the golden rule. The golden rule has the tone of a moral command about it, and that tone is intuitively inconsistent with using force in sexual activity. One does sometimes hear a defensive and unconvincing appeal to the golden rule. This occured in an interview with a physician who had done research during the communist period in East Germany in a secret program to discover how to administer anabolic steriods to East German athletes so that they would be able successfully to pass drug tests. He defended himself: "We were prepared to do to others only those things which we were prepared to do to ourselves and our families."[14] Perhaps his implication was that he did not regard the drugs as being seriously dangerous. More likely the appeal to the golden rule was merely a rationalization, alleged after the fact.[15]

This counterexample points (albeit clumsily) to a second genuine problem. People can be abusive even when they believe that they are acting in accord with the golden rule. A story of generous intentions gone awry does illustrate a limitation of the golden rule as a popular standard. A teenager who desired to wear lipstick and high heels and attend formal dances had been denied the opportunity to do these things by her mother. When this frustrated teenager became a parent, she forced her own unwilling daughter to wear lipstick and high heels and so on. The abusive mother claimed to be applying the golden rule.[16] This story, however, illustrates only a neurotically constricted application of the golden rule; someone who did live in accord with the rule would act in accord with the corollary, "Do not force others to act against their will (except to avert disaster), as you do not want others to do to you."[17] In addition, the golden rule, in its positive formulation, invites the hearer to bring to mind experiences of being treated in a satisfying way. A golden rule meditation begins with a recollection of how one has been well treated. It may continue by reflecting on how one is being well treated, or may possibly be well treated in the future. Had the abusive mother been able to recall experiences of being well treated as a girl, she would have had a suitable model for treating her daughter in accord with the golden rule.

The third problem perhaps suggested by the counterexample is that covert self-interest can invade one's motivation for using the golden rule. For example, one may be motivated by the thought of esteem from others who will notice one's golden rule conduct or by fear of the consequences of treating others offensively.[18] In a conventional process of socialization, we learn to anticipate others' feelings in order to protect ourselves from the consequences of offending others. Complying with "moral norms" all too easily becomes a defensive move. Self-interest does play a greater role in human motivation than is generally acknowledged. This fact, however, does not prove the speculative and unverifiable doctrine of psychological egoism, according to which self-interest is the dominant motive in all human behavior. Nor do the facts of covert self-interest show that motivation is never genuinely other-regarding. If we hold a background belief that we may benefit from doing good, must our motives necessarily be mixed? Since we prefer to be treated by those who genuinely care about our good, the golden rule can only be fulfilled by motivation that tips the balance of interest in a friendly and altruistic direction. If benefits to self are to be expected from the practice of the golden rule, must that prospect be totally concealed? Is it wrong to live in the hope of better times ahead? Does such hope take anything away from the recipient, or does such hope rather embrace hope for the recipient as well? A background awareness of possible benefits to self need not corrupt one's motivation to act for another's good.

In sum, the counterexample provides an occasion for recognizing that, in order for the golden rule to work reliably, one must assume that the agent has a normal capacity for sympathetic consideration for others' feelings and a reasonable sense of personal dignity.

There is one more twist to the reply. Actually, contrary to linear logic, if our sadomasochist actually set forth to follow the golden rule, he might well progress in acting more considerately and in developing self-respect. Similarly, if a suicidally depressed woman, thoroughly disillusioned with humanity, were to begin to practice the golden rule, she might well overcome self-centeredness and depression. What is of particular interest here is the possibility that the "presupposition" (self-respect) need not precede the use of the rule in personal growth. The *practice* of the rule may stimulate the growth one wants to presuppose for a theoretically sturdy golden rule. Self-respect may develop unconsciously through success in various practices.[19] This is not to say that the rule should be recommended to someone who would be tempted to use it as an excuse for wrongdoing, but just to say that the rule has considerable leverage for human growth.

In response to the standard counterexample, then, one may abandon the rule, reformulate it to make it invulnerable to such objections, or insist on interpreting it so as to conserve both the usefulness of a conventional wording and also any insights contained in the objections. I take the third way as the one best able to promote individual growth and cultural progress. I regard the rule as an overarching symbol of morality that is variously specified at different levels of growth.

CONCLUSION

As modern interpreters have emphasized, the golden rule, interpreted by moral reason, requires an even-handed consistency. Why is consistency a cardinal virtue in morality? Golden rule consistency blocks hypocrisy and promotes harmony of thought, word, and deed. In modern rational ethics, the special point of consistency is to be impartial in the application of principles.[20] Why should one care about being impartial, about not taking sides in a way that is prejudicial to the interests of any person or group? Impartiality matters only if there is a prior affirmation of the "equal, basic" worth of each person. (Basic worth, here abstracts from system differences, which make it worth guarding a nation's president more closely than most other citizens.) The golden rule asserts the equal value of self and other; but it takes progressive self-realization to discover how great that value is. Universalizability is a requirement of moral reason only if each person matters. In other words, recognition of the value of the individual is the foundation of moral reason.[21]

Technically speaking, the imperative "Do to others as you want others to do to you" does not necessarily presuppose a proposition to the effect that others are as valuable as you. In fact, the practice of the golden rule may be advocated precisely as a heuristic device to help the agent to become aware of the kinship of humankind. Nevertheless, if the giving of the imperative is not to be arbitrary, it must be based on some realization of human worth.

True, one does not need religion in order to recognize human dignity; the intuition of another person implicitly contains that recognition, and reflection on the significance of our rational powers of self-determination deepens the sense of one's own dignity and that of others. Is this acknowledgment the last word?

Suppose we have an agent with sturdy self-respect, who is minded to affirm the dignity of human beings as free, rational agents. Problems remain. First, the affirmation of human dignity flies in the face of apparent evidence to the contrary. We so often act basely. How then shall one sustain an affirmation of the dignity of each rational agent? Is it a noble gesture without a foundation? Many leading philosophers who make comparable affirmations, basing claims about human rights on claims about equal human worth, rest their arguments on unproved assumptions.[22] True, it is necessary, in any context of reasoning, to operate with certain axioms. Attempts to give reasons for a particular proposition, and to give reasons for those reasons, cannot go on forever. Shall we stipulate that the affirmation of human dignity is properly basic and call a halt to inquiry at this point?

Another problem (to repeat an observation made earlier) is that basing human dignity on rationality tends to collapse to a weaker pair of affirmations—first, all persons have the valuable *capacity* for reason, and, second, that an individual *actually* merits esteem to the *degree* that he or she lives in accord with reason. Or what if someone asserts his self-respect in a society where respect is a matter of honor, a matter of degree, a scarce commodity, a subject of competition? If one realizes that others, on the same grounds, are asserting their self-respect, why should it not be "rational" to fight rather than concede that others are worthy of the same respect?

A basis for moral reason with its clarified intuitions and considered fairness can be found by going beyond moral reason.

I would like to close on a personal note. I do not commit myself to any one intellectual formulation of the rule designed to minimize counterexamples, because I am primarily interested in the life of the rule, how the rule moves, how its various meanings weave into one another, and how working with it promotes growth. Presenting the golden rule as a principle with emotional, intellectual, and spiritual significance has become, in part, a way to recover a more adequate conception of what it means to be human and a way to move beyond theories of morality that undervalue any one of these dimensions. Because of legitimate generalizations about human growth, one may present these dimensions sequentially, though they are all always somehow co-present in the personality of the moral agent. The approach taken here sends the message, "Remember to include each of these dimensions when you want to work with the rule consciously and fully." I have no argument except against one-sidedness.

fourteen

Religious Dimensions of the Golden Rule

The children's game of leapfrog provides a metaphor of the relation between philosophical and spiritual progress. The first child goes forward by leaping over the child just in front of him. Then the first child kneels down, and the second one leaps over him. Every philosophic advance prepares a new spirititual advance, and vice versa.[1]

There are many reasons to seek a level of meaning in the golden rule beyond the level of moral reason. Sometimes even the most exhaustive study of circumstances and principles and patterns does not suffice to indicate what is to be done, and the mind seeks for wisdom from beyond itself. Moral reason points beyond itself, since it is committed to choosing the best course of action, *all things considered*. In attempting to take an ideal perspective in a complex situation, it is natural for the human mind to reach for an *actual* ideal, for God. Moreover, even when *what* is to be done is clear, the graciously spontaneous *way* to act may remain beyond one's powers. If moral decision and action is to be wholehearted, it must draw on the full range of the personality, not only the mind, and it must respond to the fullness of the other person, including the spiritual dimension. In addition, many people need religious motivation to fuel the engine of moral conduct. Indeed, a reasonable, do-your-best ethic is misleading if grace is needed to do your best. Finally, it may be that without a religiously based sense of human kinship, the drive to assert and actualize equality on other grounds runs aground. In a world where nationalism and racism and domestic violence are so widespread, given the logical and practical fragility of the affirmation of human dignity, it is worth exploring resources for an acceptable religious ethics.

THE GOLDEN RULE AND THE FAMILY OF GOD

To associate the golden rule with the concept of humankind as one family is consistent with one of the most solid points of agreement achieved in the evolution of planetary ethics. The prehistory of the golden rule is uncertain, though Edward Westermarck's generalization is plausible that in primitive societies duties had a restricted scope; one's obligations were to one's family and clan; then they expanded to include the tribe. Norms requiring humane treatment of outsiders had special leverage for the next stage in moral evolution. There might be a designated market area where raiding was prohibited so that trading could go on. There might be special consideration for the "stranger in the gate." Experiences with outsiders, in situations protected by group sanctions, probably fostered an expanding sense of identity. Gradually the sense of the in-group widened to include a sense of national identity, and on the present frontier ethical awareness encompasses all humankind.

The previous histories indicate that the golden rule is most cherished where morality is conceived primarily in terms of relationships and where people share a commitment to humankind as one family. These conditions are typically grounded in faith in a higher Source or personal God, as has been seen in Chinese, Greek, Jewish, and Christian traditions (among others). They developed the golden rule as a universal principle, and in each tradition the concept dawned, more or less clearly and prominently, of God as the universal Father of every personality. Because the experience of God includes motherly as well as fatherly love (not to mention phases that are not obviously personal), there should be no room for dogmatism about the name that someone chooses to express his or her relationship with Deity.[2] Family talk connotes personality, nearness, experienceability, and love; and it gives the golden rule new meaning: "Treat other persons as brothers and sisters, as sons and daughters of God, as you want others to treat you."

In the religious ethics of relationship proposed here, one's primary relationship is with God, the Source Personality. Put simply, the idea is this. The person is already a son or daughter of God. Once the person accepts this truth, the relationship acquires new reality and leads to new growth and a wholehearted impulse to service. God is never merely one's own Parent, but always also the Parent of others, and this is the origin of the brotherhood of man (siblinghood of humankind). A love begins to manifest whose source is deeper than the need to prop up a beleaguered affirmation of human dignity. Experiencing by faith what it is to live as a son or daughter of God, one comes to live as a brother or sister in relation to others. In this light, the golden rule becomes *the principle of the practice of the family of God*.[3]

THE GOLDEN RULE OF DIVINE LOVE

Despite the ongoing, leap-frogging realizations of philosophic meanings and spiritual values, it is possible to posit the experience of living the will and way of God as the supreme experience of living the golden rule. This spiritual interpretation, "Treat others in a Godlike way as you want others to treat you," can only be final if it is stipulated to include openhearted sympathy, respect, well-informed prudence, and philosophic insight.[4] The advance from brotherly or sisterly love to divinely fatherly or motherly love implies a higher level of commitment, parental willingness to get involved and to sacrifice that goes beyond that of a brother or sister.

The notion of a divine pattern or paradigm for golden rule living may seem odd until we recall that the rule invites the hearer to bring to mind experiences of being well treated. The rule directs us to pattern our conduct on that model of relating which we have experienced and affirm. Those who experience the goodness of God know the inspiration for living the golden rule in the highest sense. Those who know the love of God and who receive its generosities and accept its disciplines, may aspire to pass this love on to others, to become like God in a derivative and partial sense. They may choose: this is how I want to be treated; this is, in a way, how I aspire to treat others. The ambition is not to function in a superhuman role, but to be the hands and feet and spokesperson of divine love, to do the service that a human being can do.

The tendency to seek a divine paradigm for human action is widespread. In a devotional tradition of Hinduism, there is the practice of imitating and eventually living expressively the life of a heavenly character.[5] Many Buddhists regard the Buddha, Gautama Siddartha, as an incarnation of a heavenly being and as an external manifestation of the Buddha nature within. For the neo-Confucian school of Chu Hsi, the transformations of Heaven are reflected in the actions of the sage. As noted in chapter 4, the Jewish letter of Aristeas teaches golden rule conduct on the model of the way God treats us, and the tradition of Moses taught, "Be holy as I the LORD your God am holy." Islam portrays God in terms of qualities such as righteousness, mercy, and compassion that may characterize human beings, despite the abyss of difference between the Creator and the creature. The very commitment to a certain scripture as revelation implies faith that the ideals of divinity have been expressed in human language: the revealed word functions as a paradigm, a guide from the spirit world, even if no human leader has the status of a paradigm.

Jesus set forth God as the paradigm: "Be you perfect, as your Father in heaven is perfect" and "Be merciful, even as your heavenly Father is merciful." He also gave assurance that following him and living his gospel is the way of wisdom and the will of the Father. From a follower's perspective, his oneness with the Father and his identification with humanity was of such an order that at the close of his ministry he could also truly present himself as a paradigm: "Love one another as I have loved you."[6] This commandment may be regarded as Jesus' ultimate transformation of the golden rule, in conjunction with his remark, "Inasmuch as you have done it to the least of these my brethren, you have done it unto me."[7] The commandment is given not with the furrowed brow of condemnation but with an encouraging smile: Come forth! Seeking to treat others according to the will of God, the believer may inquire how Jesus would treat people in such a situation. Those for whom Jesus is the Son of Man and the Son of God find new meaning in the golden rule as the principle of the practice of the family of God.

The specifics of religion, including such commitments as faith in a divine Son of God or participation in a Muslim brotherhood, make the concept of the universal family of God more complex, if they do not obscure it altogether; but the golden rule is a balm for an overly theologized religious consciousness. So long as the development of religious consciousness functions to deepen, not discard, the concept of the universal family of God, the golden rule with its universal applicability will continue to symbolize the moral expression of religious consciousness.

ETHICAL IMPLICATIONS OF THE CONCEPT OF THE FAMILY OF GOD

The concept of the family of God illuminates some persistent problems for ethics. Experience of the goodness of the divine Parent points beyond the so-called dilemma of divine command ethics. The classic question "Is something good 'simply because' some Deity figure commands it, or does the Deity command it 'simply because' it is good?" sets a puzzle for religious reason. Linear logic, trying to isolate rationales with phrases like "simply because" only distorts the infinity of God and the complexity of creature life. The problem with the first horn of the dilemma is that, if an action is recommended "simply because" God commands it, there seems to be no defense from the arbitrary commands of a brutal god. But to know God experientially makes it unthinkable that the will of God will not ultimately be seen to be good. The problem with the second horn of the dilemma is that, if God commands something "simply because" it is good, it may seem as though we might not need recourse to God, but rather may busy ourselves directly with determining for ourselves what is good (perhaps using criteria analogous to God's). However, if our destiny is to grow in goodness, to become like God, to help others to do the same, then there is no shortcut to fulfillment that omits God. The golden rule may thus be regarded as a divine command without triggering the classic dilemma.

Next, the concept of the family of God provides a means to address the question of the proof of the golden rule. Although, logically speaking, the rule may be derived from more general principles like the categorical imperative, the question of ultimate proof still remains. In a way, the demand for ultimate proof of a fundamental moral principle is misleading, since the question "Why be moral?" cannot be answered without assuming too much or proving too little.[8] Nevertheless, there is a foundation for the golden rule: the recognition of humankind as the family of God. In a sense, the family of God is *already actual*; for example, *those are my brothers and sisters who are suffering so and abusing one another*, and that is precisely the horror of it all. The sense of the actuality of the universal family leads to a sense of its practical *potentials*—progressive individuals living in superb relationships on an advanced planet. Moral action actualizes the potentials of human kinship in the light of the actuals of the family of God.[9] This foundation of the golden rule is not a proposition, though it can be expressed in propositions.[10] Nor is there a claim here that a proposition about the family of God can function like a value-free fact, from which to derive moral propositions.[11]

The concept of the universal family also offers a clue that may be used to bridge the space between a principle in the philosophy of living and an ethics of social systems. The religious use of family terms suggests the primacy of the family as the basic institution of society, as the arena in which we learn about relationships and morality, and as the social system in which our primary human loyalties reside.

In elaborating an ethics of the golden rule, the question of completeness arises. Can the rule be taken as a guide to every sort of duty? Does it cover, in particular, the duty to worship God? Most golden rule advocates do not claim that the rule properly applies to our relationship with God, but it is interesting to consider the strongest counterargument. Such an extension of the rule is not utterly meaningless, for if God is a person, then the respect and consideration due to persons is due to God, as indicated in Paul's counsel, "Grieve not the spirit of God."[12] Therefore, employing the imaginative role reversal in the primary relationship need not be an act of impiety. Nor is it necessarily presumptuous to try to approach a divine perspective on human affairs. If God has spoken to humankind, has used human language, there is a zone of interface, and one need not pretend to transcend human limitations in approaching a divinely human perspective, the best perspective available to mortals. For a believer, to do one's utmost to determine what course of action is best in the long run, all things considered, does amount to an attempt to approximate divine wisdom. One need not assume that only heaven-storming pride, rather than a prayerful heart, would inquiringly extend to God the principle "Show adequate respect for your superiors, even as you would have your subordinates show adequate respect for you." Obviously it would be wrong to propose the corollary, "Worship God even as you desire your children to worship you," because of the difference between finite, imperfect personalities and the infinite, perfect personality. On account of this difference, it is best to think of the golden rule simply as a rule for human relationships.

SPONTANEITY AND THE PARADOX OF
THE GOLDEN RULE

There is a benign paradox in the golden rule, such that *the rule leads beyond itself.* Apply the rule recursively: Do you want to be treated by others who

are merely following a rule? Though one prefers external golden rule conformity to gross mistreatment, one's first choice is to be treated in a loving
or appropriately humane way. The paradox is reinforced by a parallel in
the command to love one's neighbor. Duty consciousness cannot carry
out the duty to love, but it can turn to the source of love where duty
consciousness is transcended. The paradox of the command to love is
that it can be fulfilled only by transcending the standpoint of obedience.
Only a spiritual transformation of morality can adequately respond to the
Nietzschean critique of the coercive tendency of moralism.

This paradox leads to a recognition that moral conduct is a consequence, an overflowing, a fruit of the spirit. Moral teaching and moral
obedience by themselves do not achieve their goal. Ethics has focused too
much on what is to be done, and not enough on how interaction goes best.
A religious ethics centered on the will of God requires, first and foremost,
the supreme desire to do the will of God. Partial devotion leads to excessive
difficulty with the "what" question and a lack of spiritual flavor in the
"how" of action. In the spirit-led agent, the golden rule can fluently direct
attention beyond self toward the other, toward an impartial third-person
perspective, and toward a divine perspective. That transfer of attention
facilitates dimensions of golden rule activation that go beyond rules. The
golden rule comes to symbolize a way of living in self-forgetfulness.[13]

If self-forgetfulness is a cardinal virtue, then the golden rule may short-
circuit excessive introspection. Traditionally, the idea of character building
has required the aspirant to exercise willpower to overcome resistance, to
do the right thing until it comes to be enjoyed as one's accustomed response. But spiritual transformation should enable the agent to enjoy even
the early steps of habit formation: first, spirit infusing mind, then, mind
over matter, so to speak.

How does responsible spontaneity operate? We enter life without deliberating and deciding in advance. A certain spontaneity is inevitable in
all of living; even when we deliberate compulsively, there is a certain
spontaneity in the instinctive, self-protective move that drives the deliberation. The ideal is that, once mature, we are ready to make decisions,
great decisions, based on our best thinking, that commit ourselves for an
unforeseeable multiplicity of future situations.[14] These decisions enable us
to act spontaneously in all such situations. When we sense that a given
situation transcends the boundaries of what we have already adequately
understood and decided, we turn to deliberate. Such deliberation does
not mean a collapse of spontaneity, inasmuch as deliberation may itself
be graced by poise as we cope with difficulties. Ideally one's decisions are
so excellent that the inclination to overturn them may be simply regarded
as temptation to betrayal. Ideally, self-mastery is so thorough and the
scope of the decisions so complete, that one can sustain them throughout
a lifetime.

CONCLUSION

Here, then, is a distillation of the main ideas of this study. The golden rule is, from the first, intuitively accessible, easy to understand; its simplicity communicates confidence that the agent can find the right way. The rule tends to function as a simplified summary of the advocate's moral tradition, and it most commonly expresses a commitment to treating others with consideration and fairness, predicated on the recognition that others are like oneself.

The golden rule is offered to those among whom a minimal sincerity may be presupposed—the hearer will not manipulate the rule in defense of patently immoral conduct. The golden rule is not best interpreted as an isolated principle in a value vacuum, to be examined as a candidate for the role of sole normative axiom in a formalized ethical theory. Nevertheless, the rule is a principle in a full sense. Even before it is formulated, its logic operates in the human mind. Once formulated, it shows itself to be contagious and quickly rises to prominence. It functions as a distillation of the wisdom of human experience and of scriptural tradition. It serves the needs of educated and uneducated people alike, and stimulates philosophers to codify its meanings in new formulations. Given the equal, basic worth of each individual, the rule implies a requirement of consistency; as Clarke put it, "Whatever I judge reasonable or unreasonable for another to do for me; that, by the same judgment, I declare reasonable or unreasonable, that I in the like case should do for him."[15] In addition, this principle of a philosophy of living carries implications for social, economic, and political realms.

Much of the meaning of the rule can be put into practice without any religious commitment, since it is a nontheologic principle that neither mentions God nor is necessarily identified with the scriptures or doctrines of any one religion. The rule is an expression of human kinship, the most fundamental truth underlying morality. From a religious perspective, the golden rule is the principle of the practice of the family of God, and it means relating with other people as a brother or sister. At the limit, it involves conduct patterned on a divine paradigm, extending to others the same attitude of service that one would welcome as the recipient of someone else's divinely parental love in the same kind of situation.

The rule cannot be captured in a static interpretation for it engages the thoughtful doer in a process of growth. To follow it to the end is to move from egoism to sympathy, to sharpen moral intuition by reason, and to find fulfillment beyond duty-conscious rule following in spontaneous, loving service. In the process of identifying maturely with others, adopting the other's perspective imaginatively may be helpful, along with every other technique of understanding and cooperating with others. Thus the unity of the rule, amid its wide diversity, is its life as a symbol of this process of growth.

Whoever practices the golden rule opens himself or herself to a process of change. Letting go of self to identify with a single other individual, or with a third-person perspective on a complex situation, or with a divine paradigm, one allows a subtle and gradual transformation to proceed, a transformation with bright hope for the individual and the planet. The rule begins by setting forth the way the self wants to be treated as a standard of conduct; but by placing the other on a par with the self, the rule engages one in approximating a higher perspective from which the kinship of humanity is evident. To pursue this higher perspective is to risk encountering the divine and the realization that every step along the forward path is illumined by the Creator.

Idealistic striving tends to generate a consciousness of levels of achievement. Talk of levels connotes the conflict required to encounter something different and finally to realize its superiority. Only at the end of a personal struggle can one speak authentically in smooth tones about integration or synthesis. It is safe to be conscious of levels when the levels are understood as phases of the realization of human kinship. The spiritual level is, in part, a way to facilitate and conduct the emotional and intellectual levels of relating. When we are spiritually engaged, love can pervade our emotional reactions to such an extent that we are able to elaborate, more or less spontaneously, an intelligent and wise affection for every person we meet. Thus emotion becomes an indicator of the degree to which the spirit pervades the entire personality. Growth is not a product we construct by adding progress on one level to progress on another level; rather, growth results unconsciously as the personality engages wholeheartedly in experience. Thus it would not improve things to replace the simple expression of the golden rule by a formulation specifying levels of realization.

Confronting the problems of modern civilization, superficial thinking looks for a panacea. A simple word of wisdom, however, cannot help with a complex problem unless its simplicity expresses a life that comes from being connected with a universal network of truths. The more deeply the golden rule is grasped, the less it seems an easy answer. But those who learn to practice it fully, conjoining material sympathy with moral reason under the guidance of spiritual love, will point the way toward a brighter future.

"Do to others as you want others to do to you" is part of our planet's common language, shared by persons with differing but overlapping conceptions of morality. Only a principle so flexible can serve as a moral ladder for all humankind.

Notes

CHAPTER ONE

1. This passage is found in the *Mahabharata*, bk. 5, chap. 49, v. 57 (in vol. 5, p. 281 of the new, but incomplete, translation by van Buitenen). I am indebted to Julian Woods for directing me to this passage as well as three similar sentences in the *Mahabharata*. "Knowing how painful it is to himself, a person should never do to others which he dislikes when done to him by others" (bk. 12, chap. 251). "A person should not himself do that act which, if done by another, would call down his censure" (bk. 12, chap. 279, v. 23). "One should never do that to another which one regards as injurious to one's own self" (bk. 13, chap. 113). The last I was able to locate in vol. 11, p. 240, in the older, complete, twelve-volume translation (of the work in eighteen books) by Pratapa Chandra Roy.

The works of Leonidas Johannes Philippidis (1929, 1933) remain fine sources for interpreting the various meanings of the golden rule in the contexts of the major world religions. Philippidis (1929) cites the German translation of the *Mahabharata* by Paul Deussen and Otto Strauss, utilizing their own system of numbering. "Do not do to anyone what you would not like another to do to you; that is the sum of the law; every other law is valid as you like [*gilt nach Belieben*] (bk. 5, vv. 1517–18). "The knowing person is minded to treat all beings as himself" (12.9923; p. 483, 10). "He who loves life himself, how can he kill another? What he wishes for himself, let him care also for the other in this regard [*dafüer sorge er auch bei den anderen*]. How can a person who lies with another man's wife reproach anyone?" (bk. 12, vv. 9250–51; p. 415, 22). "Let no one do to another what he does not want done to himself; this is the sum of righteousness" (13.5571). Philippidis also gives Yajnavalkya III, 65: "The cause of virtue is not partiality; virtue only arises when practiced. Therefore, let no one do to another what he would not welcome." I have also found references to Anusasana Parva 113.8 and Brihadaranyaka Upanishad 5.2.2.

2. This quotation is taken from the Hadith (or Traditions), records of the sayings and practices of Muhammad and his earliest followers. These traditions have a lesser authority for Muslims than that of the Qur'an; the Hadith cited here (Rost 1986, 103) is from the collection *An-Nawawi's Forty Hadith* 13 (p. 56). Rost (100) also cites the following passage from the Qur'an: "Woe to those . . . who, when they have to receive by measure from men, exact full measure, but when they

have to give by measure or weight to men, give less than due" (Surah 83, "The Unjust," vv. 1–4); the Qur'an also celebrates those who "show their affection to such as came to them for refuge and entertain no desire in their hearts for things given to the (latter), but give them preference over themselves" (Surah 59, "Exile," vv. 9). In addition, Rost records that tradition attributes the following statements to Muhammad: (1) "Seek for mankind that of which you are desirous for yourself, that you may be a believer; treat well as a neighbor the one who lives near you, that you may be a Muslim [one who submits to God]." (2) "That which you want for yourself, seek for mankind." (3) "The most righteous of men is the one who is glad that men should have what is pleasing to himself, and who dislikes for them what is for him disagreeable." According to Rost, the last four quotations are nos. 14, 21, 63, and 306 in the Sukhanan-i-Muhammad (Teheran, 1938; Rost cites Donaldson 1963, 82).

I am grateful to Abrahim H. Khan at the University of Toronto for sharing with me an unpublished paper titled, "The Golden Rule as Moral Bedrock in Religious History?," which includes a section on Islam (the paper was written in 1993). Following Alvin Gouldner's functionalist approach, Khan proposes that the golden rule has conduced to social cohesion in religious communities whose forms of life are so different that the rule cannot be regarded as a universal principle with common meaning. Nevertheless, the rule promotes social cohesion in all societies, which require reciprocity (the exchange of benefits), beneficence (e.g., toward the very young and the very old, who cannot repay benefits), and moral absolutism (the dangerous demand for conformity to the social norms). Khan finds the functions of the golden rule expressed in the moral institution of Hisba, integral to socioeconomic fairness in Islamic society. He also cites the constitution that Muhammad worked out in Medina for all groups, including Muslim and Jewish ones, specifying rights and responsibilities involved in the mutual defense of their city. He cites Muhammad's last testament to his community, given shortly before he died, in which he concluded with a reminder that Muslims are all brothers. Islamic morality, however, is first and foremost an affair of obedience to divine command. Khan gives an illustration from Ibn al-'Arabi's "Instructions to a Postulant," where one reads: "All the commandments are summed up in this, that whatever you will like the True One to do to you, that do to His creatures, step by step" (cited in Jeffery 1962, 647).

3. One example of the golden rule drawn from Buddhism states: "Hurt not others in ways that you yourself would find hurtful" (Udana-Varga, 5.18). Additional references include the Sutta Nipata 705; Samyutta Nikaya 353; the Dhammapada 129–30; the Acarangasutra 5.101–2; and the Majjhima Nikaya i.415. The Jainist Sutrakritanga contains the admonition that one should "treat all beings as he himself would be treated" (1.10.13). The standard citation from Zoroastrianism is from the Dadistan-i-Dinik: "That nature only is good which shall not do unto another whatever is not good for its own self" (94.5) The Christian writer Garcilaso de la Vega (1961, p. 9) reported of the Inca leader Manco Capac that he taught his subjects that "each one should do unto others as he would have others do unto him" (cited in Alton 1966, 111).

4. I owe the keen recognition of this problem to Alton (1966, 14–19). His dissertation is outstanding in both comparative historical and analytic philosophic virtues. Alton, now affiliated with Trinity College, the University of Toronto, has in many ways been of help in my own work.

5. Indeed, the very effort to make clear the importance of differences presupposes that differences can be understood. The cultural barriers are explained in a single language, and the listener/reader is expected to understand both sides of the "divide." Moreover not every intercultural discovery is a discovery of difference. These ideas are developed in several essays contained in Larson and Deutsch's *Interpreting across Boundaries*. In the interfaith dialogue movement, participants have sometimes remarked that they feel they have more in common with kindred minds or kindred spirits in other religions than with those in their own tradition who are resistant to dialogue.

6. Paul Tillich, *The New Being*, 30–32, cited in Phipps 1982.

7. Some writers, alienated by the sentimental or Christian connotations of the word "love," prefer the term "caring"; others speak of doing "good" to others.

8. Shaw 1930, 217. This quote is taken from the appendix to *Man and Superman*, entitled "Maxims for Revolutionists."

9. Melville 1967, 54. As Alton has pointed out, a deeper problem is raised by this story on account of the wide cultural difference between the two characters. How is it possible to apply the golden rule across such a barrier without falling either into cultural imperialism or naive cultural relativism? The progressive interpretations of the rule provide a bulwark against both extremes, but it would be folly to claim that even a marvelously conceived principle would, in and of itself, dissolve such knotty problems.

10. A few examples will serve to illustrate imaginative perspective-taking. The first case goes something like this: "Remember, our Indian colleague coming for dinner is a Hindu; think how she would feel if we served beef." Immediately one grasps the point: of course, we will not serve beef. No foray of imaginative speculation has been undertaken about how one would feel about being served objectionable food. Given the habit of consideration for friends, what suffices is a simple reminder about the Hindu restriction regarding beef. The thinking is in accord with the golden rule, though no reversal of roles has occurred.

In a second case, Alicia promises Margo that she will call her after work. By the time she gets home, Alicia is very tired and doesn't feel like calling Margo. As she sinks down on the couch, she takes a moment to rethink her disinclination to call her friend. She realizes that Margo will worry that something may have happened to her on the way home, and she thinks to herself, "I know how I would feel if Margo didn't call me after having promised to do so." Alicia thus momentarily imagines such a scenario and lets herself experience, in a preliminary way, the feelings associated with the imagined situation. This imagining, which only lasts a few seconds, brings to mind thoughts of the uncertainties of urban life and the vulnerability of women. Margo's probable concern becomes vividly understandable. Alicia gets up and places the call.

In a third case, Alicia knows that Margo is easily provoked to extreme worry. Here the role reversal might involve Alicia's imagining not how *she* herself would feel but how upset *Margo* would be if the expected phone call did not occur. These last two cases illustrate the two standard variations on the imaginative role reversal involving a single recipient.

11. The original source of this quote is C. C. Claridge, *Wild Bush Tribes of Tropical Africa* (n.p.), 248 and 259; cited in Hertzler 1934, 419. Claridge also relates that the Ba-Congo have a general formulation of the golden rule: "O man, what you do not like, do not to your fellows." An internet search by Harry Gensler turned up

a Nigerian Yoruba proverb: "One going to take a pointed stick to pinch a baby bird should first try it on himself to feel how it hurts."

12. I am grateful to Sioux Harvey for gathering this information. There are many versions of this prayer or motto, and no original author can be identified. The quotation given in the text is derived from the St. Francis Indian Mission, where Rev. R. M. Denmaier has testified that this statement is especially important among the Indians of the northern plains. The *World Treasury of Religious Quotations* includes the following prayer: "Great Spirit, Help me never to judge another until I have walked two months in his moccasins." Another version contains the following variables: "Don't judge a man until you have walked a mile (or a hundred miles) in his shoes (or moccasins)."A final version, cited in the *International Thesaurus of Quotations* as being supplied by the Indian Committee of the National Council of Churches, runs as follows: "Don't judge any man until you have walked two moons in his moccasins"—a quotation free of "miles" and "months," both European measures.

13. It is not my intent to suggest a limited model of religion here, at least in terms of my use of the term "faith." Wilfrid Cantwell Smith (1979) has adequately demonstrated the significance and operation of faith in Buddhism, Hinduism, Islam, and Christianity.

14. I have located but been unable to read writings in Hebrew and Finnish.

CHAPTER TWO

1. *Analects* 2.4, Confucius 1979.

2. For present purposes, I forbear to probe reflections on the golden rule by the other major neo-Confucian thinker, Wang Yang-ming (1472–1529), whose inspiring life and teachings on moral and spiritual insight and bold action make him an enduringly compelling figure.

3. *Analects* 15.23; tr. Wing-tsit Chan, included in Chan 1963, 44 (the numbering of the *Analects* varies slightly from one translation to another). Shu is pronounced in a clipped way with a descending intonation. The most common current translation for *shu* is "empathy," but this rendering lacks the active, ethical connotations of *shu*, so "consideration" is preferable. The lack of uniformity among translations creates extra difficulty for the student.

4. One variation on the golden rule directs the agent to satisfy the recipient's opinions and desires: "Do not do to others whatever they do not want you to do." Mencius (1970) coins a similar formula to promote conformity with public opinion and common valuations: "Do not do what others do not choose to do; do not desire what others do not desire" (7A17). Advising rulers, Mencius expresses democratic sentiments. The ruler desiring to win the people's hearts should "amass what they want and not impose what they dislike" (4A10). "The people will delight in the joy of him who delights in their joy, and will worry over the troubles of him who worries over their troubles" (1B4). "Heaven sees with the eyes of the people" (5A5).

5. Chung, usually translated "loyalty," is pronounced "joong" in a clipped way in a high tone, neither rising nor falling.

6. Chan 1963, 27. I am indebted to Jie Yang of the University of Calgary for the observation that the term "thread" is supplied in the tradition of English trans-

lation, the image being that there is a *one* that goes *through* something else, as through a coin with a hole in the center.

7. I owe this observation to John C. Meagher.

8. Loyalty and consideration have the same lower character. A. C. Graham collects this text from "the fullest collection of early Confucian definitions, by Chia Yi in the second century B.C.E.: "Concern for and benefiting issuing right from the centre of you is called *chung*" ("Lore of the Way") in the *Chia Yi hsin shu* (B, 32A) *Tao shu* (Graham 1989, 20–22).

9. Scholars disagree on whether these connotations inhere in the terms *loyalty* and *consideration*, but not on the importance of these obligations in Confucian society. On this point I follow Nivison's interpretation, whose 1984 paper is forthcoming in a collection of Nivison's papers edited by Brian Van Norden. References to Nivison in this chapter (except as otherwise noted) are to this 1984 paper and quotations are by permission. My chapter takes a different direction from Nivison's, but I owe to him the discovery of the social symmetry of loyalty and consideration and Chu Hsi's metaphysical transformation of these concepts.

10. D. C. Lau uses this entire sentence to translate expansively the single word *shu* in *Analects* 4.15.

11. *Analects* 5.12; Chan 1963, 28.

12. *Doctrine of the Mean*, section 13. The translation is adapted from Nivison 1984.

13. I would usually translate *jen* by "humanity," except that it might cause confusion, since I use "humankind" so often. It is tricky to translate *jen* (pronounced "ren," with a rising intonation). In ordinary language, when a man is praised for his *humanity*, or as being "truly humane," or as a person "of great humanity," the sense of *jen* is present, and many translators have used this term. The term *cohumanity* has several advantages, and is increasingly used by translators despite the fact that it is a neologism. "Cohumanity" renders a significant feature of the etymology in Chinese: *jen* is written with two characters—the character for "person" followed by the character for "two." The virtues that illustrate cohumanity involve relationships between two persons. Cohumanity is the person-to-person virtue par excellence. The term *benevolence* is a good translation, so long as it is not associated with diffuse and passive wishing. Using the term *love* as a translation has been suspect during the past century on account of its Christian overtones, which do not fit Confucius. Obviously, one can go overboard both in using and in forbidding the use of English terms that suggest similarities between classical Chinese and Christian experience.

14. See, e.g., Cua 1984.

15. *Analects* 12.2, Chan 1963, 39.

16. *Analects* 6.28, Chan 1963, 31. The last sentence is variously rendered. Nivison translates, "The ability to make a comparison (sc. with the other person) from what is near at hand (sc. from your own case) can be called the method of (attaining) benevolence." Herbert Fingarette gives, "To be able from what is close to take analogy, *that* way is where *jen* is" (Fingarette 1980, 380). Leonidas Johannes Philippidis cites Wilhelm's translation—"being able to take the near (= oneself) as example"—and puts his own summary in a single phrase, "consciousness of likeness" (*Bewusstsein der Gleichheit*) (Philippidis 1933, 43 and 50).

17. Mencius 1970, 7A4.

18. Chu Hsi 1973, 435.

19. Chan 1963, 91.

20. Relying on the intuitive character of interpersonal understanding, the scientific component of understanding, so prominent in Chinese tradition, is missing in the traditional texts on the golden rule. It is puzzling why the notion of "the investigation of things," regularly highlighted in discussions of self-cultivation, was never used to develop the concept of interpersonal comparing.

21. Chuang Tzu 1968, 218–19.

22. Ch'en Ch'un 1986, 89.

23. Fingarette 1980, 381.

24. Mencius 1970, 1A7.

25. Mencius, as translated in Wu 1986, 77.

26. I believe that a contemporary Confucianism should acknowledge Mo Tzu as one of its intellectual ancestors. Mo's doctrine of universal love, so controversial in its day for its alleged disregard of filial piety, was largely accepted by the neo-Confucians. Chu Hsi's criticism was that Mo's doctrine needs to invoke a second principle (in addition to universal love) to undergird filial piety, whereas if one starts from filial piety, one can generate universal love by extending that one foundation (see Chu Hsi 1967, II.89.80).

27. Mo Tzu 1963, sec. 16.

28. Ultimately, for Mo Tzu, it is a matter of identifying with the will of Heaven.

29. Mencius 1970, 4B4.

30. Is the description of such a level of experience an invitation to disregard social proprieties? No, because the Way is understood to include situation-specific implications for action, and the agent's grasp of the Way is based tacitly on the agent's perception of the other-in-context.

31. *Analects* 12.5.

32. Chan 1963, 107, sec. 20.

33. Chan 1963, 497.

34. Yang-ming draws on classical teachings here (Wang Yang-ming 1963, I.142.118; the numbering means pt. I, sec. 142, p. 118).

35. Chu Hsi and Lu Tsu-Chien 1967, I.20.19.

36. Wing-tsit Chan explains Chu Hsi's concept of the mutual reflection as suggesting "perfectly clear mirrors without any dust (selfishness) on them reflecting each other" (Chu Hsi 1963, I.20.19).

37. Chu Hsi 1963, II.89.77.

38. *The Doctrine of the Mean*, chap. 20; Chan 1963, 107.

39. Hsun Tzu 1963, 157.

40. Mencius 1970, 1A7.

41. Suzuki 1952, 607.

42. Fung 1953, II, 393.

43. Nivison 1956, 68.

44. Mencius 1970, 2A6.

45. Mencius 1970, 2B2.

46. Chu Hsi 1963, I.32.26.

47. I owe this idea to Nivison. Chu Hsi wrote, "*Chung* means 'facing the Lord in Heaven' all day long" (Chu 1963, I.19.17). Commenting on *Analects* 4.15, he wrote, "Fully realizing the self is called *chung*; extending the self is called *shu*"; then

he quotes Cheng I for the point: Chung is the Way of Heaven; shu is the Way of Man. Chung means absence of error; shu is how we put chung into practice. Chung is t'i (essence or 'substance'); shu is (yung) ('function'). The one is the 'great root'; the other is the realized Way." (Chu Hsi, quoted and translated by Nivison [1984]; cf. Chu Hsi and Lu Tsu-Chien 1967, II.52.62.)

48. Chan 1963, 633.

49. Ching 1972, 17, Letter 9 (1511).

50. Allinson 1985.

51. Allinson 1985, 308.

52. Ch'en Ch'un 1986, 89.

53. Ch'en Ch'un 1986, 91. I have substituted the word "consideration" for the original translator's "empathy."

CHAPTER THREE

1. Homer 1949, bk. V, vv. 184–91, p. 62.

2. Diogenes Laertius, 1905, ix.i, "Life of Thales," 19; in Alton 1966, 98.

3. Herodotus 1859, bk. III, chap. 142; vol 2, p. 435.

4. Dover 1974, 182.

5. Dihle (1962) challenges the interpretations given above of the golden rule expressions found in Homer and Herodotus. To appreciate the magnitude of his book, consider that in Die goldene Regel he collects and analyzes the occurrences of the golden rule and related phrases in Greek, Hebrew, Christian, and Roman antiquity. His thesis is that in these civilizations the golden rule evolved from, and remained bound to, the archaic Greek concept of justice, whose popular and crude morality of returning good for good and evil for evil spread thence to the rest of the Mediterranean world. He collects a great variety of specific maxims, suppressing crucial differences, in order to make his argument.

Despite the fact that Dihle argues that the Greek golden rule remained captive to repayment thinking, he records that as Greek culture progressed, the principle of retaliation, based on calculations about outward fact, was progressively abandoned as understanding gained new depth. Inner intentions were increasingly weighed, and the degree of the agent's responsibility was considered (18–19). Forgiveness was recommended. It was recognized that it is wise to check the impulse to judge and to repay in kind and that tragic protagonists suffer in ways that simple retaliation does not explain (52–56).

6. Dihle 1962, 80–81.

7. Dihle 1962, 85–87.

8. Robinson 1966, 86.

9. Westermarck 1906, 77, 102–5; cited in Hans Reiner 1977, 236.

10. An example of a psychological observation is found in a letter to a ruler and friend: "Deliver your citizens from their many fears, and be not willing that dread should beset men who have done no wrong; for even as you dispose others toward you, so you will feel toward them" (Isocrates 1928; vol. 1, "To Nicocles," 23).

11. Isocrates 1928, vol. 3, "Aegineticus," 51.

12. Isocrates 1928, vol. 1, "To Demonicus," 14. Cf. "Whatever advice you would give to your children, consent to follow it yourself" (Isocrates 1928, vol. 1, "To Nicocles," 38).

13. Isocrates 1928, vol. 1, "To Nicocles," 24, translation revised. Isocrates uses a similar phrase in his *Panegyricus* in praising Athens for passing the test of a great civilization—exercising power without abusing it (Isocrates 1928, vol 1, 81).

14. From this standpoint, he admonishes the king's subjects to behave among themselves according to the exemplary behavior they think appropriate on the part of their king: "You should be such in your dealings with others as you expect me to be in my dealings with you" (Isocrates 1928, vol. 1, "Nicocles," 49–50).

15. Isocrates 1928, vol. 1, "Nicocles," 61.

16. Dihle 1962, 101; Alton 1966, 84.

17. Dihle 1962, 21–22.

18. The *good* of Plato's *Republic* may be identified with the *beautiful* of the *Symposium* and with the *one* of the *Parmenides*; of these only the last offers a fully philosophical exposition.

19. *Crito* 49d; *Meno* 71e; *Gorgias* 474b-481b; cf. Dihle 1962, 5–6 and 62–65.

20. *Crito* 50a5–8. I use the translation of the *Crito* and the *Phaedo* by Tredennick in the *Collected Dialogues of Plato* (Plato 1961).

21. Scholars debate whether *phroura* is correctly translated here as "guard post" or "prison." The latter translation brings to mind not only the literal imprisonment of Socrates (Gallop 1975, 83) but also the Orphic-Pythagorean doctrine, relevant to later discussion in the *Phaedo*, that the soul is imprisoned in the body as a punishment, a sentence to be endured before the soul can return on high (cf. *Cratylus* 400c, *Gorgias* 493a). Rendering *phroura* as "prison" is favored by John Burnet (1937, 22) and R. Hackforth (1972, 36) (cf. Jaeger 1947, 55–72 and 83–86).

Ronna Burger makes use of both meanings in her study (1984, 32). For Burger, the notion of the body as prison connotes the (for Plato) illegitimate craving of the soul to be free of the body to experience realities directly, which is precisely what she says Socrates learned not to do through his earlier flirtation with the method of Anaxagoras; rather, in his second approach to the issue, Socrates learns to persist in examining *logous*, arguments. The notion of life as guard duty points to Socrates' tenacity in playing the role of gadfly in Athens and to the legitimate conviction of the philosopher that the *logos* is to be pursued and that the *logos* is separable from the "things themselves"—even as the *Phaedo* may be studied though Socrates has died.

I do not claim that the meaning "prison" is absent in the term *phroura*; but new meaning is surfacing, as Burger observes, in the term "guard post." It would be foolish to neglect the Orphic-Pythagorean background of Socrates' interlocutors—though Hans-Georg Gadamer has argued that Simmias and Cebes represent more the mentality of a scientific enlightenment (1969, 22–38). The final word in this debate is given by Socrates, who, after referring to our life in a *phroura*, immediately sets aside the controversial mystical connotations in order to identify what is essential for his *logos*: that we belong to the gods.

22. *Phaedo* 62c1–3.

23. Cf. the appeal for consideration in Ephesians 4:30: "Grieve not the spirit of God."

24. *Laws* 913a, tr. A.E. Taylor (Plato 1961); cited by Alton 1966, 99.

25. Plato's primary term, which is commonly translated as "form," is *eidos*, which is based on the past participle of the verb "to see." *Eidos* might be etymologically rendered, "that into which there has been insight." The insight, once

achieved, is unchallengeable, not in the sense that others may not raise objections, but in the sense that the protests do not shake the insightful person. Cosmic reality has been recognized.

26. *Republic* 504c, tr. Paul Shorey in Plato 1961.

27. Katherine M. Nickras, a student at Kent State University, made the connection that Socrates in the *Apology* directs Athenians to treat his sons as he has treated his fellow citizens. In addition, at the close of the *Phaedo*, Socrates exhorts his friends to treat one another as he has been treating them.

28. Diogenes Laertius 1905, XI.v, 88 (cited in Alton 1966, 100).

29. Aristotle 1985, 1167a23–1167b15.

30. Aristotle 1985, 1166a31. The translator's use of the masculine pronoun is harmonious with the fact that Aristotle writes more about men; nevertheless, he cites the love of a mother for a child as a paradigm of "friendship."

31. Aristotle 1985, 1161b28.

32. Aristotle 1167a2.

33. Aristotle 1985, 1169a20. The excellent person chooses for himself noble deeds above all (1169a 9–25).

34. Aristotle records the reasons for the custom of helping friends and harming enemies.

> For people seek to return either evil for evil, since otherwise [their condition] seems to be slavery, or good for good, since otherwise there is no exchange; and they are maintained [in an association] by exchange. Indeed, that is why they make a temple of the Graces prominent, so that there will be a return of benefits received. For this is what is special to grace; when someone has been gracious to us, we must do a service for him in return, and also ourselves take the lead in being gracious again. (Aristotle 1985, 1132b35–1133a5)

35. Aristotle 1985, 1155b33, 1163a2, 1164b1.

36. Aristotle 1985, 1124b11.

37. Aristotle 1991, 1381a8–11, cited in Pakaluk 1991, 72–73.

38. Aristotle 1991, 1384b3–5.

39. "The remarks he is willing to hear made are of the same sort, since those he is prepared to hear made seem to be those he is prepared to make himself" Aristotle 1985, 1128b28.

40. Aristotle 1985, 1161b7. Of course Aristotle was not the first of the Greeks to begin to envisage a common humanity in a way that challenged popular prejudice. Aeschylus in *The Suppliant Maidens* had presented an argument that Greeks and black Egyptians were kin in virtue of derivation from a common deity. Plato in the *Meno* had presented a slave boy as endowed with reason and capable of mathematics.

41. Aristotle 1985, 1155a16–23.

42. "Again and again in his letters [Seneca] speaks of a holy spirit living within our bodily frame" (Rist 1969, 267). According to Marcus Aurelius, "This *daimon* [indwelling spirit] is each man's mind and reason." He continues:

> Live with the gods. But he is living with the gods who continuously exhibits his soul to them, as satisfied with its dispensation and doing what

the *daimon* wishes, the *daimon* which is that fragment of himself, which Zeus has given to each man as his guardian leader." (*Meditations* 5.27; cited in Rist 1969, 269)

43. Inwood 1985, 106.
44. Seneca 1928, On Anger III.12.2, 3.
45. Seneca 1928, On Benefits II, i, 20.
46. Seneca, *Epistle to Lucius* I, 307; cited in Alton 1966, 100.
47. Griffin 1976, 256–85.
48. "In exile he had put his literary talent and philosophical training at the service of adulation in an attempt to return [to office]" Griffin 1976, 135.
49. Epictetus, n.d. Fragment 42, 462.
50. There are exceptions (except in cases of actions whose description implies wrongdoing, e.g., adultery, theft, and murder). Aristotle 1985, I.3 and II.6 1107a11.
51. Robert Sokolowski (1985) makes this point as follows:

The Stoics shift the substance of moral virtue from the external performance to the mental attitude because they want to attain independence in human action, but the autonomy they seek cannot be achieved by human agents. The Stoics want the kind of autonomy that is only possible in the life of thinking, which can be extremely independent of externals. They confuse contemplative and practical thinking and want to provide the latter with the independence of the former. (198)

It is a commonplace that Stoic cosmopolitanism was in part a defensive reaction to the destruction, by imperial powers, of the opportunities for vital, local, political involvement that had been enjoyed in many of the city-states of ancient Greece. The philosophic advance to cosmopolitan thinking was thus often accompanied by withdrawal from vital engagement in the here and now, with living not into and through, but over and above local affairs.

CHAPTER FOUR

1. "Torah" means, literally, "teaching," especially the scriptures, especially the first five books of the Bible.
2. Gen. 1.26.
3. Exod. 20; Deut. 5.
4. 2 Sam. 12.1–7. The New Revised Standard (NRSV) translation is used unless otherwise noted. Gensler (1977) notes similar stories in 2 Sam. 14.1–13 and 1 Kings 38–42. I am indebted to Torsti Äärelä for a major contribution to my perspective in this chapter, including, initially, the observation that this biblical text may well date from after the sixth century. The scholars' debate about who had the golden rule first, and who did or did not get it from whom, and which origins are original, is one that I cannot adjudicate. Moreover, there is often an unrecognized assumption in such questions, namely, that the earliest recognitions of the golden rule do not predate the most ancient extant texts. In his critique of an earlier draft of this chapter Äärelä emphasized the conservative Jewish origins of the exemplars I cite: Ben Sira exalts the wisdom of God in opposition to human wisdom, and Hillel is a Babylonian rabbi at the origin of the Pharisaic movement.

Thus Dihle's portrait of the Jewish golden rule as a Hellenistic import is problematic, though possible; Hellenistic Judaism, centered in Alexandria, arose in response to the Greek influence in Palestine after the conquest by Alexander the Great in 333 B.C.E.

5. Philippidis finds a remark in the oldest of books (2300 B.C.E.), the Sumerian epic of Gilgamesh, which tells of the friendship between Gilgamesh and Enkidu. Before they depart on a dangerous venture, the queen, the mother of Gilgamesh, gives Enkidu instructions, including the line "You shall love him as yourself" (Philippidis 1933, 33). I have been unable to confirm this in the English translations I have checked.

6. Charles 1913, 739.

7. Blenkinsopp 1983, 17. Some scholars, he notes, interpret *mashal* (proverb) emphasizing the sense of standard of "comparison" or "model."

8. Wisdom literature includes the core books of Job, Proverbs, and Ecclesiastes; more widely defined, it includes the Psalms, the Wisdom of Solomon, Ben Sira (Ecclesiasticus), and Tobit.

9. Pro. 16.18.

10. Pro. 15.17.

11. Ps. 1.

12. Deut. 4:29. Blenkinsopp 1983, 100. ("Wisdom," in Latin, is *sapientia*.)

13. Ben Sira, also known as Ecclesiasticus, is regarded by Protestants as apocryphal and by Roman Catholics as deuterocanonical, i.e., accepted among the second group of books regarded as canonical by the church.

14. Ben Sira 28:1–4.

15. Compare Matt. 6:12 and Luke 11:4

16. Ben Sira 31:12–18.

17. Translation adapted from Meecham 1935, sec. 207, 60. The text is grouped with the Old Testament Pseudepigrapha—pseudonymous, noncanonical, Jewish writings.

18. Tobit is another text not in the canon of the Hebrew Bible, and regarded by Christians as deuterocanonical or apocryphal.

19. Tobit 4:14–15.

20. Deut. 6.4. The Ten Commandments formed the core of the religious legislation that Moses presented to his followers to form them into a community. There are also versions at Exod. 19–20 and Exod. 34. Moses also gave instructions for organizing the worship of the fledgling community (though how much of these derive from later sources is debated). The Deuteronomic code (Deut. 12–26) gives the impression of a very severe code, yet one aiming at justice.

21. Lev. 20.7; cf. 20.26.

22. Lev. 19.18. In its entirety, the verse reads as follows: "You shall not take vengeance or bear a grudge against any of your people, but you shall love your neighbor as yourself: I am the Lord."

23. Lev. 19.34.

24. Edward Schillebeeckx cites Deut. 6.4–5; 6.6; 5.10; 7.9; 10.12; 11.1,13,22; 19.9; 30.6; especially 6.4–5 with 26.26; 2 Kings 23.25 (1981, 249).

25. See the Book of Jubilees 20.2 and 36.8. Regarding this book, classified among the Pseudepigrapha, I rely on Flusser 1990.

26. Quoted in Flusser 1990, 235.

27. I owe this grammatical point to Hal Warlock of High Point College.

28. Alton noted that the law of love needs a logical qualification, which the golden rule does not: there are ways in which we care for ("love") ourselves that would not be suitable to do to others [except those who cannot care for themselves] (Alton 1966, 68–69).

29. The *Palestinian Targum* (commentary), also known as the *Jerusalem Targum*. David Flusser (1990) gives another, later example:

> It is interesting to note the following from an old Hebrew translation of *Tales of Sanbar* (ed. Morris Epstein, Philadelphia 1967, p. 296). Toward the end of the story, the hero advises the king, "What you yourself hate, do not do to your neighbor; and love your people as yourself." So runs one group of mss.; and it is clear that we are dealing with a translation from some other language. In a second group of mss. the Golden Rule and the quotation about loving one's neighbor have been corrected to conform with the classical biblical and talmudic formulations—with the Golden Rule quoted in the Aramaic formulation of Hillel: "What is hateful to you do not do to your fellowman, and you shall love your neighbor as yourself." (228)

30. *The Testament of Naphtali*, quoted in Flusser 1990, 231n.

31. It has been suggested that positive rules pertain to our obligations to God and negative rules to our obligations toward humankind.

32. Rabbi Simmler, in the Babylonian Talmud *Makkoth* 23b-24a (quoted in Abrahams, 1967, 23).

33. Matthew's translation into Greek at 22.36—"commandment" (*entole*)—did not preserve this sense; though Flusser notes that Philo's translation did and that Paul overcame this linguistic difficulty in Rom. 13.9 and Gal. 5.14 (1990, 228n).

34. *Shabbath* 31a.

35. Gerhardsson 1987, 168.

36. Rehm 1060, 118, cited in Flusser 1990, 226n.

37. The record of the wisdom of the early rabbis, *Pirke 'Abot, The Chapters of the Fathers* shows applications of golden rule thinking in words of wisdom attributed to Rabbi Eleazar ("Let the honor of thy fellow be as dear to thee as thine own") and Rabbi Jose "Let thy fellow's property be as dear to thee as thine own"; Rabbi Eliezer teaches, "Let the honor of thy fellow be as dear to thee as thine own" (Nathan 1955, 235).

The Jewish Platonist Philo (13 B.C.E.–50 C.E.), who envisioned universal patterns expressed in the Torah, wrote, "What you hate to suffer, you must not do to others." The rule is attributed to Philo by Eusebius, in the *Praeparatio Evangelica*, viii.7.6 (included in Philo of Alexandria 1941); he there quotes from a lost work of Philo, the *Hypothetica*.

Flusser notes that such one-principle simplifications are also found in the New Testament:

> Owe no one anything, except to love one another; for he who loves his neighbor has fulfilled the law. The commandments, "You shall not commit adultery, You shall not kill, You shall not steal, You shall not covet," and any other commandment, are summed up in this sentence, "You shall love your neighbor as yourself." Love does no wrong to a neighbor; therefore love is the fulfilling of the law. (Rom. 13.8–10)

For the whole law is fulfilled in one word, "You shall love your neighbor as yourself." (Gal. 5.14)

If you really fulfill the royal law, according to the scripture, "You shall love your neighbor as yourself," you do well. (James 2.8)

Such simplifications presuppose that loving God is a tacit condition for love of one another: "for love is of God, and he who loves is born of God and knows God" (1 John 4:7). Although the golden rule summarizes both Jewish and Christian moral teachings regarding conduct toward human others, it arguably does not really summarize the first table of the Ten Commandments regarding the relationship toward God. The rule is not, except at the margin, a guide for the believer's relation with God.

38. *Abot de Rabbi Nathan*, ed. Schechter (2nd ed., n.d.) chap. 26, p. 53, quoted in King 1928, 268.

39. Schillebeeckx 1981, 249–50.

40. See David Winston's article, "Wisdom in the Wisdom of Solomon" in Perdue, Scott, and Wiseman 1993. Philo synthesized the concept of philanthropy from Greek and Jewish sources.

CHAPTER FIVE

1. It is customary to refer to the first four books of the New Testament as, e.g., "the Gospel According to Matthew." Actually, the phrase "the Gospel" is an interpolation; the Greek simply has "According to Matthew."

2. Matt. 11.28–30. The New Testament quotations use the New Revised Standard Version.

3. See Amos Wilder's history of the interpretation of the Sermon on the Mount regarding this issue in his article in *The Interpreter's Bible* 7, 160–61. Cf. Lerne 1970 and Bauman 1985.

4. The Beatitudes are the teachings on happiness, Matt. 5.3–12, promising blessings on the poor in spirit, those who mourn, the meek, those who hunger and thirst for righteousness, the merciful, the pure in heart, the peacemakers, and those who endure persecution.

5. This is no trivial point for the discussions in philosophy that use action theory primarily as a vehicle for the mind–body problem, neglecting the interpersonal significance of action.

6. Judgments differ on how much of the previous text the rule is intended to summarize; for Dale C. Allison Jr., 7.12 can be read as a summary of 6.19–7.12 and also of the central core of the sermon, 5.17–7.12 (Allison 1987, 436). Since the rule is presented as such a general principle, it is difficult to limit the scope of what it may be taken to summarize. At the same time, its immediate bond is important, which attaches it directly to the preceding verse about how the Father answers prayer. In Luke the rule functions centrally in a coherent section, 6.27–38.

7. Luke 11.1–13.

8. Matt. 7.1–5.

9. Matt. 7.21; cf. 12.50.

10. Isa. 55.9.

11. Matt. 5.17.

12. Matt. 22.40. The phrase occurs once more in Matthew: "For all the prophets and the law prophesied until John came" (11.13).

13. This remains true, despite the places where Matthew refers to Gentiles in a derogatory way: 5.47, 6.7, 6.32, 10.22, 15.21, 18.7 and 17.

14. Matt. 5.45.

15. Luke 10.30–37.

16. Matt. 23.9.

17. A version of this argument may be found in Abrahams 1967.

18. The *Letter of Aristeas* has been cited. Bruce Alton (1966) has collected examples of several early Christian varieties of the golden rule. The early Christian *Didache* uses a negative version (appropriated from the *Two Ways*) (in Schopp 1947, 357); *The Teaching of the Twelve Apostles* (a version of the *Didache*) has the same version of the golden rule (cited in Alton 1966, 47) that is also found in the *Apostolic Constitutions* vii, 2.1 and in the *Apology* of Aristides (*The Ante-Nicene Fathers* IX, 257). The "Western" manuscripts of the Book of Acts (e.g., "D," Codex Bezae) insert the golden rule in a negative formulation into Acts 15.20.

19. Matt. 5.21–22a.

20. Cf. Prov. 20.22: "Do not say, 'I will repay evil'; wait for the Lord, and he will help you."

21. Exod. 21.23; cf. Lev. 24.19 and Deut. 19.19.

22. Lev. 23.4–5; Prov. 25.21.

23. Job 33.27f; Ps. 32; Isa. 43.25.

24. Cf., e.g., Deut. 32.

25. Clement, cited in Alton 1966, 41.

26. Malina 1981, 80. He adds that it was a widespread custom for pairs of individuals, social equals and unequals, to begin a mutually beneficial, open-ended relationship of doing things for the other.

27. Matt. 5.47.

28. Jeremias 1971, 216.

29. Matt. 5.38–39.

30. Luke 9.51–56.

31. Blenkinsopp 1983, 79.

32. Cf. the Parable of the Talents, Matt. 25.15–28). Grundel (1970) takes the bull by the horns and accepts the term *talio* as a legitimate characterization of God's last, "eschatological" judgment, rewarding and punishing, beyond the capacity of human wisdom, especially of a single individual. In support he cites Matt. 4.25, 6.14–15, 8.38, 10.33, 18.35; Rom. 2.1, 2.12; 2 Cor. 9.6; and 2 Tim. 2.12. The golden rule of the New Testament should not be interpreted as requiring an extraordinary and impossible level of love; the rule "places individuals in connection with the people of God and his thinking and acting in eschatological connection with the coming judgment" (112). The golden rule is a worldwide principle (and a principle of natural law) "since the thought of human *talio* is one of the essential bases of our consciousness of what is right and fair" (112). The golden rule is a principle, not of radical *agape* love, but of *philia*, friendly relations within divinely ordained and politically secured orders (pertaining to property rights, family life, etc.). There love may be practiced, when each person's home space (*Beheimatung*) is secured (136).

33. Matt. 7.24–27.

34. The parable of the talents, Matt. 25.15–28.

35. Luke 22.42–43.

36. Luke 23.28, 34, 43.

37. Because of the role this parable has played in contemporary ethics since R. M. Hare drew on it in his influential *Freedom and Reason* (1963) to produce an illustration of the logic of the golden rule, I cite it here in full:

> The kingdom of heaven may be compared to a king who wished to settle accounts with his slaves. When he began the reckoning, one who owed him ten thousand talents was brought to him; and, as he could not pay, his lord ordered him to be sold, together with his wife and children and all his possessions, and payment to be made. So the slave fell on his knees before him, saying, "Have patience with me, and I will pay you everything." And out of pity for him, the lord of that slave released him and forgave him the debt. But that same slave, as he went out, came upon one of his fellow slaves who owed him a hundred denarii; and seizing him by the throat, he said, "Pay what you owe." Then his fellow slave fell down and pleaded with him, "Have patience with me, and I will pay you." But he refused; then he went and threw him into prison until he would pay the debt. When his fellow slaves saw what had happened, they were greatly distressed, and they went and reported to their lord all that had taken place. Then his lord summoned him and said to him, "You wicked slave! I forgave you all that debt because you pleaded with me. Should you not have had mercy on your fellow slave, as I had mercy on you?" And in anger his lord handed him over to be tortured until he would pay his entire debt. (Matt. 18.23–34)

In their discussion of the golden rule in Matthew, Little and Twiss (1978) claim that the parable of the unforgiving servant shows that the lord is bound by the principle of golden rule fairness. Thus there is not only an "authoritarian" system of justification for morality in Matthew—teachings validated by the power and greatness of God—but also a "formalistic" system of justification, "a combination of versions of the law of reciprocity" (180). They conclude:

> We can see in the Gospel of Matthew, then, the roots of a long-standing ambivalence in the Christian tradition regarding the grounds of Christian action. "Is something right because God wills it, or does he will it because it is right?" turns out to be a dilemma springing directly from the Gospel of Matthew itself, and from the competing patterns of justification contained in that book. Both patterns, though with their different emphases and implications, are at home in, and sustained by, a similar set of cosmological and anthropological beliefs. (206)

38. Josh. 24.15.

39. Matt. 7.17.

40. Matt. 10.28.

41. Matt. 13.12.

42. To judge, in Hebrew (din), is also to discern.

43. Matt. 23.

44. Cf. Matt. 21.33–41. Despite its militance, the rebuke is limited. At the opening of the discourse Jesus admonished the people to obey those who sit on Moses' seat and in closing he expressed his "mother hen" attitude to the people.

The discourse led to no further action. Jesus simply walked out. He uttered no further rebuke during his trial and crucifixion. Despite these facts, and despite reason and the golden rule, the chap. 23 discourse has been used against Jews in the twentieth century, though it contains nothing anti-Jewish. Davies has pointed out that there were Jewish sects of the period that used similarly heated language to condemn the corruption of the politically appointed priesthood of that day.

45. Matt. 5.38–48.

46. Communication theory distinguishes a speaker's primary audience from audiences that are secondary in the speaker's intention.

47. Matt. 5.1.

48. Matt. 7.28.

49. Matt. 5.14.

50. Williams 1990, 164.

51. Luke 6.13.

52. Eschatology is the doctrine concerning the "last things," matters pertaining to the end of the age, or to a glorious, divinely inaugurated, planetary future.

53. Matt. 4.8.

54. Matt. 5.38–41; cf. 1 Cor. 6.1–6.

55. See Coppenger 1990. Faced with the question "What would I want others to do if I were to join in the military service of murderous tyrants?" Coppenger writes, "the Christian answer seems clear—'Stop me! Do not let me succeed in my efforts at establishing or defending a malevolent regime'" (1990, 296–97).

56. Luke 7.1–10.

57. Matt. 5.3–12, 6.25 (cf. Luke 12.22).

58. Matt. 6.25–33.

59. Luke 18.22.

60. Luke 22.35–36.

61. Davies 1964, 387, quoting C. H. Dodd.

62. Jeremias 1971, 230; for a view interpreting Matthean perfection in terms of the law of the community see Davies 1953, 115–116.

63. Matt. 6.24.

64. Matt. 6.25–33.

65. Matt. 5.3.

66. Matt. 4.17, 18.4.

67. Matt. 16.24–25.

68. Luke 10.3–4. According to the view developed here, the refusal to bear arms would be appropriate, necessarily, for those who function as ministers, whose lives are to symbolize a better age, but it would not necessarily be appropriate for believers in general.

69. Borgen (1966) summarizes the sense of the Matthean golden rule thus:

In the Gospel of Matthew the golden rule is in the service of Jesus' messianic interpretation of the will of God, with the purpose of wholehearted obedience shown by disciples. The meaning of the golden rule in Matthew is: With his natural self-love in the background, that which a disciple expects from others, he will, in obedience to the will of God, turn into that which he does to others. Instead of making demands, disciples will be unstintingly obedient to the will of God, above anything else. This obedience to God characterizes those to whom the kingdom of God has been promised, who are the light of the world, and whom the kingdom of God already concerns.(140)

70. Dihle interpreted the golden rule (in Luke) as an illustration of what Jesus intended to reject, rather than propose (1962, 113). It is grammatically possible for the term *poiete* ("do") in the second clause to be indicative as well as imperative. On the new reading, the sentence describes how "you" in fact behave, not how "you" ought to behave. "As you want men to treat you, so you treat them." Then 6.31 may be read as the first of a series of descriptions of how sinners behave, loving only those who love them, etc. James Robinson (1966) criticizes Dihle's grammatical analysis of Luke 6.31. He puts his key point as follows:

> Yet the fact that one has a chain of coordinated sayings connected with each other by "kai" makes it difficult to find a basis for the adversative meaning at verse 32 that this interpretation calls for (the word "but" in the translation above). Rather than verse 31 portraying the situation criticized in verses 32–34, the situation to be criticized is given in the conditional clauses introducing the critical statements in each of the verses 32–34. (87)

Merkelbach (1973) (without having read Robinson) develops Dihle's position by proposing the modifications in the text of Luke that would be necessary to make this reading grammatically plausible. The sole motive for Merkelbach's reconstruction, however, is to save an interpretation that has more plausible alternatives. It should be noted that Robinson praises Dihle for his exemplary methods, focusing on language and on cultural presuppositions; Dihle, according to Robinson, shows how a deep tendency can explain appearances without having to rely primarily on hypotheses of diffusion or borrowing.

71. Luke 16.16.

72. Ricoeur 1990, 395.

73. Ricoeur 1990, 396.

74. Ricoeur 1990, 396–97.

75. Ricoeur 1989, 8.

76. Ricoeur 1990, 397.

77. Luke 4.16–20, 6.20 and 24, 7.22, 12.34, 13.15, 14.12–14, 16.13–14, 19.8, 27.26–37.

78. Jeremias 1971, 221. Jeremias notes that Matthew's conception is more spiritual than Luke's—"Blessed are the poor in spirit" (Matt. 5.3) rather than "Blessed are the poor"—and argues, correctly, in my opinion, that Matthew's understanding of "poverty" is closer to that of Jesus. He is able to do this, in part, by interpreting the passage in Luke where Jesus announces his mission in terms of Isa. 61: "The Spirit of the Lord is upon me, because he has anointed me to preach good news to the poor. He has sent me to proclaim release to the captives and recovering of sight to the blind, to set at liberty those who are oppressed, to proclaim the acceptable year of the Lord" (Luke 4.18–19). A look at what Jesus did supports Jeremias's reading. This understanding of Jesus does not carry immediate, detailed political implications.

79. Luke 19.1–10.

80. Malina 1981, 85.
81. Luke 4.43; cf. Mark 1.32–38.
82. Luke 6.40.
83. Luke 10.17.
84. Acts 6–7.
85. Luke 11.13.
86. Luke 17.21. The NRSV presents this translation as an alternate to another one—"the kingdom of heaven is among you"—which also has its point.
87. Luke 15.
88. Acts 2.17.

CHAPTER SIX

1. See Ex. 20.21–22; Luke 15; Gal. 3.28.
2. For Latin Christian literature generally, I rely especially on the bibliography provided in Reiner 1951, 178–292; Reiner 1954/55; and Reiner 1964, 186–95.
3. Reiner 1954/55, 551, 544. Justin writes (160 C.E.): "God makes known the way of righteousness to every race of men and every race recognizes that adultery and theft and murder and everything similar is wrong, even if everyone were to do them" (Dialogue with Tryphon, chap. 93).
4. Tertullian, quoted in Alton 1966, 50, with citation to Migne 1879, vol. 2, 427.
5. Reiner 1954/55, 549. Origen saw the golden rule as expressing both the precepts written in the heart and the scriptural law: "What is so close to natural experience as that people may not do to others what they do not want to see done to themselves?" The self-evident quality of the rule bolstered the claim that the human mind is blessed with natural ethical knowledge (Reiner 1954/55, 549–51).
6. Augustine, Confessions I.18, cited in Alton 1966, 55.
7. Reiner 1954/55, 551–52. Reiner refers to Augustine, De sermone Domine in monte (c. 394) II, 9, 32; Contra Faustum (c. 398) XIX, 2.
8. This comment on Matt. 7.12 is found in The Lord's Sermon on the Mount II, 22 (sec. 74) (Augustine 1948, 161–62). In the following section, Augustine argues that the golden rule "pertains to the love of neighbor and not also to the love of God," primarily because Jesus did not say, "All things whatsoever you would should be done to you, this do you also."

According to Karl F. Morrison (1988), the effort to understand divine truth by means of the adventure of interpreting scripture is comparable, for Augustine, to the effort to understand another person by interpreting what they say. Augustine regarded interpretation as risky and described it with metaphors of games. Interpretation can only attain understanding insofar as the interpreter receives "powers, insights, or visions that did not originate in the interrogator, but that came to him by empathetic participation in another" (Morrison, 191). Such participation carries with it not only the possibility of approximately satisfactory understanding but also the possibility of fusion with the other. Sympathy between persons is enhanced by common descent from the original parents of humankind, by shared feeling about something, and by shared commitments for example on intellectual or political matters. But something closer than sympathy is possible. "The bonding of identities that [Augustine] taught occurred when one person participated in (partook of) the feelings of another and so the two become one in spirit" (Morrison, 95). Thus participation transcends interpretation.

9. In Sermon 192 Augustine quoted the rule in wording close to that of Matthew.

10. Cf. Augustine, The City of God, bk. XIV, sec. 8 (1950, 450).

11. Augustine 1948, 163.

12. Augustine 1948, 161.

13. Augustine, cited by Bishop William, 1679, 12.

14. Lactantius gives the rule special praise at least twice:

The taproot of justice and the entire foundation of equity consists in not doing to another what you would not endure yourself, measuring your own feelings by those of your neighbour. If it is bitter to tolerate a wrong, and the doer appears unjust, transfer to another what you are yourself feeling, and to yourself what you judge concerning another; you will then understand that you are acting as unjustly if you hurt another as another if he hurts you. If we ponder this, we will hold fast to innocence, which is the first stepping-stone of justice. The first stone is "hurt not," the next "be helpful." (Epitome of the Divine Institutes, 108; quoted in Alton 1966, 55, with citation to the translation of E. H. Blakeney [London: S.P.C.K., 1950], 108)

Let us consider ourselves in the other's place. For the height of justice is this: that you do not do to another what you yourself would not want to suffer from another. (Divinae institutiones, vi, 23; quoted in Alton 1966, 56, with citation to The Fathers of the Church. [Washington, D.C.: Catholic University of America Press, 1964], XLIX, 461)

15. Reiner 1954/55, 556.

16. Reiner 1964, 189, provides the references: Anselm—Liber de voluntate Dei, in Migne 1879, vol. 158, 582; William of Champeaux—Dialógus inter Christianum et Judeum, in Migne 1879, vol. 163, 1051; Peter Lombard—In Epistolam ad Romanos, in Migne 1879, vol. 191, 1345; Hugh of St. Victor—Dialogus de sacramentis legis naturalis et scriptae, in Migne 1879, vol. 176, 351; John of Salisbury—Polycraticus, lib. IV, in Migne 1879, vol. 199, 527; Bonaventure—Compendium theologiae veritatis, lib. V, cap. II; Matthaeus ab Aquasparta—Quaestiones disputatae, Quaestiones de legibus, Codex 159 Assisi; Johannes Duns Scotus—Opus Oxoniensis IV, distinctio 21, quaestio 2, n. 8.

17. Spendel 1967, 498.

18. See Thomas Aquinas, 1951, chap. 7, sec. 6, remark 648, p. 102. He associates Matt. 7.12 with Matt. 6.12, "Forgive us our debts as we have forgiven our debtors."

19. Thomas Aquinas 1969, 1a2ae (question 99, art. 1, reply to objection 3), vol. 29, 35; cited in Alton 1966, 114. This article examines "whether only a single precept is contained in the old law." The answer is that the law is multiple in terms of the means employed, and one in terms of the end or goal to be attained by those means:

For all law tends of its nature to establish harmonious relationships between man and man or between man and God. For this reason the whole of the law is summed up in this single commandment, Thou shalt love thy neighbour as thyself, as the end to which, in a certain sense, all the commandments are directed. For when one loves one's neighbour for God's sake, then this love of neighbour includes the love of God also. (1a2ae. 99, I, reply to objection 3)

Aquinas takes the golden rule as a gloss on the commandment of love for the neighbor.

20. Love as an infusion of grace is the theme of Thomas's Summa theologica, 1a,2ae, questions 62–65 and 2a2ae, question 24.

21. 2a2ae, question 25, article 4.

22. Summa theologica, 1a2ae, question 62, article 1; the quotation is from 2 Pet. 1.4. Cf. 1a2ae, question 66, article 6: Charity brings one close to God, "for what is loved is in a certain way in the one who loves, and also the one who loves is drawn by affection to a union with what is loved." Thomas refers to John 4.16, which reads, "God is love, and he who abides in love abides in God, and God abides in him." The act of unitive love—Thomas is consistent with Chinese tradition—"no longer has the quality of being difficult" (2a2a3, question 23, article 6).

23. 2a2ae, question 26, article 2. Thomas is no friend of sinners. They are to be loved solely for their capacity to ascend to God. (One thinks of Kant's clarification that respect for persons reduces to respect for the moral law [Kant 1983, 401n.].) Thomas is also prepared to speak for the state, that sinners who fall into great wickedness and become incurable must be put to death for the protection of others. Thomas anticipates Luther on this extension of theology into politics.

24. 2a2ae, question 26, article 4. For a discussion of the Platonic theme of participation in Thomistic metaphysics, see Rolnick, 1993.

25. I am indebted to George L. Murphy, theologian, physicist, and pastor of St. Mark Lutheran Church in Tallmadge, Ohio, for bringing two sermons of Luther on the golden rule to my attention and for a helpful critique of this section of this chapter. The sermon summarized here is found in Luther 1959, vol. 51, 5–13.

26. "The Freedom of a Christian," in Luther 1970, 297.

27. Luther expressed the gratitude of a believer thus:

Hard on this faith there follows, of itself, a most sweet stirring of the heart, whereby the spirit of man is enlarged and enriched (that is love, given by the Holy Spirit through faith in Christ), so that he is drawn to Christ, that gracious and bounteous testator, and made a thoroughly new and different man. Who would not shed tears of gladness, indeed, almost faint for joy in Christ, if he believed with unshaken faith that this inestimable promise of Christ belonged to him? How could he help loving so great a benefactor, who of his own accord offers, promises, and grants such great riches and this eternal inheritance to one who is unworthy and deserving of something far different? ("The Babylonian Captivity of the Church," in Three Treatises, in Luther 1970, 158.)

28. "The Babylonian Captivity of the Church," in Luther 1970, 202.

29. "The Freedom of a Christian," in Luther 1970, 277.

30. Referring to the critical edition of Luther's works, the 1883 [1966] Weimarer Ausgabe (WA), Raunio (1987) cites the following passages: WA, vol. 4, pp. 590–95; WA, pp. 56, 197–200, 482–85; WA, vol. 1, p. 502, 16–26; WA, vol. 2, pp. 577–82; WA, vol. 17 II, pp. 88–104; WA, vol. 32, pp. 494–99; WA, vol. 40 II, pp. 144–46.

31. Laulaja 1981, 6. This book in Finnish offers a brief summary in English

and an extended summary in German. Heckel (1952) expands on and incisively presents the twist and turns of Luther's commentary on the golden rule as part of his 1515/16 lectures on Paul's Letter to the Romans (Rom. 12.10 in particular). It is the *unconditional* character of self-love that we fail to extend to the neighbor; thus the law condemns us. Only on the basis of the destruction of selfish love can spiritual love animate us. Thus, to interpret the golden rule as presupposing the possibility of a facile equation of self and other is infinitely remote from an honest encounter with the command of God which Matthew 7.12 presents.

32. Laulaja 1981, 266.

33. Laulaja 1981, 278.

34. Laulaja 1981, 274–77.

35. Luther 1959, Vol. 21, 235–241.

CHAPTER SEVEN

1. Hobbes 1909, pt. 1, chap. 14, 100. The principle of equal liberty "is that Law of the Gospell; *Whatsoever you require that others should do to you, that do ye to them. And that Law of all men, Quod tibi fieri non vis, alteri ne feceris.*" In chap. 15, concluding pt. 1, "Of Man," Hobbes presented nineteen specific laws of nature pertaining to justice, equity, modesty, mercy, and certain essentials of judicial procedure, such as "No man is his own judge." Hobbes allowed that most people are too busy or negligent to grasp the many laws of nature, yet every member of civil society is obliged to obey them. "To leave all men unexcusable," the laws

> have been contracted into one easy sum, intelligible even to the meanest capacity; and that is, "Do not that to another, which thou wouldst not have done to thyself"; which sheweth him that he has no more to do in learning the laws of nature, but, when weighing the actions of other men with his own, they seem too heavy, to put them into the other part of the balance, and his own into their place, that his own passions, and self-love, may add nothing to the weight; and then there is none of these laws of nature that will not appear unto him very reasonable. (Pt. 1, chap. 15, 121)

Alton (1966) identified five claims about the golden rule in Hobbes: "that it summarizes the 'laws of nature'; that it provides a method for deducing those laws; that this method is rational; that it operates by excluding self-interest; and (by implication) that these laws are laws of justice, balance, or order" (116).

2. The last of these four publications, a book by Benjamin Camfield (1638–1693) I discovered too late to include in this study. It is titled *A Profitable Enquiry into That Comprehensive Rule of Righteousness Do as You Would Be Done By. . . . Being a Practical Discourse on S. Matt. vii 12* (1679).

3. For Boraston, the rule is one of "those natural notions interwoven in our make and constitution" (1684, 1); children appeal to it to protect themselves. The simplicity of the golden rule makes it valuable for adults as well. Since human reason errs, and because of "the shortness of human life, and the difficulty and tediousness of learning, and the intricacy of knowledge, and the multiplicity of particular cases, exceptions, and restrictions" (10) we have need of an infallible, revealed guide—an aphorism, axiom, or summary to give us "the substance, pith, and marrow" of our duties (10). Boraston's formulation of the rule's sense antici-

pates that of Samuel Clarke. Boraston writes: "Our own regular and well-governed desires, what we are willing that other men should do, or not do to us, are a sufficient direction and admonition, what we in the like cases, ought to do or not to do to them" (4). "Every man doth naturally seek his own preservation and welfare"; this provides "a pattern for the exercise of charity and justice to all other men;" for the golden rule obliges us to treat others "as if we had exchanged persons and circumstances with them and they were in ours" (5). Boraston proclaims the universal scope of the rule, requiring us to follow the example of Christ in virtuous conduct toward all. After pages of using the rule in symmetrical relationships to show how, specifically, we should treat others as we want to be treated, Boraston shifts toward the end to interpreting the rule asymmetrically regarding political authority: "We should obey our superiors with the same willing subjection with which we desire our children and servants should obey us" (21).

4. Goodman (1688) noted counterexamples to the rule (a drunkard, a lascivious person, a skillful pickpocket, and persons who would wish to be given an undue proportion of a rich man's wealth or wish for laws in their self-interest; so he regarded the golden rule as a measure of how much we should do for the other rather than as a law. Here is his formulation.

> My obligation from this rule principally lies in this, that I both do, or refrain from doing (respectively) toward him, all that which (turning the tables and then consulting my own heart and conscience) I should think that neighbour of mine bound to do, or to refrain from doing toward me in the like case. (26)

The rule binds the prince as well as the private man, for its import is "antecedent to the several ranks and distinctions of man." It applies between citizens of different nations and believers in different religions, "for our Saviour hath shewed us that all Mankind are to be esteemed our neighbours." Although God had erected a barrier between Jews and Gentiles, "when our Saviour came, that wall of partition was pulled down, and all the world were made one people" (31–33, adapting Eph. 2.14).

Goodman argued that the rule does not govern our relation to God, "for he being infinite in all perfections, there is nothing in us that we can appeal to as a measure of what is due towards him." We must love God "better than we love our selves." In addition, if the golden rule were our whole duty, it would render the Bible superfluous; the heathen, having the light of nature, would have the essential (16, 19).

Goodman concludes his book with a list of vices (reminding his readers that, as they would not be treated in such a way, they should not treat others thus) and with a list of advantages of following the golden rule, including giving Christianity a good reputation, obtaining success in one's prayers, and reaping the inner peace of a clear conscience (though it is "selfish and stingy" to do good "upon the motive, and in expectation" of benefits) (36–37, 80–86).

5. The earliest use of golden rule noted in the Oxford English Dictionary (2nd ed.) goes back to the fourteenth century and refers to a ruler in the sense of a carpenter's tool. The Latin word for rule, regula, had had just that sense (regere means to make or lead straight). The many senses of rule go back to that same period of the English language.

The OED gives a 1674 use: "Whilst forgetting that Golden Law do as you would be done by, they make self the center of their actions" (cited to R. Godfrey, *Inj. & Ab. Physic* 54). Terminology remained flexible in the next century, as is shown by a 1741 reference to that "golden principle of morality" (cited to Watts, *Improv. Mind* I.xiv.8).

6. William 1679, 53. On p. 212 of this book is the earliest use of the term *golden rule* (as the name of a *moral* principle) I have found.

7. William 1679, from his preliminary words to "the Christian reader."

8. William 1679, 69.

9. William 1679, 63–67.

10. William 1679, 33.

11. William 1679, 57.

12. William 1679, 54.

13. William 1679, 61.

14. William 1679, pp. 38–52.

15. William 1679, 81–86.

16. William 1679, 81.

17. William 1679, 90.

18. William 1679, 91.

19. William 1679, 58.

20. William 1679, 77–80.

21. William 1679, 60, 61 [misnumbered as 63].

22. William 1679, 146–53.

23. William 1679, 212.

24. Locke 1959, bk. I, chap. 2, sec. 4, p. 68. Sec. 7 in the same chapter includes this remark: "The great principle of morality, 'To do as one would be done to,' is more commended than practised. But the breach of this rule cannot be a greater vice, than to teach others, that it is no moral rule, nor obligatory." (71)

25. Leibniz 1981, 91–92, bk. 1, chap. 2, sec. 4.

26. Clarke 1969, 192.

27. Clarke 1969, 192.

28. Clarke 1969, 207.

29. The quotations cited in this paragraph come from Clarke 1969, 208–9.

30. Pietism was a Protestant movement that emphasized devoted religious living—prayer, the study of scripture, and moral action—over dogmas, creeds, and rituals.

31. Kant speaks of the need for sanctions in the *Grounding of the Metaphysics of Morals*: while it is crucial that reason, not desire or fear, determine what the agent will do, Kant acknowledges the need of feelings (based in moral reason) to motivate conduct. "In order to will what reason alone prescribes as an *ought* for sensuously affected rational beings, there certainly must be a power of reason to infuse a feeling of pleasure or satisfaction in the fulfillment of duty, and hence there has to be a causality of reason to determine sensibility in accordance with rational principles" (460; page numbers cited are the standard page numbers of the Prussian Academy edition). Kant also notes that a "power of judgment sharpened by experience" is required to influence the will to put moral laws into practice (389). Further citations from Kant refer to the *Grounding* [1785].

32. Kant 1983, 421. If duty is to be determined not by (mere momentary) desire, but by reason, what does that entail? We are to will in accord with the laws proper to willing. Just as things of nature act according to the laws appropriate to

them, so there is a type of law appropriate to willing. Moral rationality requires the impartial application of universal principles. One must apply moral rules consistently, without making special exceptions for oneself.

For Kant, the maxims on which we act must be capable of functioning as universal principles. A maxim is a proposition expressing the commitment that determines our action. Whenever we act, we have a motive. If we take the trouble to express that motive as a proposition (and Kant holds that we can never be absolutely sure of our motive), we can formulate it as a policy or "maxim." On one interpretation, a maxim, fully expressed, states three things: the action to be performed, the conditions under which it is appropriate to perform this action, and the motive. In contemporary terms, a maxim takes the form "Whenever I am in a situation of type S, I will perform an action of type A on account of consideration C." For example, "Whenever I am invited to cheat, I will refuse in order to preserve my reputation." The motive of self-interest, for Kant, makes the maxim submoral. An example of moral motivation would be to refuse to cheat from fidelity to truth.

33. Kant 1983, 429.

34. Kant 1983, 431, 433.

35. How can we tell which maxims stand up under rational scrutiny? Kant's leading criterion is whether the agent can consistently will for everyone to act on the same maxim. We sometimes initiate critical reflection by asking, "What if everyone did that?" As a first approximation, that question unlocks the door to Kant's idea of moral rationality; but the categorical imperative does not merely an appeal to the *desirability* of the *consequences* of making a given maxim into a rule for everyone. He notices that in some cases it would be *logically incoherent* for a person to will that his maxim be universal law. To make a deceptive promise to borrow money, for example, involves a maxim that, if made universal law, would render impossible the very practice of borrowing and lending in which the deceptive person is engaging. In contemporary terms, the universalizability test shows that such an immoral maxim cannot be universalized, cannot be coherently willed as a principle for everyone to act on. Regarding duties of love to others, as quoted above, Kant says that a man initially willing to universalize his maxim about not benefiting others must reflect that he will one day stand in need of others' help, and so recognize that to universalize his maxim would bring him into contradiction with his own desire for help.

36. Kant 1983, 429.

37. Kant 1983, 430. In 1769 Kant read Leibniz's critique of the golden rule (Leibniz 1981, xiii), and it is tempting to consider the production of the categorical imperative as having been prompted in part by the need to reform the golden rule. Kant used the term "strict" (or "perfect") duty to refer to those duties to which no exceptions are permitted are any circumstances, such as the duty of respect for self and others. Strict duties contrast with "wide" duties, which are not binding in every situation to which they might apply, such as the duty to improve oneself or to do good to others. Though one must do all the good one can, one need not give to *every* charity, or cultivate oneself unceasingly. There are four types of duties, perfect and imperfect duties to self and to others. Kant's critique of the golden rule is that it "contains the ground" for none of these.

38. In addition to Clarke, see Whately 1857 for another clear resolution of this problem. According to Whately, the rule presupposes our first notions of justice.

39. Mill 1987, 288 (*Utilitarianism*, chap. 2).

40. Kant (1983) writes, "Morality and humanity, insofar as it is capable of morality, alone have dignity" (435). At one point, he clearly reveals that he does not provide the respect for *persons* that many people have seemed to find in his ethics: "All respect for a person is properly only respect for the law (of honesty, etc.) of which the person provides an example" (402n).

41. Kant 1983, 406 (the opening paragraph of sec. 2).

CHAPTER EIGHT

1. Because of the importance of the religious concept of the family in this chapter and in this book, an extended, critical note about the social psychology of that concept is in order. Historical realism adds a note about how social-psychological concerns influenced the theology of the fatherhood of God and the brotherhood of man in America. Janet Fishburn shows in *The Fatherhood of God and the Victorian Family: The Social Gospel in America* (1980) that religious doctrine was related to the anxieties and conflicts of the men of that generation. The golden rule in the King James version of the Gospel according to Matthew might appear to envision primarily males: "Therefore all things whatsoever ye would that men should do to you, do ye even so to them; for this is the law and the prophets." Nevertheless, the Victorians regarded men and women as enjoying perfect "equality" through their complementary functions in their special spheres of life. Women were seen as more intuitive, moral, and spiritual; whereas men fought the battles of the public realm (Fishburn 1981, 27f).

The full achievement of manhood, however, had become more difficult in this period, and family life less rewarding. Regarding the middle class in Chicago in the 1870s and 1880s, Richard Sennett writes:

> The nuclear family was used as a refuge from the city, rather than as an adaptive mechanism. Consequently, this family form infringed upon the authority of the father, trapped its members in mother-dominated households, and undermined the sons' chances for social mobility. In times of crisis, "intense nuclear families" were singularly unequipped to deal with urban violence and the general fear of social breakdown. (quoted in Hareven 1971, 221)

Peter G. Filene writes that at the turn of the century men were finding it acutely difficult to "be a man" (1986, chap. 3, "Men and Manliness," 69–93). The ideal of manhood involved superb self-mastery and righteously won success in an individual who would exercise a benevolent and just leadership in the family. But employment took the man away from home for more hours of the day; work was less rewarding economically and its satisfactions were far from the popular image of "the strenuous life" advocated by Theodore Roosevelt—vitalistic, militaristic, and victorious. For the 1890s saw a cult of Napoleon in popular magazines. And Luther H. Gulick promoted an athletic "muscular Christianity" with the YMCA, in which "working out on the mats and bars or playing the newly invented game of basketball [would develop] altruism, cooperation, and self-control." Look to Jesus, Gulick advised, if you want an example of "magnificent manliness" (quoted in Filene 1986, 75). Women, meanwhile, became stronger, having been encouraged since the mid-nineteenth century in novels celebrating their ability to make themselves and society better. They became involved in crusades against vices that were more or less associated with men. Their emerging sexuality was sometimes felt as a threat to male health and to the balance of male energies (Filene 1986, 92). Moreover, the industrial revolution gave women an alternative to the home; the right to vote came in 1921; it was an age of progress for women. Thus it is understandable according to Fishburn (1981), that for those who could not prove their manhood by economic success the heroic ideals of the Social Gospel preachers combatted the effeminate image of Christianity (165–66).

Fishburn (1981) gives the following account: the preachers of the social gospel portrayed God as the immanent source of natural order, evolutionary progress, and the moral law; and also as a source of motherly forgiveness: "God the Father who creates and sustains and loves and forgives reflects the two halves of a Victorian marriage. He contained the male powers of procreation and sustenance and the female virtue of pure love" (141). Through the light of the indwelling spirit, God was understood to minister to each person, aiding them in the struggle against temptation. In any situation calling for action, the intuition of what to do and the power to accomplish it would be provided from within by the power of the spirit of Jesus (167). People were thus "reassured that they were children of a personal God to whom they could go in prayer for comfort and power amid the hard work, moral demands, and stress of life" (141). Religious self-examination became obsolete, as the new concept of God consigned the older Calvinist doctrine of a judging, punishing God to the less highly evolved stages of human history.

The picture of a divine Father utterly free of any authoritarian sovereignty may represent, according to Fishburn, a reaction against the harshness of fathers during the early Victorian period (161). The proclamation of the fatherhood of God and the brotherhood of man symbolized "the 'new' worldview of a large and ambitious American middle class" (89, 162–63). Social gospel preacher Walter Rauschenbusch deliberately crafted his concept of God from the ideals implicit in human relations in order to provide leverage for social progress (138–42). Fishburn estimates that Rauschenbusch's accommodation to middle-class values finally deprived him of any genuine power to change the society (175). The family imagery spoke differently, however, to lower-class listeners; for them, the Father was a God of justice on the model of the God who punished the Pharaoh and liberated Moses' people from Egypt.

For the social gospel movement, "[t]he spirit of love and brotherhood learned in a stable, loving family was expected to flow naturally through the family" into American society and thence into the rest of the world (23). Fishburn recounts the extensive use of "the fatherhood of God" by labor leaders and politicians and the confusion between the kingdom of God and manifest destiny (the idea that America was obviously destined to lead the world); racial doctrines were sometimes associated with the social gospel (15, 90). The emphasis on reforming America and on America's role among nations sometimes got more genuine attention than the relationship to God, which became a means to the desired end. It may be said, then, that in the proclamation of the fatherhood of God and the brotherhood of man, overemphasis on the connection of advanced religion with advanced civilization obscured the very spiritual equality of humankind which that gospel meant to convey.

Fishburn criticizes the proponents of the social gospel for confusing the best experiences of family life with the divine ideal. The transcendence of God and the sense of difference between God and historical process was compromised. In theological terms, Rauschenbusch's God concept "reduces a religious symbol to a metaphor"; its analogical power to indicate something beyond what it can express is lost: "analogy becomes identity" (171) In other words, to regard the father concept of God as a metaphor is to envision primarily a human father and transfer that image to God. To think analogically is to think of God as the pattern imperfectly represented by human fathers; it regards the fatherhood of God as the pattern imperfectly represented by human fathers (cf. Rolnick 1993). A symbol expresses more than social science, philosophy, and theology can explicate.

2. Tolstoy, 1930.

3. Kant, Ritschl found, was "the first to perceive the supreme importance for ethics of the 'Kingdom of God' as an association of men bound together by laws of virtue" (quoted in Welch 1972–85, 18). Ritschl developed a modernized Lutheranism in which God's healing of a person's sin and guilt (justification) opened the believer to the universal love of the neighbor (reconciliation).

4. Harnack 1957.

5. This was clear from the opening address by C. C. Bonney: "We seek in this congress to unite all religion against all irreligion; to make the golden rule the basis of this union; and to present to the world the substantial unity of many religions in the good deeds of the religious life (Neely 1894, 40). Bishop Arnett of the African Methodist Episcopal Church looked forward to a liberated Africa, "whose cornerstone will be religion, morality, education, and temperance, acknowledging the fatherhood of God and the brotherhood of man; while the ten commandments and the golden rule shall be the rule of life in the great republic of redeemed Africa" (Neely 1894, 70; Arnett refers again to the rule on 155).

6. In Neely 1894: for Confucianism, see 150; for Judaism 147, 213, 376–77; and for Christianity 40, 69, 70, 196, 285, 645, 687, 843. Harvard professor D. G. Lyon, in his talk "Jewish Contributions to Civilization," said, "Our church and Christian charities are but the embodiment of the golden rule as uttered by a Jew" (377). Among the reasons why Christianity can be expected eventually to triumph in Japan, according to Nobuta Kishimoto, is this: "Christianity teaches love to God and love to man as its fundamental teaching. The golden rule is the glory of Christianity, not because it was originated by Christ—this rule was taught by Buddha and Laotse many centuries before—but because He properly emphasized it by His words and by His life" (quoted in Neely 1894, 796).

7. Commager 1950, 13–39.

8. Spencer 1892, 201.

9. Spencer 1892, 194.

10. Spencer 1892, 200 and 204.

11. John Hay, from his speech, "American Diplomacy," quoted in Huffman 1966, 315. The Monroe Doctrine insisted that no European power shall establish a sphere of influence in the Americas.

12. For a discussion of parallel developments in English and German theology, see Welch 1972–85.

13. Smith 1879. Richard Hofstadter (1955) summarizes Goldwin Smith's 1879 article:

Religion, Smith believed, had always been the foundation for the western moral code; and it would be idle for positivists and agnostics to imagine that while Christianity was being destroyed by evolution the humane values of Christian ethics would persist. Ultimately, he conceded, an ethic based upon science might be worked out, but for the present there would be a moral interregnum, similar to those which had occurred in past times of crisis. There had been such an interregnum in the Hellenic world after the collapse of its religion brought about by scientific speculation; there had been another in the Roman world before the coming of Christianity gave it a new moral basis; a third collapse in western Europe following the Renaissance had produced the age of the Borgias and Machiavelli, the Guises and the Tudors; finally, Puritanism in England and the Counter Reformation in the Catholic Church had reintroduced moral stability. At present another religious collapse is under way:

> What, then, we ask, is likely to be the effect of this revolution on morality? Some effect it can hardly fail to have. Evolution is force, the struggle for existence is force, natural selection is force. . . . But what will become of the brotherhood of man and of the very idea of humanity? (quoted in Hofstadter 1955, 87)

14. In his 1896 book, *The Golden Rule in Business*, Charles Fletcher Dole set forth his belief that the rule must be intelligently applied in a law-governed universe; that a businessman should be willing to make a somewhat costly moral investment at the start of a farsighted venture; and that certain changes would follow the widespread adoption of the rule:

> [T]he great bulk of mercantile transactions has to be reasonably near the lines of justice and of human service. The margin of dishonesty is somewhat narrow and dangerous. The Golden Rule, aiming at the utmost human welfare, is so deep in nature that it commands a sort of conformity, long before men have fairly caught its spirit. It is possible, if all the men in New York to-morrow adopted the Golden Rule that the figures of prices, values, and profits might not have to undergo very great change. It is likely that the services of few of us are worth much more than we get. The adoption of the Golden Rule would lessen great sources of waste; it would increase the grand product out of which we all live; it would correct certain sad abuses and injustices; but its chief gain would be on the side of our humanity, in the quickened sense of our brotherhood, lifting the ordinary relations of trade to the same level with the ministrations of the teacher, the physician, the poet and artist, the friend and the patriot.

Douglas Firth Anderson tells the story of the San Francisco Presbyterian preacher, J. E. Scott (1836–1917), who advocated Christian socialism during the middle of his career. Like many others of his generation, Scott could be critical of contemporary industrial society on the basis of his memories of life on the family farm and the ideals implicit in it (Anderson 1989, 234). He dissociated himself from Marxist socialism, affirming nonpartisan gradualism in the social approach to an order in which competition and unequal distribution would be eliminated. He appealed to the intelligent middle-class with his message of the "Kingdom of

Socialism" in terms of which the golden rule (symbolizing the ideals of the Sermon on the Mount) would be practiced. Scott's priorities were social, though he, unlike some who left the ministry upon joining a socialist group, retained his function as a religious spokesperson:

> Suppose the health of a city were suffering from bad sewerage, would the mere fact of the religious conversion of every man, woman and child make the sewerage conditions any better? A new machine is introduced in the factory that renders unnecessary the work of half those previously employed. Will the mere fact even of universal individual reformation or regeneration give those men a new job and make them again as independent and self-sustaining as before? If all the people in the Southern states before the rebellion had been "born again," would that fact have abolished African slavery? These and many like conditions are what call for "Social Reform" in distinction from individual reform. Which should come first? A Kourdish bandit can never become a true Christian till he stops plundering; and he will never stop while plundering is recognized as a respectable business. (Anderson 1989, 240)

For an unselfconscious and effective golden rule ministry, see Buzzell n.d.

15. Seward n.d., 7.
16. Seward n.d., 39.
17. Neely 1894, 509.
18. Seward n.d., 29.
19. Seward n.d., 55.
20. Reed and Duckworth 1967, 46 and 151–59.
21. Seward n.d., 47.
22. Seward 1901, 41–43. Silverman's address to the Parliament of Religions had focused on anti-Judaism (Neely 1894, 636).
23. Simmons 1981, 19. Herron wrote, "The real problem of inspiration is not as to the manner in which holy men of old were inspired, but whether there are now holy men willing to be inspired and consumed in the service of truth and justice" (quoted in Frederick 1976, 21).
24. Simmons 1981, 23.
25. Simmons 1981, 30.
26. Simmons 1981, 29.
27. Smith 1988, 49.
28. Simmons 1981, 2.
29. Jones's treatment of prostitution was controversial:

> When a woman of the town was arrested for relieving a customer of his watch and wallet, Jones questioned the man, and when it was found the accuser was a respectable man of family, he refused to listen to a word against the woman, simply saying to her, "Go and sin some more!" And the Mayor added, quietly, "Vice cannot be exterminated until the respectable element quits paying good money to surreptitiously support it." He then fined the man ten dollars, on his own confession, for patronizing a house of ill-fame. (quoted in Simmons 1981, 43)

Jones did not enforce laws against gambling and he let the saloons operate on Sunday. Statistics indicate that crime declined during his tenure, though that may be due to the fact that, as one judge recalled, "they always found some reason or other for letting all the culprits go." A tramp arrested for drunkenness was let free after Jones smashed the loaded revolver that had been found in his pocket. Jones said, "I have done by the unfortunate men and women who have come before me in this court just as I would have another judge do by my son if he were a drunkard or a thief, or by my sister or daughter, if she were a prostitute" (Simmons 1981, 61).

30. Research by Marcia Carolyn Kaptur summarized by Simmons 1981, 94.

31. Nash 1930 (the second, 1930, edition includes a final chapter, added by Philip I. Roberts, a Nash associate, completing the account Nash originally set down in the 1923 edition); and Penney, 1950.

32. Nash 1930, 10f. He writes at length about his saintly mother and her influence upon him.

33. Nash had the formative experience of working when he first lived in Detroit with an inspirational woman outside his church. Agnes d'Arcambal had organized a halfway house for released convicts and was widely acknowledged as an extraordinarily uplifting individual. Days after her death, he was asked by a supervising elder whether it was possible that this woman could be saved. He boldly defended her eternal prospects and resigned from the church before the Conference Committee of the Disciples of Christ called to investigate him could begin. Then, thoroughly disillusioned, he left religion for the second time, noting in passing in his autobiography that he went through a period of years in "sin and degradation," wandering throughout the Midwest from one odd job to another (Nash 1930, 11).

Later, during the first three years of World War I, he blamed Christianity bitterly for what was happening in Europe. Then in 1917, a minister friend who was planning to be out of town invited Nash to occupy the pulpit one Sunday in his absence. The minister invited him to present his criticisms of Christianity to his congregation. Researching intensely for two months in preparation for his diatribe, he discovered the life and teachings of Jesus as he never had in seminary, and he was ennobled and empowered by the spiritual reality of the ideals that he now saw brightly.

34. Nash 1930, 51–53.

35. Early in 1919, they began production and business more than doubled over the previous year. In 1920, business tripled. In 1921 business increased by a third and they reached the limits of their plant capacity. In 1922, business increased by 50 percent to $3 million dollars. He made some innovations in labor relations and was on the very cutting edge of farsighted, ethical management.

36. The business innovations of the golden rule are largely set forth in a report done on the A. Nash Company by Rev. F. Ernest Johnson, secretary of the Commission on the Church and Social Service, of the Federal Council of the Churches of Christ in America, chap. 6 in Nash 1930.

37. Nash 1930, 79.

38. One testimonial is a piece of investigative reporting done by Ruth White Colton, a black woman who represented herself to the "Golden Rule Factory" as Hattie Clark, poor and needing work. She recorded the outpouring of generosity that greeted her, as several employees offered her lodging. When a man who had robbed the company was caught and sentenced, some of the workers told the group that the man had a wife and four children and that they (the workers) wanted to do something for them. They agreed to give the mother a job and

assigned to Clark the supervision of funds for the family. After she disclosed her true identity and purpose, she was warmly invited to go ahead with her investigation and interview as she pleased, and she gathered story after story of lives dramatically touched by this group devoted to living the golden rule.

39. *Nash Journal* 1, no. 2 (December 13, 1926): 1, 3. These comments appear to respond to the August 1926 account of his success by Silas Bent (pp. 18–19) arguing that the primary factors responsible for Nash's success had to do with his business acumen.

40. Penney 1950, 245. We should not imagine that the son's experience of his father was dominated by harshness. Penney recalls when his father was excommunicated from the church he had served so long over a controversy regarding Sunday School. While the boy was filled with resentment over the incident, his father said, "Don't harbor bitterness, Jim. People see things as they see them. It takes time for ideas to take hold" (Penney 1950, 21).

> From the time I was a young boy I had understood, that though he worked at two separate callings, by his way of working at them he made them interchangeable. He was a farmer and he was a preacher, and to him there was no real difference in what these two occupations demanded of a man. He plowed, planted, harvested—and then, when he preached his sermons, applied his industry with the same quality of feeling so that, in effect, he had one over-all ministry: to serve. (Penney 1950, 64)

41. Penney 1950, 44.

42. Penney 1950, 47.

43. Penney 1950, 48.

44. Penney 1950, 75.

45. Penney 1950, 58 and 74. A cardinal principle was reposing confidence in people: "Men who came into the J. C. Penney Company with me have never been put under surety bond. Men who must have halters around their necks to make them do the right thing were not the men for us. I have always preferred letting men know that I rely on them. Those who proved unworthy only caused the others, who far outnumbered them, to stand out.

46. Penney 1950, 104.

47. Penney 1950, 118.

48. Penney 1950, 219.

49. Penney 1950, 52.

CHAPTER NINE

1. I am grateful Daniel Batson, who responded in detail to an earlier version of this chapter. Though I cannot claim his support for the line of thought presented here, he helped by giving a seasoned perspective, clarifying issues, correcting errors, and indicating bibliographic resources. His many books and articles, including *The Religious Experience* (1982), *The Altruism Question* (1991), and his new book, *Religion and the Individual* (1993), have been particularly helpful.

2. Piaget 1965, 78.

3. Piaget 1965, 56.

4. Piaget 1965, 78.

5. Piaget 1965, 111.
6. Piaget 1965, 53, 77.
7. Piaget 1965, 28.
8. Piaget 1965, 295.
9. Piaget 1965, 95–96.
10. Piaget 1965, 107.
11. Piaget 1965, 72, 73.
12. Piaget 1965, 323–24.

13. It may be questioned whether Kohlberg's earliest stages represent moral reasoning at all, rather than rationales for conformity. Nor is it clear that asking young children how to resolve complex adult issues such as the Heinz dilemma gives appropriate access to their moral consciousness. What if genuinely moral decisions involve a recognition of meanings and values of relationships, such that mere conformity with authority or with one's social group hardly expresses what is genuinely moral about young persons' emerging morality? From the perspective of a faith that morality ultimately means doing the will of God, stage 2 behavior to please parents might show more than merely "preconventional" significance. Could there be a spiral pattern in the sequence from parental influence to peer influence, such that religious "authority" returns, transformed into cooperation, in the growing adult? What if moral principles are the propositional forms of ideas that can indeed be grasped by a child of six? What if full moral development involves a grasp of spiritual meanings and values, followed by a supreme commitment to live by them, and, finally, the integration of the whole of one's life in accord with that commitment?

14. Kohlberg 1981, 202.
15. Kohlberg 1981, 202.
16. Kohlberg 1981, 149–50.
17. Kohlberg 1981, 197.

18. Kohlberg 1981, 199. Kohlberg surprisingly regarded his procedure, moral musical chairs (with its built-in appeal to "the prior claim to justice"), as equivalent to the decision procedures advocated by R. M. Hare (1963) and John Rawls (1971) (which are not circular in this way). According to Hare, morality requires one to imagine oneself in the position of each person affected by an action and then act so as to maximize the total satisfaction of desires and interests of those involved. According to Rawls, one must act according to principles that would be selected by a group of individuals that may be imagined to be (1) ignorant of what characteristics they will have in the society to be structured by the principles they will choose, and (2) desirous to maximize their own interests.

19. Kohlberg, with Clark Power, "Moral Development, Religious Thinking, and the Question of a Seventh Stage," in Kohlberg 1981. The authors work with stages of faith as developed by James Fowler, in which the highest stage of faith, Fowler's sixth stage, is here set forth as Kohlberg's seventh stage.

20. One social psychologist who connected the golden rule with the ability to take the perspective (or role) of other persons was George Herbert Mead. He envisioned the golden rule as the rule of conduct for a future global society, and he gave a social-psychological interpretation of the religious factor in altruism (see Mead 1934, 19). Mead taught that our self-concept is generated in large measure by learning to take the perspective of others on the self. Social maturity develops along with the capacity for imaginative role taking, identifying with progressively

wider circles of persons—family, neighborhood, nation, and with humankind as one family. Mead, a social psychologist and philosophical pragmatist envisioned religious living as an extension of sympathy. For Mead, in the evolution of a universal society, religion plays an important role, but not a foundational role, since religion is just one of the factors conducing to this goal; other factors include the logic of science, the conception of democracy, and the tendency of market exchange to develop into global trade. For Mead, the truths of social-psychological responses to others harmonize with the religious regard for all humankind as one family. While recognizing that Christianity is not the only religion with a universal vision, he repeatedly cites the teachings of Jesus. Mead commented that, in the parable of the good Samaritan, "Jesus took people and showed that there was distress on the part of one which called out in the other a response. . . . This is the basis of that fundamental relationship which goes under the name of 'neighborliness.' It is a response which we all make in a certain sense to everybody. The person who is a stranger calls out a helpful attitude in ourselves, and that is anticipated in the other. It makes us all akin" (Mead 1962, 272). Religion built along these lines, for Mead, remains limited to the sympathetic response to distress or to emotional relationships. It takes social integration of the many dimensions of human relationships in order to make fully concrete the religious ideal of humankind as one family.

21. Gilligan (1982) initially set forth women's development as following a different sequence of stages from Kohlberg's stages for men. On the basis of a study that she did, she proposed the following scheme: (1) "an initial focus on caring for self in order to ensure survival"; (2) "a new understanding of the connection between self and others" in which the concept of responsibility is associated with a "maternal morality that seeks to ensure care for the dependent and unequal"; and (3) realizing that the self, as well as the other, merits care, a new sense of morality remains focused on "relationships and response but becomes universal in its condemnation of exploitation and hurt" (74). Research has not, on the whole, supported Gilligan's initial generalizations, and she now talks about justice and caring as concerns for both men and women.

22. Erikson 1963. Erikson challenged the assumption that the sense of trust and the other virtues are achievements, "secured once and for all at a given state. In fact, some writers are so intent on making an achievement scale out of these stages that they blithely omit all the 'negative' senses (basic mistrust, etc.) which are and remain the dynamic counterpart of the 'positive' ones throughout life" (Erikson 1963, 273–74).

23. Erikson 1964, 222, quoted in Conn 1977, 251.

24. Erikson 1964, 243; quoted in Conn 1977, 261. Unconscious, moralistic rage, for Erikson, justifies a call for advanced techniques of self-scrutiny.

25. Erikson 1964, 165; quoted in Conn 1977, 258.

26. Erikson 1964, 233; quoted in Conn 1977, 258.

27. This formulation is generally attributed to Islam, not to Hinduism.

28. Erikson 1964, 243.

29. Conn 1977, 259.

30. Gal. 6.2; Isa. 63.9.

31. Wispé 1986, 314; Wispé has campaigned for a conceptual and terminological distinction between sympathy and empathy, a campaign that has had only marginal success among experimental psychologists. See Hoffman 1984 for a

highly differentiated account of stages of development of empathy, combining affective and cognitive factors in many stages of development. The terms "empathy" and "sympathy" have a variety of meanings in the literature, and researchers disagree about how similar the feeling of empathetic person is to the feeling of the other person, and about the extent to which "empathy" (as the etymology implies) specializes in emotion or feeling (*pathe*). Note also that talk of *imagining* oneself in another person's situation implies a cognitive concession, an acknowledgment that what one desires to grasp is a bit out of reach because it is a possibility, not an actuality—how would I feel if I *were* in that situation, or how would the other person be affected if I *were* to do a particular action?

32. Alper 1985, 14.

33. Strayer 1987, 222.

34. Sigmund Freud, "The Unconscious," in *The Standard Edition*, vol. 14, 169; quoted in Katz 1963, 60.

35. Katz 1963, 167.

36. Katz 1963, 145, 179.

37. Katz 1963, 184.

38. Katz 1963, 17.

39. See Hughes, Carver, and MacKay 1990, 107.

40. Hughes, Carver, and MacKay 1990, 110.

41. Hughes, Carver, and MacKay 1990, 112.

42. It would be interesting to investigate how this program could be adapted to a culture that relies more heavily on nonverbal communication.

43. Burrow quoted in Katz 1963.

44. Douglas Adams of the Graduate Theological Union in Berkeley, California, has pioneered the use of dramatic role reversals in response to works of art. For example, his students take the positions of individuals represented in sculpture or move about to embody the vectors in a painting, and discuss their experiences.

45. Reported in *Morning Edition*, National Public Radio, May 19, 1992.

46. Lahr 1993, 90.

47. Lahr 1993, 93.

48. Lahr 1993, 94.

49. Davis 1994, 144.

50. Krebs and Russell 1981, p. 162.

51. Wispé 1986, 317. Nancy Eisenberg has found that subjects who report feeling very upset by witnessing another's suffering, often do little to help, and when they do help, they appear often to be motivated more by desire for personal relief than by concern for the one suffering. She has found that these more egoistical "altruists" tend to be compliant and nonassertive. Furthermore, those who feel bad from self-concern are less altruistic; while those who feel bad out of concern for others show enhanced altruism (Eisenberg 1986).

52. "Arousal," of course, is a term that covers many phenomena. Arousal can be produced by extraneous environmental factors that impede altruism. It is not difficult to guess the effect of heightened pedestrian and traffic flow, abundance of visual stimuli, and a constantly high noise level on altruistic behavior (Moser 1988). Nor will we be surprised at the following report:

[Princeton Theological Seminary students were] asked to prepare and deliver a short talk on the parable of the Good Samaritan and then to deliver their talks in another building, requiring a short walk between campus buildings. Darley and Batson used the walk as an analogue of the road between Jerusalem and Jericho, and to complete the scenario, positioned a student confederate along the way who was slumped over, shabbily dressed, coughing and groaning. Darley and Batson wanted to see how much the students would help the "victim." The factor that made a large difference in helping behavior was the time pressure put on the subjects. (Rest et al. 1986, 17)

Moreover, arousal may connote the positive mobilization of one's powers stimulated by a good mood. People who feel good as the result of succeeding at a task, thinking happy thoughts, reading "elation" statements, receiving unexpected gifts, or finding money, subsequently show increased altruism. See Rosenhan 1980.

53. See Rigby and O'Grady, 1989, 726. See Batson et al. 1986 for evidence that even in situations where it is easy to reduce personal distress by escaping from the distressing situation, subjects with a high degree of experimentally induced empathy tend to show an accompanying high tendency toward helping behavior.

54. Batson Schoenrade, and Ventis 1993, chap. 10.

55. Rembert 1983, 101.

56. Du Bois 1990, 8–9.

CHAPTER TEN

1. Sidgwick 1962, 379–80.

2. I must also mention Paul Weiss's 1941 article on the golden rule, which was revised and enlarged for his 1950 book, *Man's Freedom*; but the treatment was not sufficiently close to existing discussions to draw responses from other philosophers.

3. Singer 1985, 47.

4. See Singer 1961, chap. 2.

5. Singer 1963, 310.

6. Singer 1967, 365–66.

7. Singer 1961, 16. Singer later says that the relation between the golden rule and the generalization principle has not been definitively worked out (Singer 1985, 47).

8. Singer's move had been clearly anticipated by Arthur T. Cadoux, who had written of "the plane of more general thinking which is [the rule's] natural level. Browne may like his name spelled with an "e," but he must generalize this desire into the wish for a correct spelling of his name before he can apply the Rule" (Cadoux 1911/12, 276).

9. These principles are the generalization principle, the generalization argument, the principle of consequences ("If the consequences of A's doing x would be undesirable, then A ought not to do x"), and the categorical imperative ("Act only on that maxim whereby you can at the same time will that it should become a universal law") (Singer 1961, 336).

10. Singer 1961, 144.

11. *Freedom and Reason* (1963), my primary source for Hare's theory, was preceded by *The Language of Morals* (1952) and followed by *Moral Thinking* (1981) and by many articles.

12. Hare 1975b, 45.

13. Hare 1975a, 208.

14. The continuation of Hare's argument is murky. If someone who is not glad to have been born appeals to the golden rule to justify an abortion, Hare objects that this person had the *potential* for happiness, and should therefore keep similar potentials alive for others. Hare leaves open the possibility of abortion in cases where there is no prospect of a happy life. Hare writes:

> If the present fetus is going to be miserably handicapped if it grows into an adult, perhaps because the mother had rubella, but there is every reason to suppose that the next child will be completely normal and as happy as most people, there would be reason to abort this fetus and proceed to bring to birth the next child, in that the next child will be much gladder to be alive than will this one. (1975b, 209)

Potential persons who, as a result of some act or omission (the distinction is trivial according to Hare), are not brought into existence may be said to be harmed. And Hare is not only talking about embryos but also about those who could be brought into existence if copulations were to occur. His utilitarian theory makes it a duty to have as many children as possible, until the brink of overpopulation, defined as the point after which additional births reduce the sum total of happiness (Hare 1975b, 208).

Mary Anne Warren (1977) challenged Hare's notion that aborting a fetus amounts to harming a person at all; a person never was a fetus, and so something done to a fetus is not, ipso facto, something done to a person. Gensler (1986) has recast Hare's argument more rigorously, an effort criticized by Brian Wilson (1988).

Corradini (1994) argues that Hare's application of the golden rule to solve the problem of abortion relies on an "empiricist" concept of the person such that one person may substitute for another rather than an "ontological" concept of the person such that each person is unique.

15. Hare 1963, 31–32.

16. Hare 1963, 91–92, 94. The original story is found in Matt. 18.

17. Gensler 1976. Cf. Singer 1961, 40. Hans-Ulrich Hoche (1983), developing Hare's theory, replied that the creditor's disinclination to be thrown into prison is surely stronger than his inclination to throw his debtor into prison, so he will, if reasoning properly, draw the correct conclusion. Hoche also proposes another line of defense. Again, on Hare's 1963 account, all the creditor can conclude, strictly speaking, is that he is not *obliged* to put his debtor in prison; whereas the real question is whether it is morally *permissible* to put his debtor in prison. The way to find out, according to Hoche, is to test the contrary hypothesis, "I am obliged not to put my debtor in prison" (equivalent to "I'm not morally permitted to put my debtor in prison"). The test operates as before, imagining the intensity of one's preferences in a situation where the roles are reversed. If one of the hypotheses to be tested runs afoul of inclinations, that is an indication to embrace the other hypothesis. Ralf Kese (1990) has criticized Hoche's defense as question begging, since the inclination whose moral worth is to be tested is utilized in the very test of the contrary hypothesis.

18. Hare's interpretation of universalizability leads to utilitarianism, since he appeals to desires and interests for the content of the singular prescriptions that the agent is then to go on to universalize. For Hare, "To have an interest is, crudely speaking, for there to be something which one wants, or is likely in the future to want, or which is (or is likely to be) a means necessary or sufficient for the attainment of something which one wants (or is likely to want)" (1963, 122). In *Freedom and Reason*, however, he does not embrace a thoroughgoing utilitarianism, inasmuch as he acknowledges that our decisions are prompted by ideals as well as utilitarian considerations.

19. Hare 1963, chap. 9.

20. Hare 1963, 105–6.

21. Hare 1981, chap. 10.

22. See C. C. W. Taylor's 1965 review of R. M. Hare's *Freedom and Reason*; cf. Wiseman 1978.

23. MacKay 1986, 322. Cf. Brülisauer (1980).

24. MacKay 1986, 308.

25. Hare 1963, 206–7.

26. Piper 1991, 738.

27. One example is the interfaith dialogue movement, where conference organizers involve members of other faiths early in the planning stage, instead of designing the conference in accord with the ideas of a single tradition and then inviting representatives of other traditions to fill in slots that have already been shaped for them.

28. Habermas 1990, 233. I am grateful to Norman Fischer for sharing this article with me.

29. Habermas 1990, 231, summarizing Scanlon.

30. Habermas 1990, 234.

31. Habermas 1990, 233–34.

32. Mead, *Mind, Self, and Society* (1934), p. 379, cited in Habermas 1990, 241.

33. Habermas 1990, 245.

34. Habermas 1990, 236.

35. Habermas 1990, 242.

36. Habermas 1990, 246.

37. Alton 1966, 225. This is but one of a cluster of golden rule type metaethical rules that Alton produces.

38. Gensler did a dissertation on the golden rule (1977) and has published three books and several articles on logic and several articles on ethics. Gensler's *Formal Ethics* combines logical complexity with user-friendly, down-to-earth clarity, and I am learning very much from his work.

39. Gensler precedes this statement with the following one as a part of the universalizability axiom: "If act A ought to be done (would be all right), then there's some conjunction F of universal properties such that: act A is F, and in any actual or hypothetical case every act that is F ought to be done (would be all right)." A universal property is "a nonevaluative property expressible without proper names (like *Gensler, Chicago,* or *IBM*) or pointer words (like I, *this,* or *now*)." An evaluative property is one, like *wrong,* which represents an all-things-considered evaluation.

CHAPTER ELEVEN

1. The account here is based primarily on Husserl's posthumous writings on intersubjectivity. Husserl's position on this topic is normally criticized on the basis of his fifth Cartesian meditation; this is unfortunate, since that text exhibits reflection closer to the brink of solipsism than the bulk of his other writings.

2. Ricoeur will add that I cannot claim to know that the other's experience is similar to my own simply because the other's verbal expressions are similar to my own. The other's experience remains the other's, not mine. The marvel is the very recognition that the other is also a self, also a center of consciousness: "Like me, the other thinks, desires, enjoys, suffers" (Ricoeur 1993, 335).

3. Stein's writings on the role of women anticipate many contemporary feminist ideas, and her religious perspective balanced the two major themes of gender relations, equality and complementarity.

4. Stein 1956, 13–14. Stein wrote books of religious philosophy and translated *Disputed Questions on Truth* of Thomas Aquinas. She has been recently made a saint.

5. Stein 1964, 4.

6. Stein 1964, 14.

7. Stein 1964, 6–7.

8. Stein 1964, 10.

9. Stein 1964, 20; cf. 10.

10. Stein 1964, 16.

11. Stein 1964, 12.

12. Stein 1964, 16–17. The phenomenologist Max Scheler had emphasized the importance of such emotional "contagion" of mood, conveyed beneath the conscious transactions that occur between people. The contagious enthusiasm of a crowd is a favorite example, but the phenomenon occurs as well between just two persons. According to Scheler, this level of shared emotion is an enduring and essential stratum of human unity, never completely lost, although severely constricted in modern Western society. In adult life, according to Scheler, primal undifferentiated emotional sympathy remains the affective bond underlying other human bonds. It is a residual capacity less common in the average civilized adult than "in primitive peoples, children, dreamers, neurotics of a certain type, hypnotic subjects and in the exercise of the maternal instinct" (Scheler 1954, 31).

13. Stein 1964, 22–23.

14. Stein 1964, 14.

15. Stein 1964, 14.

16. Scholarship in German on the golden rule has unfolded in five phases: (1) the encyclopedic study of the golden rule in the world's religions by Leonidas Johannes Philippidis (1929, supplemented in 1933); (2) persistent philosophical articulation and increasingly detailed historical research by Hans Reiner (1948, 1951, 1954/55, 1964, 1977), whose conception of the golden rule has become a standard reference for German philosophers and theologians (writings that build on Reiner's work include Spendel 1967; Langer 1969; Lesnik 1975; Hoche 1978; Schüller 1980; Brülisauer 1980); (3) Albrecht Dihle's 1962 book, previously discussed, which has been influential, despite some criticisms (Lutz 1964; Reiner 1977; cf. also Robinson 1966; Lerne 1970, Wattles 1993); (4) continuing engagement, by Hans-Ulrich Hoche and others, in the discussion of questions raised by

Hare's *Freedom and Reason* and other writings (Hans-Ulrich Hoche 1978 and 1983; Hörster 1974; Kese 1990; Corradini 1994); (5) social and political philosophy, which though creative in developing Kantian ethics, has had little explicit reference to the golden rule, except in Craemer-Ruegenberg (1975).

17. Historically, the golden rule has been associated with the conviction of the profound and equal basic dignity of each person. In the wake of Stoicism, Roman legal theory had three branches: laws pertaining to citizens of Rome, laws pertaining to those living within the empire, and "natural law," pertaining to human beings as such. The resulting conception of natural law has generated evolutionary and revolutionary tensions in systems with gross inequalities. The golden rule is central to Middle Age and modern natural law tradition, which emphasizes the limited powers of rulers and the obligations of rulers toward the governed, an obligation sometimes thought to be grounded in a contract between the citizens or in the consent of the governed. Natural law doctrines were radical and unhistorical, by virtue of their appeal to eternal (though nontheocratic) principles, which indicated an ideal to be approximated. According to the early modern conception of natural law political theory, human beings "were originally free and equal, and therefore independent and isolated in their relation to one another." The contemporary importance of this tradition is that it is the source of human rights talk today.

18. Reiner observed that Kant's derogatory footnote about the golden rule footnote had extinguished interest in the rule among German philosophers for 150 years. His historical research, much of which has been incorporated into earlier chapters, will not be summarized here.

19. Reiner 1948, 80.
20. Reiner 1948, 84.
21. Reiner 1948, 85–86.
22. Reiner writes:

In praise and blame of another's conduct and in our requirements directed to him, we have recognized the rightness of certain ethical valuations and their connection with corresponding requirements. This means that we have therein expressed that we ourselves will that action be in accord with these valuations and requirements. Since we have done this, however, as free people and with our free personality at stake, we have taken upon our autonomous personality ethical requirements which originally arise from *values*. (Reiner 1948, 90)

23. Reiner 1948, 101.
24. Reiner 1948, 101.
25. Reiner 1951.
26. Reiner 1964.
27. Reiner 1977.
28. Wyschogrod 1990, 27.
29. I am grateful for permission to use a copy of David Goicoechea's unpublished paper, "Beyond the Golden Rule with Levinas," presented at the Canadian Council for the Study of Religion, June 7, 1993.
30. Ricoeur 1993, 320.
31. Ricoeur 1993, 119.
32. Ricoeur 1993, 72.

33. Ricoeur 1993, 168.

34. Ricoeur 1993, 161.

35. Ricoeur 1993, 145.

36. Ricoeur 1993, 144. Philosophic terms for interaction represent a compromise. Instead of using "agent and recipient," one might use either "agent and patient" (the type of case which Ricoeur has in mind) or "donor and recipient" (the happy possibility which he neglects). Talk of donor and recipient, however, connotes a distance between interacting persons, as though the transfer of a thing necessarily mediates the relationship; therefore, "agent" is preferable to "donor." And talk of patients connotes an extreme that obscures interaction; therefore, "recipient" is preferable to "patient."

37. Ricoeur 1993, 190.

38. Ricoeur 1993, 181.

39. Ricoeur 1993, 193.

40. Ricoeur 1993, 189; cf. 307; 180.

41. This idea is signaled by the fact that Kant's second formulation of the categorical imperative elaborates meanings not explicit in the first formulation (Ricoeur 1993, 211).

42. Ricoeur 1993, 222.

43. Ricoeur 1993, 220–21.

44. Ricoeur 1993, 219.

45. Ricoeur 1993, 274.

46. Ricoeur 1993, 286.

47. Ricoeur 1993, 330. Mark Hunyadi (1994) finds in *Oneself as Another* reasons to criticize the golden rule. Ricoeur, in moving from the ethical orientation to the good to the moral orientation to obligation, claims to discover a phenomenological stratum of pre-interactional sympathy and solicitude that grounds the later recognition of the need to impose the golden rule as a universal moral "no" to the potentials of violence that permanently haunt interaction. But neither the notion of a pre-interactive self nor the notion of interaction as involving power-over are satisfactory; and the golden rule, used in such a Hobbesian framework of assumptions, remains trapped in a self-centered orientation, despite Ricoeur's anti-Cartesian narrative of the self. It is more faithful to the otherness of the other to change the rule: "Do not do to the other as he or she does not want done to him or her."

In response to Hunyadi's critique, it may be observed, first, that the problem of persistent self-centeredness may be alleged even in the alterity rule: it is the self who must interpret the expressions of what the other does not want. Second, insofar as ethical and moral growth are concerned, the self cannot grow for the other, nor can the self act to promote the other's growth without applying, with some degree of specificity, the self's own standards.

The ideal solution is to find within the self a transcendent source of guidance whose leading is identical in both self and other.

48. Ricoeur 1993, 259, 268, 269, 274, 272.

CHAPTER TWELVE

1. Cadoux 1911/12, 277–78.

2. Cadoux 1911/12, 280.

3. Cf. du Roy 1970, 24:

Childhood is lived under the sign of the law. But training is bit by bit tempered by the educational admiration by which the child identifies with his parental models. Adolescence is also often the age of the ideal. Adulthood is beyond virtue. Only the love of others goes to the limits of the human when it decenters moral consciousness of itself in order to open to the very goal of law and virtue: the other, every person, humankind.

Later, du Roy, adapting Reiner's three levels of the golden rule, will articulate three stages of moral education: sympathy or affective fusion, law (droit), and communion. He leaves these two models without a synthesis.

4. Du Roy 1970, 44.

5. A more articulate exposition of a sequence of levels, moving through sympathy and morality to a spiritual level, may be found in The Urantia Book 1955, 1650–51.

6. Thomas 1970, 199.

7. Thomas 1970, 195.

8. Balthasar 1981, 76.

9. Rost's 1986 book, The Golden Rule, written during his years at Kenyatta University College in Kenya, is replete with quotations from many world religions.

10. Rost 1986, 148.

11. Cf. Ronald Green's 1973 article.

CHAPTER THIRTEEN

1. A claim to insight, therefore, is a claim about the future as well as about the present. Using the language of quest, adventure, and approximation, however, may mislead, if it is interpreted as simply erecting an empirical, scientific model of truth as provisional and revisable in the light of new experience. The empirical model of truth does not do justice to the philosophic level of truth as insight (e.g., the insight that empirical generalizations are revisable), or to the spiritual experience of truth as the divinely social enjoyment of the interplay of all these levels of truth.

2. The higher levels of self-realization may, of course, be only potential, not actual, in the recipient (as in the agent).

3. The saying is adapted from The Great Learning (Chan 1963, 88).

4. The fact that voluntariness is an ideal that admits of degrees does not make coherent institutional policies impossible, e.g., in a health care setting with patients who are not fully able to consent to treatment.

5. Such an evolutionary perspective does not, of course, require blindness to symptoms of civilizational decline; but decline does not go on forever. Sooner or later we will find the inspired leadership and teamwork to reorient our planetary course, and who can say whether that reversal is not already under way? It is no simple matter to generalize regarding the countless ups and downs that simultaneously and continuously reshape the present and future. During the years when I taught world history, I arrived at the conviction that history is like a decathlon in which the power of love competes with the forces of self-centeredness and materialism and destruction; I am not in doubt about the ultimate triumph of love, though in any given event on the horizon, there is uncertainty. There are so many positive persons to work with and so many promising projects to join that

courage and faith can dispel anxiety and cynicism. Nevertheless, I believe that nothing short of a spiritual renaissance will have the power to remotivate and redirect our planetary course. Moral teaching and religious doctrine are not enough.

6. One form of this objection is the critique, made by Jean-Paul Sartre, of the very idea of a common human nature. Rather, according to Sartre, what we are we determine moment to moment in radical freedom. This proposal, however, merely amounts to a *different* conception of what it means to be human: we are to affirm that each human being is free and faces certain basic alternatives, for example, whether or not to be lucid about our freedom.

7. Jer. 17.9.

8. Consider Ronald M. Green's definition of humility:

As the voluntary renunciation of the special advantages or "merit" provided by the accidents of birth or fate, and as a recognition of the contingency of all one's accomplishments, humility has a fundamental role in prompting the individual to adopt the moral point of view in the first place. (1978, 130)

9. Take, for example, Socrates' encounter with Cephalus in bk. 1 of *The Republic*, where the definition of justice implicit in Cephalus' conversation is disposed of with a single counterexample.

10. In the halo effect, the observer has an initial positive (or negative) first impression of someone or something and then extends that favorable (or unfavorable) impression to the whole person or object. Thus a positive first impression of a person inclines us to interpret charitably the same person's gaffe noticed later. Guilt by association is another example of the halo effect.

11. Mill 1987, chap. 2, 296.

12. *Ad hominem* arguments are classified as fallacies, since they attack the person, not the argument: "You'd better not be swayed by that rich man (poor man); of course he'd speak in opposition to (in favor of) socialized medicine."

13. Groth 1979, 26–30.

14. Interview with Mike Wallace, in the CBS coverage of the Winter Olympics, February 14, 1992.

15. If it is possible to mention a contrasting case without overtones of political polemics, consider the very different example of James Schlesinger, who, as chairman of the Atomic Energy Commission in 1971, was so convinced of the safety of a particular underground nuclear test, the Cannikin Test, that he went with his wife and two children to Amchitka Island in the Aleutian Islands of Alaska where the test took place. I am grateful to Dr. Schlesinger for responding in a telephone conversation to my request for details.

16. Moffett 1975.

17. A team of diversity consultants, who teach employees how to avoid saying offensive things to women and minorities, instruct their classes to avoid the golden rule and to use the "platinum rule," to treat others as *they* [their recipients] want to be treated (from the McNeill/Lehrer News Hour on PBS, March 17, 1994).

18. The more abuse a person has sustained, the more difficult it may be to awaken the memories, realizations, or imaginations that will provide suitable models of being well treated.

19. There may be, then, a reciprocal influence of factors in personal growth.

Alternatively, growth in those factors may be regarded as resulting from the growth of the person as a whole.

20. Impartiality has been expressed as omnipartiality; the point is not cold-heartedness but equal interest in each person involved. Matters are of course more complex than that. Michael Slote (1984) has noted that ordinary morality recognizes several asymmetries between self and other that are not foreseen by the impersonal standpoint of utilitarian or Kantian ethics. Ordinary morality accords a slight preference for altruism, for benefiting the other. Moral intuition permits agents to choose careers of their own preference or to make sacrifices in ways that do not satisfy the greatest total good. I may run risks for myself that I may not run for others. The impersonal standpoint makes special commitments between family members seem anomalous. If persons are so valuable, it might be acceptable on an impersonal standpoint, in contrast to common morality, to kill one to save five. Slote concludes that ordinary morality is more complex and more difficult to justify and to generalize in theory than had been thought. He does not claim that the principle of impartiality requires the agent to attempt to dispense equal benefits to all possible recipients; his point is that applying the same standard to oneself and others involves complexities unsuspected in much of modern ethics.

21. If this argument is correct, Kant's mistake in the Groundwork was to try to reverse matters, to try to base respect for persons on a notion of legal consistency. He would have done better to reverse the sequence (in the Groundwork) of his first two formulations of the categorical imperative and to take the dignity of humanity as an axiom than to try to demonstrate it rationally.

22. Louis J. Pojman's 1992 article, "Are Human Rights Based on Equal Human Worth?" examines ten strategies for basing equal human rights on equal human worth and treats R. S. Peters, Stanley Benn, Monroe Beardsley, E. F. Carritt, James Rachels, Ronald Dworkin, Kai Nielsen, Robert Nozick, David Gauthier, Gregory Vlastos, Joel Feinberg, Peter Singer, Alan Gewirth, Thomas Nagel, and John Rawls. His purpose, as he says, is to show "how little attention has been paid to justifying the egalitarian plateau."

Another argument that should also be noted is Hume's, that in conventional judgments of moral character we approve of characteristics of others that bring no benefits to ourselves, and that this fact gives evidence that the sentiment of care for the welfare of humanity is well-nigh universal (however often it be overpowered by other sentiments). This argument, however, also leaves open the question of a possible foundation for the spark of goodness within each person.

CHAPTER FOURTEEN

1. Let me clarify the meaning I associate with spiritual by contrast with the meaning I associate with religious. Talk of spiritual experience affirms that spiritual realities are in play, God and the indwelling spirit gift of God. Talk of religious experience acknowledges the role of religious tradition in interpreting and preparing that experience.

My working definition is that the spiritual is that level of reality, different from matter, which transcends mind, such that as we grow toward it, the more we become like the divine paradigm along the path from being spirit-taught to being spirit-led and spirit-filled. To speak of spiritual experience is to report a discontinuity from the "merely" intellectual level. Indeed, until one moves beyond the level of mind, as it were, one cannot meaningfully label it as such. If the discontinuity were absolute, of course, there would be no personality continuity and perhaps no human, conscious awareness of the spiritual.

2. To avoid misunderstandings, it is important to emphasize that,in the religious philosophy proposed here, God is the pattern for human parents; the father concept is not a metaphor in which human parents are taken as the basis for an understanding of God; rather, human parents, at their best, participate in and express the parental love of God. The fatherhood of God, far from supporting patriarchal domination, provides ultimate leverage for moving beyond patriarchy. See Ricoeur 1974; Visser't Hooft 1982; Hamerton-Kelly 1979; and Rolnick 1993.

3. Those who deny that unbelievers are the sons and daughters of God may regard humankind as a neighborhood rather than a brotherhood. But the experience of loving others as oneself makes it reasonable to conceive others in terms of their continuities with oneself, rather than in terms of discontinuities, apparent or real. It matters little what vocabulary we choose, but a lot how we treat one another. The validity of the concept of the brotherhood of man (the siblinghood of humankind) depends upon the answer to the question, who are the sons and daughters of God? It is the multiplicity of meanings of this term that makes the concept of the family of God irridescent and dynamic. Though Christians acknowledge Jesus of Nazareth as the Son of God in a unique sense, there are other meanings that are interrelated in a full concept of the family of God.

First, we are the sons and daughters of God if we through faith and by grace accept the truth of the family of God. Faith enables truth to be consciously, enduringly, and increasingly effectively experienced.

In a second sense, perhaps none of us is a son or daughter of God yet. Jesus said, "Blessed are the peacemakers, for they shall be called sons of God" (Matt. 5.9) and "Love your enemies and pray for those who persecute you, so that you may be sons of your Father who is in heaven" (Matt. 5.43–44). The future tense suggests a fullness of relationship that is sealed only beyond the earth life.

In a third sense, all humankind are the sons and daughters of God. The Hebrew Bible and the New Testament provide many supports for this affirmation. Job defended his treatment of his servants this way: "If I have rejected the cause of my male or female slaves, when they brought a complaint against me; what then shall I do when God rises up? When he makes an inquiry, what shall I answer him? Did not he who made me in the womb make them?" (Job 31.13–15). The Creator proposed, "Let us make humankind in our image" (Gen. 1.26). "The spirit in man is the candle of the Lord, searching all the inward parts" (Prov. 20.27); the spirit has been "poured out upon all flesh" (Acts 2.17); the kingdom of heaven is within us (Luke 17.21). It does not compromise the requirement that faith is the price of salvation to affirm all humankind as the family of God. Jesus spoke of God to everyone he met as the Father, my Father, our Father, and your Father. He said to the crowds, "Call no man father, for you have one Father, who is in heaven" (Matt. 23.9). God goes forth in search of every "lost sheep," awaits the return of every "prodigal son," does not want any to perish" (Luke 15). The scriptures portray a Creator who loves each one of us with an infinite love.

Analytically, one might distinguish families of God: the family of the faithful, the heavenly family, and the family of humankind as a whole. The vitality of the full concept of the family of God is that each of these distinguishable families is embraced in it.

4. In placing sympathy and other achievements before the spiritual level, I do not wish to imply any prejudgment regarding the theological question of whether divine grace is needed for even the exercise of sincere sympathy. By placing a God-centered *ethics* at the pinnacle of human development, I do not imply that God-centered *religion* is not needed in earlier levels of "ordinary" human living.

5. This practice is discussed in Haberman 1988.

6. John 15.12.

7. Matt. 25.40.

8. Various replies have been proposed to answer the question "Why be moral?"

A. People are moral because of social influences on their development. This purported *explanation* of behavior, even if it were correct, would prove too little, since it only touches outward conformity to social norms, not the inner, purposive core of moral experience.

B. People should be moral because it is in their best interests to be so, or because one feels most personally fulfilled by moral rather than by immoral living. This answer also proves too little, since it reduces morality to intelligent egoism, whereas morality pertains to norms that transcend personal interest. Aristotle's rejoinder, that self-love only has a bad name because it is so often practiced in a materialistic way—and that one's own happiness requires devotion to friends—remains inadequate. Even if the command to be perfect be acknowledged as supreme, one cannot flourish with that principle alone without other principles taken as equally important.

C. People should be moral because society presupposes trustworthiness among its members; the alternative is a state of nature—"solitary, poor, nasty, brutish, and short" (Hobbes). This answer, like (B), proves too little.

D. People should be moral because some authority (e.g., God) commands it. If this answer is not to be interpreted as another variation on (B), it must presuppose that whatever God commands is moral—which assumes too much for the purpose of giving an answer to the question, "Why be moral?"

9. I do not assume that "human effort alone" (if such a thing were conceivable) can achieve an advanced civilization.

10. There is today a widespread critique of foundationalism defined as any attempt to provide self-evident, clear, definite, rational foundations for philosophy. Such an error allegedly obscures the dependence of any putative foundation on the wider web of human ideas and language. Moreover, foundationalism allegedly masks our inability to know the truth of any great and fundamental doctrine. The kind of foundation proposed here is illustrated in a passage from *Works of Love* by Søren Kierkegaard (1962): "Spiritually understood, what are the ground and foundation of the life of the spirit. . . ? In very fact it is love; love is the origin of everything, and spiritually understood love is the deepest ground of the life of the spirit" (205).

11. I would propose that only a *combined* recognition of fact and experience of value counts as a realization of the family of God. Consciousness of fact is marked by a definite stability, whereas consciousness of (spiritual) value is marked

by a fluid vitality. In any given conceptual moment, one of these phases is in the focus of consciousness, one is in the background, and each theme (the fatherhood of God and the kinship of humankind) may be grasped as fact or value. The effective margin of consciousness is such that no sense of self-correction is involved when an item in the effective margin moves into focus.

12. Eph. 4.30.

13. It remains true that in situations where fairness is the value in question, the rights of the self are not excluded from consideration.

14. A model for such decisions is reported in Matt. 4. Jesus made decisions that structured his subsequent career in a nonviolent, nonpolitical ministry, not based on appeal to miracle, in a life that accepted the full limitations of humanity.

15. Clarke 1969, 208.

Bibliography

Abrahams, I. 1967. *Studies in Pharisaism and the Gospels*. Library of Biblical Studies. New York: Ktav.

Ahlstrom, Sydney E. 1972. *A Religious History of the American People*. New Haven: Yale University Press.

Allinson, Robert E. 1982. On the negative version of the golden rule as formulated by Confucious. *New Asia Academic Bulletin* 3: 223–32.

———. 1985. The Confucian golden rule: A negative formulation. *Journal of Chinese Philosophy* 12: 305–15.

Allison, Dale C., Jr. 1987. The structure of the Sermon on the Mount. *Journal of Biblical Literature* 106 (5): 423–44.

Alper, Joseph. 1985. Is empathy innate? *Science* 85 (March): 70–76.

Alton, Bruce. 1966. "An Examination of the Golden Rule." Ph.D. diss. Stanford University.

Anderson, Douglas Firth. 1989. Presbyterians and the golden rule: The Christian socialism of J. E. Scott. *American Presbyterians* 67 (3): 231–43.

An-Nawawi. 1976. *An-Nawawi's Forty Hadith*. Tr. Ezeddin Ibrahim and Denys Johnson-Davies. Damascus: Holy Koran Publishing House.

Aristotle. 1985. *Nicomachean Ethics*. Tr. Terence Irwin. Indianapolis: Hackett.

———. 1991. *Rhetoric* (selections). Tr. Terence Irwin. In *Philosophers on Friendship*, ed. Michael Pakaluk. Indianapolis: Hackett.

Atkinson, David. 1982. The golden rule. *Expository Times* 93 (11): 336–38.

Augustine, St. 1948. *The Lord's Sermon on the Mount*. Vol. 5 of *Ancient Christian Writers: The Words of the Fathers in Translation*. Ed. Johannes Quasten, Joseph C. Plumpe, and John J. Jepson. Westminster, Md.: Newman Press.

———. 1950. *The City of God*. Tr. Marcus Dods. New York: Random House.

Bachmeyer, T. J. 1973. The golden rule and developing moral judgment. *Religious Education* 68 (May–June): 348–65.

Baier, Kurt. 1958. *The Moral Point of View*. Ithaca: Cornell University Press.

Balthasar, Hans Urs von. 1981. Neun Sätze zur christlichen Ethik. In *Prinzipien Christlicher Moral*, ed. Joseph Ratzinger. Einsiedeln: Johannes Verlag.

Barach, Jeffrey, and John B. Elstrott. 1988. The transactional ethic: The ethical foundations of free enterprise reconsidered. *Journal of Business Ethics* 7 (July): 545–51.

Bartsch, H.-W. 1984. Traditionsgeschichtliches zur "goldenen Regel" und zum

Aposteldekret. *Zeitschrift für die neutestamentliche Wissenschaft und die Kunde des Ur-christentums* 75 (1–2): 128–32.

Batson, C. Daniel. 1991. *The Altruism Question*. Hillsdale, N.J.: Erlbaum.

Batson, C. Daniel, Patricia Schoenrade, and W. Larry Ventis. 1993. *Religion and the Individual*. New York: Oxford University Press.

Batson, C. Daniel, and W. Larry Ventis. 1982. *The Religious Experience*. New York: Oxford University Press.

Batson, C. Daniel, et al. 1986. Where is the altruism in the altruistic personality? *Journal of Personality and Social Psychology* 50 (1): 212–20.

Bauer, Walter. [1959] 1979. *A Greek-English Lexicon of the New Testament and Other Early Christian Literature*. Tr. William F. Arndt and F. Wilbur Gingrich. Chicago: University of Chicago Press.

Bauman, Clarence. 1985. *The Sermon on the Mount*. Macon, Ga.: Mercer University Press.

Becker, Lawrence C. 1986. *Reciprocity*. Chicago: University of Chicago Press.

Behnisch, Martin. 1985. The golden rule as an expression of Jesus' preaching. *Bangalore Theological Forum* 17 (1): 83–97.

Bent, Silas. 1926. The golden rule, plus sound business. *Nation's Business* (August): 18–19.

Blackstone, W. T. 1965. The golden rule: A defense. *Southern Journal of Philosophy* 5 (Winter): 172–77.

Blenkinsopp, Joseph. 1983. *Wisdom and Law in the Old Testament*. New York: Oxford University Press.

Blundell, Mary Whitlock. 1989. *Helping Friends and Harming Enemies: A Study in Sophocles and Greek Ethics*. Cambridge: Cambridge University Press.

Boraston, George. 1684. *The Royal Law, or the Golden Rule of Justice and Charity*. London: Printed for Walter Kettilby.

Borgen, Peder. 1966. Den såkalte gyldne regel (The so-called golden rule; tr. Seppo Kanerva). *Norsk Teologisk Tidsskrift* 9: 129–46.

Brook, Richard. 1987. Justice and the golden rule: A commentary on some recent work of Lawrence Kohlberg. *Ethics* 97 (January): 363–73.

Brülisauer, Bruno. 1980. Die goldene Regel. *Kant-Studien* 71: 325–45.

Burger, Ronna. 1984. *The Phaedo*. New Haven: Yale University Press.

Burnet, John, ed. 1937. *Phaedo*. In *Platonis Opera*. Oxford: Clarendon Press.

Buzzell, Rev. G.W. n.d. *Story of Good Will Institute and Golden Rule Farm Homes*.

Cadoux, Arthur T. 1911–12. The implications of the golden rule. *International Journal of Ethics* (then *The Ethical Record*) 22: 272–87.

Camfield, Benjamin. 1679. *A Profitable Inquiry into that Comprehensive Rule of Righteousness*. Printed by William Leach.

Cary, Alice S. 1953. Economic freedom and the golden rule. *Christianity and Crisis* 13 (11): 84–86.

Chan, Wing-tsit. 1963. *A Source Book in Chinese Philosophy*. Princeton: Princeton University Press.

Charles, R. H., ed. 1913. *The Apocrypha and Pseudepigrapha of the Old Testament*. Oxford: Clarendon Press.

Ch'en Ch'un. 1986. *Neo-Confucian Terms Explained (The Pei-hsi Tzu-i)*. Tr. Wing-tsit Chan. New York: Columbia University Press.

Chu Hsi. 1973. *The Philosophy of Human Nature*. Tr. J. Percy Bruce. New York: AMS Press.

Chu Hsi and Lu Tsu-Chien. 1967. *Reflections on Things at Hand*. Tr. Wing-tsit Chan. New York: Columbia University Press.

Chuang Tzu. 1968. *The Complete Works of Chuang Tzu*. Tr. Burton Watson. New York: Columbia University Press.

Clarke, Samuel. [1705] 1969. *A Discourse of Natural Religion*. In *British Moralists 1650–1800*, ed. D. D. Raphael. Oxford: Clarendon Press.

Commager, Henry Steele. 1950. *The American Mind*. New Haven: Yale University Press.

Confucius. 1979. *The Analects*. Tr. D. C. Lau. Harmondsworth: Penguin Books.

Conn, Walter E. 1977. Erik Erikson: The ethical orientation, conscience and the golden rule. *Journal of Religious Ethics* 5 (2): 249–66.

Coppenger, Mark. 1990. The golden rule and war. *Criswell Theological Review* 4 (Spring): 295–312.

Corradini, Antonella. 1994. Goldene Regel, Abtreibung und Pflichten gegenüber möglichen Individuen. *Zeitschrift für philosophische Forschung* 48 (1): 21–42.

Craemer-Ruegenberg, Ingrid. 1975. *Moralsprache und Moralität*. Freiburg: Verlag Karl Alber.

Cua, Antonio S. 1984. Confucian vision and human community. *Journal of Chinese Philosophy* 11: 227–38.

Davies, W. D. 1964. *The Setting of the Sermon on the Mount*. Cambridge: Cambridge University Press.

Davis, Mark H. 1994. *Empathy: A Social Psychological Approach*. Madison, Wis.: Brown and Benchmark.

De Bary, William Theodore. 1975. Neo-Confucian cultivation and the seventeenth-century "enlightenment." In *The Unfolding of Neo-Confucianism*, ed. de Bary. New York: Columbia University Press.

Dihle, Albrecht. 1962. *Die goldene Regel*. Gottingen: Vandenhoeck & Ruprecht.

Diogenes Laertius. 1905. *The Lives and Opinions of Eminent Philosophers*. Vol. 9. Tr. C. D. Yonge. London: George Bell & Sons.

Dole, Charles F. 1896. *The Golden Rule in Business*. New York: Thomas Y. Crowell.

Donaldson, Dwight M. 1963. *Studies in Muslim Ethics*. London: S.P.C.K.

Dover, K. J. 1974. *Greek Popular Morality in the Time of Plato and Aristotle*. Berkeley and Los Angeles: University of California Press.

Du Bois, W. E. B. 1990. *The Souls of Black Folks*. New York: Vintage Books.

Du Roy, Olivier. 1970. *La Reciprocité*. Paris: Éditeurs Epi.

Eisenberg, Nancy. 1986. *Altruistic Emotion, Cognition, and Behavior*. Hillsdale, N.J.: Erlbaum.

Eisenberg, Nancy, and Janet Strayer, eds. 1987. *Empathy and Its Development*. New York: Cambridge University Press.

Epictetus. n.d. *The Discourses of Epictetus with the Encheiridion and Fragments*. Tr. George Long. London: Chesterfield Society.

Erikson, Erik H. 1963. Eight ages of man. In *Childhood and Society*. New York: W. W. Norton.

———. 1964. The golden rule in the light of new insight. In *Insight and Responsibility*. New York: W. W. Norton.

Evans, Donald. 1993. *Spirituality and Human Nature*. Albany: State University of New York Press.

Evans, Owen E. 1951. The negative form of the golden rule in the Diatessaron. *Expository Times* 63, no. 1 (October): 31–32.

Filene, Peter G. 1986. *Him/Her/Self*. 2nd ed. Baltimore: Johns Hopkins University Press.

Fingarette, Herbert. 1980. Following the "one thread" of the *Analects*. *Journal of the American Academy of Religion* 47 (3): 372–405.

Fishburn, Janet Forsythe. 1981. *The Fatherhood of God and the Victorian Family*. Philadelphia: Fortress.

Flusser, David. [1985] 1990. The Ten Commandments and the New Testament. In *The Ten Commandments in History and Tradition*, ed. Gershon Levi. Jerusalem: Magnes Press, The Hebrew University.

Frederick, Peter J. 1976. *Knights of the Golden Rule*. Lexington: University Press of Kentucky.

Freud, Sigmund. 1953–1974. *The Standard Edition of the Complete Psychological Works of Sigmund Freud*. Ed. James Strachey. 24 vols. London: Hogarth.

Fung, Yu-lan. 1953. *A History of Chinese Philosophy*. Princeton: Princeton University Press.

Gadamer, Hans-Georg. 1969. *Dialogue and Dialectic*. Tr. P. C. Smith. New Haven: Yale University Press.

Gallop, David. 1975. *Plato's Phaedo*. Oxford: Clarendon Press.

Gensler, Harry J. 1976. The prescriptivism incompleteness theorem. *Mind* 85, no. 340 (October): 589–96.

———. 1977. The Golden Rule. Ph.D. diss. University of Michigan.

———. [1984] 1986. A Kantian argument against abortion. *Philosophical Studies* 49: 83–98.

———. *Formal Ethics*. London: Routledge.

Gerhardsson, Birger. 1987. Agape and imitation of Christ. In *Jesus, the Gospels, and the Church*, ed. E. P. Sanders. Macon, Ga.: Mercer University Press.

Gewirth, Alan. 1978. The golden rule rationalized. *Midwest Studies in Philosophy* 3: 133–47.

Gilligan, Carol. 1982. *In a Different Voice*. Cambridge: Harvard University Press.

Goicoechea, David. 1993. Beyond the golden rule with Levinas. Unpublished paper.

Goodman, John. 1688. *The Golden Rule; or, The Royal Law of Equity Explained*. London: Printed by Samuel Roycroft for Robert Clavell.

Gould, James. 1963. The not-so-golden rule. *Southern Journal of Philosophy* 5: 10–14.

———. 1983. The golden rule. *American Journal of Theology and Philosophy* 4, no. 2 (May): 73–79.

Graham, A. C. 1989. *Disputers of the Tao*. La Salle, Ill.: Open Court.

Green, Ronald. 1973. Jewish ethics and the virtue of humility. *Journal of Religious Ethics* 1: 53–63.

Griffin, Miriam T. 1976, *Seneca*. Oxford: Clarendon Press.

Groth, A. Nicholas. 1979. *Men Who Rape*. New York: Plenum Press.

Grundel, Johannes. 1970. Die goldene Regel und die Situationsethik. In *Ethik ohne Normen?*, ed. Hendrik van Oyen and Johannes Grundel. Freiburg: Herder.

Haberman, David L. 1988. *Acting as a Way of Salvation*. New York: Oxford University Press.

Habermas, Jürgen. 1990. Justice and solidarity: On the discussion concerning stage 6. In *The Moral Domain*, ed. Thomas Wren. Cambridge: MIT Press.

Hackforth, R. 1972. *Plato's Phaedo*. Cambridge: Cambridge University Press.

Hamerton-Kelly, Robert. 1979. *God the Father*. Philadelphia: Fortress.

Hare, R. M. 1963. *Freedom and Reason*. Oxford: Clarendon Press.

———. 1975a. Abortion and the golden rule. *Philosophy and Public Affairs* 4, no. 3 (Spring): 201–22.

———. 1975b. Euthanasia: A Christian view. *Proceedings of the Center for Philosophic Exchange* 6: 43–52.

———. 1981. *Moral Thinking*. Oxford: Clarendon Press.

Hareven, Tamara K. 1971. The history of the family as an interdisciplinary field. In *The Family in History*, ed. Theodore K. Rabb and Robert I. Rotberg. New York: Harper & Row.

Harnack, Adolf. [1900] 1957. *What Is Christianity?* Tr. Thomas Bailey Saunders. Harper Torchbooks. New York: Harper & Row.

Heckel, Theodor. 1952. Regula aurea. In *Zur politischen Predigt*, ed. Evang.-Luth. Dekanats München. Munich: Evang.-Luth. Dekanats München.

Herodotus. 1859. *The History of Herodotus*. Tr. George Rawlinson. 4 vols. New York: D. Appleton.

Hertzler, J. O. 1934. On golden rules. *International Journal of Ethics* 44: 418–36.

Hobbes, Thomas. [1651] 1967. *Leviathan*. Oxford: Clarendon Press.

Hoche, Hans-Ulrich. 1978. Die goldene Regel. *Zeitschrift für Philosophische Forschung* 32, no. 3 (July–September): 355–75.

———. 1982. The Golden Rule. Tr. J. Claude Evans. In *Contemporary German Philosophy*, vol. 1, ed. Darrell E. Christiansen et al. University Park: Pennsylvania State University Press.

———. 1983. Zur logischen Struktur von "Goldene-Regel" Argumenten im Sinne Hares. *Kant-Studien* 74 (4): 453–78.

Hodges, Donald Clark. 1957. The Golden Rule and Its Deformations. *The Personalist* 38 (April): 130–48.

Hoerster, Norbert. 1974. R. M. Hares Fassung der goldene Regel. *Philosophisches Jahrbuch* 81: 186–96.

Hoffman, Martin L. 1984. Interaction of affect and cognition in empathy. In *Emotions, Cognition, and Behavior*, ed. Carroll E. Izard, Jerome Kagan, and Robert Zajonc. Cambridge: Cambridge University Press.

Holoviak, Stephen J. 1993. *Golden Rule Management: Give Respect, Get Results*. Reading, Mass.: Addison-Wesley.

Homer. 1949. *Odyssey*. Tr. W. H. D. Rouse. New York: New American Library.

Huffman, James Floyd. 1966. John Hay, the poetic trumpet: The rhetoric of "the statesman of the golden rule." Ph.D. diss. Michigan State University.

Hughes, Jean R., E. Joyce Carver, and Ruth C. MacKay. 1990. Learning to use empathy. In *Empathy in the Helping Relationship*, ed. Ruth C. MacKay, Jean R. Hughes, and E. Joyce Carver. New York: Springer.

Hunyadi, Mark. 1994. La règle d'or: L'effet-radar. *Revue de theologie et philosophie*. 126 (3): 215–22.

Inwood, Brad. 1985. *Ethics and Human Action in Early Stoicism*. Oxford: Clarendon Press.

Isocrates. 1928–1945. *Isocrates*. Tr. George Norlin, vols. 1–2. Tr. Larue Van Hook. Loeb Classical Library. Cambridge: Harvard University Press.

Ivanhoe, Philip J. 1990a. Reweaving the "one thread" of the *Analects*. *Philosophy East and West* 40 (1): 18–33.

Jaeger, Werner. 1947. *The Theology of the Early Greek Philosophers*. Oxford: Clarendon Press.

Jeffery, Arthur, ed. 1962. *A Reader on Islam*. The Hague: Mouton.

Jeremias, Joachim. 1971. *New Testament Theology*. Tr. John Bowden. New York: Scribner's.

Justin Martyr. 1971. *An Early Christian Philosopher: Justin Martyr's Dialogue with Trypho*. Ed. J. C. M. van Winden. Leiden: Brill.

Kant, Immanuel. 1983. *Ethical Philosophy*. Tr. James W. Ellington. Indianapolis: Hackett.

Katz, Robert L. 1963. *Empathy*. Glencoe, Ill.: Free Press.

Kese, Ralf. 1990. Zur Methodologie und Logik von "Goldene-Regel" Argumenten. *Kant-Studien* 81 (1): 89–98.

Khan, Abrahim H. 1993. The golden rule as moral bedrock in religious history? Unpublished paper.

Kielkopf, Charles F. 1974. Possible world problems with the golden rule. *Proceedings of the Ohio Philosophical Association*. 96–108.

Kierkegaard, Søren. [1847] 1962. *Works of Love*. Tr. Howard Hong and Edna Hong. New York: Harper & Row.

King, George Brockwell. 1928. The "negative" golden rule. *Journal of Religion* 8: 268–79.

Kohlberg, Lawrence. 1981. *The Philosophy of Moral Development: Moral Stages and the Idea of Justice*. Vol. 1 of *Essays on Moral Development*. San Francisco: Harper & Row.

Krebs, Dennis, and Cristine Russell. 1981. Role-taking and altruism. In *Altruism and Helping Behavior*, eds. J. Philippe Rushton and Richard Sorrentino. Hillsdale, N.J.: Erlbaum.

Lahr, John. 1993. Under the skin. *New Yorker*, June 28, 90–94.

Langer, Adalbert. 1969. Die goldene Regel—Ein Schlussel zum Frieden. In *Kirche, Recht, und Land*, ed. Franz Lorenz. Munich: Sudetendeutschen Priesterwerkes.

Larson, Gerald James, and Eliot Deutsch. 1988. *Interpreting across Boundaries*. Princeton: Princeton University Press.

Laulaja, Jorma. 1981. *Kultaisen Saannon Etiikka*. Helsinki: Missiologian Ja Ekumeniikan Seura R. Y.

Leibniz, G. W. [1765] 1981. *New Essays on Human Understanding*. Tr. Peter Remnant and Jonathan Bennett. Cambridge: Cambridge University Press.

Lerne, Ernst. 1970. Realisierbare Forderungen der Bergpredigt? *Kerygma und Dogma* 16: 32–48.

Lesnik, Siegfried Alfons. 1975. *Die goldene Regel: Prinzip der neuen Menschlichkeit in Naturrechtlicher und biblischer Auffassung*. Gutenberg: Self-published.

Little, David, and Sumner Twiss. 1978. *Comparative Religious Ethics*. San Francisco: Harper & Row.

Locke, John. [1690] 1959. *An Essay Concerning Human Understanding*. New York: Dover.

Luther, Martin. [1883] 1966. *D. Martin Luthers Werke*. Kritische Gesamtausgabe. Weimarer Ausgabe. Weimar: H. Böhlaus Nachfolger. Reprint Graz, Austria: Akademische Druck-u. Verlagsanstalt.

———. 1959. *Luther's Works*. Vol. 51, *Sermons*. Tr. and ed. John Doberstein. Philadelphia: Fortress.

———. 1970. *Three Treatises*. Rev. ed. Tr. Charles M. Jacobs, A. T. W. Steinhäuser, and W. A. Lambert. Philadelphia: Fortress.

Lutz, Adolf. 1964. Diskussion: Die goldene Regel. *Zeitschrift für philosophische Forschung* 18: 467–75.

McGray, James W. 1989. The golden rule and paternalism. *Journal of Interdisciplinary Studies* 1: 145–61.

MacKay, Alfred F. 1986. Extended sympathy and interpersonal utility comparisons. *Journal of Philosophy* 83, no. 6 (June): 305–22.

The Mahabharata of Krishna-Dwaipayana Vyasa. [1883–1896.] Tr. Pratap Chandra Roy. Calcutta: Oriental Publishing Co.

Mahabharata. 1906. *Vier philosophischen Texte aus des Mahabharatam.* Tr. Paul Deussen and Otto Strauss. Leipzig: F. A. Brockhaus.

Mahabharata. 1978, Vol. 5. Tr. J. A. B. van Buitenen. Chicago: University of Chicago Press.

Malina, Bruce J. 1981. *The New Testament World.* Atlanta: John Knox Press.

Mayhew, Edward, ed. 1896. *Golden Rules for the Treatment of Horses and Other Animals.* Philadelphia: Women's Pennsylvania Society for the Prevention of Cruelty to Animals.

Mead, George Herbert. 1934. *The Social Psychology of George Herbert Mead.* Ed. Anselm Strauss. Chicago: University of Chicago Press.

———. [1934] 1962. *Mind, Self, and Society.* Ed. Charles W. Morris. Chicago: University of Chicago Press.

Meecham, Henry G. 1935. *The Letter of Aristeas: A Linguistic Study with Special Reference to the Greek Bible.* Manchester: Manchester University Press.

Melville, Herman. [1851] 1967. *Moby-Dick.* Ed. Harrison Hayford and Herschel Parker. Norton Critical Edition. New York: W. W. Norton.

Mencius. 1970. *Mencius.* Tr. D. C. Lau. Harmondsworth: Penguin.

Merkelbach, Reinhold. 1973. Über eine Stelle im Evangelium des Lukas. *Grazer Beiträge* 1: 171–75.

Metzger, Bruce M. 1958. The designation "the golden rule." *Expository Times* 69 (July): 304.

Migne, J. P., ed. 1879. *Patrologia Latina.* Paris: Garnier Fratres.

Mill, J. S., and Jeremy Bentham. 1987. *Utilitarianism and Other Essays.* Ed. Alan Ryan. London: Penguin.

Mo Tzu. 1963. *Mo Tzu.* Tr. Burton Watson. New York: Columbia University Press.

Moffett, Judith. 1975. The habit of imagining. *Christian Century,* 24 December, 1176–79.

Morrison, Karl F. 1988. *"I am you": The Hermeneutics of Empathy in Western Literature, Theology, and Art.* Princeton: Princeton University Press.

Moser, Gabriel. 1988. Urban stress and helping behavior: Effects of environmental overload and noise on behavior. *Journal of Environmental Psychology* 8: 287–98.

Mulholland, Leslie A. 1988. Autonomy, extended sympathy and the golden rule. In *Inquiries into Values,* ed. Sander H. Lee. Lewiston, N.Y., and Queenston, Ont.: Edwin Mellen.

Nash, Arthur. 1926–27. *Nash Journal* (company newsletter). Cincinatti: A. Nash Co.

———. [1923] 1930. *The Golden Rule in Business.* 2nd ed. New York: Fleming H. Revell.

Rabbi Nathan. 1955. *The Fathers According to Rabbi Nathan.* Tr. Judah Goldin. New Haven: Yale University Press.

Neely, F. Tennyson. 1894. *Neely's History of the Parliament of Religions and Religious Congresses at the World's Columbian Exposition.* Ed. Walter R. Houghton. Chicago: F. Tennyson Neely.

Nivison, David S. Forthcoming. Golden rule arguments in Chinese moral philosophy. In David S. Nivison, *The Ways of Confucianism.* Ed. Bryan Van Norden. La Salle, Ill.: Open Court.

Noble, Miriam. 1931. *Golden Rules of World Religions.* Los Angeles: Ivan Deach, Jr.

Penney, J. C. 1950. *Fifty Years with the Golden Rule.* New York: Harper.

Perdue, Leo G., Bernard Brandon Scott, and William Johnston Wiseman, eds. 1993. *In Search of Wisdom*. Louisville: Westminster/John Knox Press.

Philippidis, Leonidas Johannes. 1929. *Die "goldene Regel" religionsgeschichtlich Untersucht.* Leipzig: Adolf Klein Verlag.

———. 1933. *Religionswissenschaftliche Forschungsberichte über die "goldene Regel."* Athens: n.n.

Philo of Alexandria. 1941. *Philo.* Vol 9. Tr. F. H. Colson. Loeb Classical Library. London: Heinemann.

Phipps, William E. 1982. The glittering rule. *Theology Today* 39, no. 2 (July): 194–98.

Piaget, Jean. 1965. *The Moral Judgment of the Child.* Tr. Marjorie Gabain. New York: Free Press.

Piper, Adrian M. S. 1991. Impartiality, Compassion, and Modal Imagination. *Ethics* 101 (July): 726–57.

Plato. 1961. *The Collected Dialogues of Plato.* Ed. Edith Hamilton and Huntington Cairns. New York: Bollingen Foundation.

Pojman, Louis P. 1992. Are human rights based on equal human worth? *Philosophy and Phenomenological Research* 52, no. 3 (September): 605–22.

Quinn, Phil E. 1989. *The Golden Rule of Parenting.* Nashville, Tenn.: Abingdon.

Raunio, Antti. 1987. Die "goldene Regel" als theologisches Prinzip beim jungen Luther. *Thesaurus Lutheri.* Ed. Tuomo Mannermaa, Anja Ghiselli, and Simo Peura. Helsinki: Finnische Theologische Literaturgesellschaft and Luther-Agricola-Gesellschaft.

Rawls, John. 1971. *A Theory of Justice.* Cambridge, Mass.: Harvard University Press.

Reed, Henry Hope, and Sophia Duckworth. 1967. *Central Park.* New York: Clarkson N. Potter.

Rehm, B., ed. 1969. *Die Pseudoklementinen.* Vol. 1, Homilien. Berlin: n.p.

Reiner, Hans. 1948. Die "goldene Regel": Die Bedeutung einer sittlichen Grundformel der Menschheit. *Zeitschrift für philosophische Forschung* 3: 74–105.

———. 1951. *Pflicht und Neigung.* Meisenheim am Glan: Westkulturverlag Anton Hain.

———. 1954/55. Antike und Christliche Naturrechtslehre. *Archiv für Rechts- und Sozialphilosophie* 41: 528–61.

———. 1964. *Die philosophische Ethik.* Heidelberg: Quelle & Meyer.

———. 1977. Die goldene Regel und das Naturrecht. *Studia Leibnitiana* 9: 231–54.

Rembert, Ron B. 1983. The golden rule: Two versions and two views. *Journal of Moral Education* 12, no. 2 (May): 100–3.

Rest, James, et al. 1986. *Moral Development.* New York: Praeger.

Reuter, Hans-Richard. 1982. Bergpredigt und politische Vernunft. In *Die Bergpredigt,* ed. Rudolf Schnackenburg. Schriften der Katholischen Akademie in Beyern, vol. 107. Dusseldorf: Patmos Verlag.

Ricoeur, Paul. 1974. Fatherhood: From phantasm to symbol. Tr. Robert Sweeney. In *The Conflict of Interpretations,* ed. Don Ihde. Evanston, Ill.: Northwestern University Press.

———. 1989. Entre philosophie et théologie: La Règle d'or en question. *Revue d'Histoire et de Philosophie Religieuses* 69 (1): 3–9.

———. 1990. The golden rule: exegetical and theological perplexities. *New Testament Studies* 36: 392–97.

———. 1993. *Oneself as Another.* Tr. Kathleen Blamey. Chicago: University of Chicago Press.

Rigby, Paul, and Paul O'Grady. 1989. Agape and altruism. *Journal of the American Academy of Religion* 57 (4): 719–37.

Rist, J. M. 1969. *Stoic Philosophy.* Cambridge, Mass.: Cambridge University Press.

Robins, Michael H. 1974. Hare's golden-rule argument: A reply to Silverstein. *Mind* 83: 578–81.

Robinson, James. 1966. Review of Albrecht Dihle, *Die goldene Regel. Journal of the History of Philosophy* 4: 84–87.

Rolnick, Philip A. 1993. *Analogical Possibilities.* Academy Series. Atlanta: Scholars Press.

Rosenhan, David. 1980. Focus of attention mediates the impact of negative affect on altruism. *Journal of Personality and Social Psychology* 38 (2): 291–300.

Rosmarin, Aaron. 1947. *Golden Rules.* New York: OM Publishing.

Rost, H. T. D. 1986. *The Golden Rule: A Universal Ethic.* Oxford: George Ronald.

Rowley, H. H. 1940. Chinese sages and the golden rule. *Bulletin of the John Rylands Library* 24: 321–52.

Scheler, Max. [1913] 1954. *The Nature of Sympathy.* Tr. Peter Heath. Hew Haven: Yale University Press.

Schillebeeckx, Edward. 1981. *Jesus: An Experiment in Christology.* Tr. Hubert Hoskins. New York: Random House.

Schmidt, K.O. n.d. *Die goldene Regel und das Gesetz der Fülle.* Pfullingen in Württ: Baum-Verlag.

Schlopp, Ludwig, ed. 1947. *The Fathers of the Church.* Vol. 1. New York: Christian Heritage.

Schmitz, Philipp. 1977. Die goldene Regel—Schlussel zum ethischen Kontext. In *Christlich Glauben und Handeln,* ed. K. Demmer. Dusseldorf: Patmos Verlag.

Schüller, Bruno. 1980. *Die Begründung sittlicher Urteile.* Düsseldorf: Patmos Verlag.

Schultz, Joseph P. 1974. Reciprocity in Confucian and rabbinic ethics. *Journal of Religious Ethics* 2 (1): 143–50.

Seneca, L. Annaeus. 1887. *On Benefits.* Tr. Aubrey Stewart. London: George Bell.

———. 1928. *Moral Essays.* Tr. John W. Basore. Loeb Classical Library. London: Heinemann.

Seward, Theodore F. n.d. *The Golden Rule Brotherhood.* New York: The Golden Rule Brotherhood.

Shaw, Bernard. 1930. Man and Superman. In *Collected Works of George Bernard Shaw,* Vol 10. New York: W. H. Wise.

Shubik, Martin. 1984. A Note on Biology, Time, and the Golden Rule. Cowles Foundation Discussion Paper No. 696. New Haven: Cowles Foundation for Research in Economics at Yale University.

Sidgwick, Henry. [1907]. 1962 *The Methods of Ethics.* 7th ed. Chicago: University of Chicago Press.

Silverstein, Harry S. 1972. A note on Hare on imagining oneself in the place of others. *Mind* 81, no. 323 (July): 448–50.

Simmons, Donald B. 1981. A Rhetorical History of Samuel "Golden Rule" Jones. Ph.D. diss. Ohio University.

Singer, Marcus George. 1961. *Generalization in Ethics.* New York: Alfred Knopf.

———. 1963. The golden rule. *Philosophy* (Journal of the Royal Institute of Philosophy) 38 (146): 293–314.

———. 1967. The golden rule. In *Encyclopedia of Philosophy,* ed. Paul Edwards. New York: Macmillan.

———. 1985. Universalizability and the generalization principle. In *Morality and Universality,* ed. Nelson Potter and Mark Timmons. Dordrecht: D. Reidel.

Slote, Michael. 1984. Morality and self-other asymmetry. *Journal of Philosophy* 81, no. 4 (April): 179–92.

Smith, Goldwin. 1879. The prospect of a moral interregnum. *Atlantic Monthly* 44, no. 265 (November): 629–42.

Smith, Robert M. 1988. Beyond progressivism. *Midwest Review* 10: 43–54.

Smith, Wilfrid Cantwell. 1979. *Faith and Belief*. Princeton: Princeton University Press.

Sokolowski, Robert. 1985. *Moral Action*. Bloomington: Indiana University Press.

Spencer, Herbert. 1892. *The Principles of Ethics*. New York. D. Appleton.

———. 1967. *The Evolution of Society*. Ed. Robert L. Carneiro. Chicago: University of Chicago Press.

———. [1850] 1970. *Social Statics*. New York: Robert Schalkenbach Foundation.

Spendel, Günter. 1967. Die goldene Regel als Rechtsprinzip. In *Festschrift für Fritz von Hippel zum 70. Geburtstag*, ed. Josef Esser and Hans Thieme. Tübingen: J. C. B. Mohr (Paul Siebeck).

Spooner, W. A. 1928. Golden rule. In *Encyclopedia of Religion and Ethics*, ed. James Hastings. New York: Scribner's.

Stein, Edith. 1956. *Writings of Edith Stein*. Tr. and ed. Hilda Graef. Westminster, Md.: Newman Press.

———. 1964. *On the Problem of Empathy*. Tr. Waltraut Stein. The Hague: Martinus Nijhoff.

Stewart, R. W. 1950. The golden rule. *Expository Times* 62: 115–17.

Strayer, Janet. 1987. Affective and cognitive perspectives. In *Empathy and Its Development*. Ed. Nancy Eisenberg and Janet Strayer. New York: Cambridge University Press, 1987.

Strecker, Georg. 1981. Compliance—Love of one's enemy—The golden rule. *Australian Biblical Review* 29(October): 38–46.

Suzuki, D. T. 1952. Ethics and Zen Buddhism. In *Moral Principles of Action*, ed. Ruth Ananda Anshen. New York: Harper.

Taylor, C. C. W. 1965. Review of R. M. Hare's *Freedom and Reason*. *Mind* 74: 280–98.

Thomas, S. B. 1970. Jesus and Kant. *Mind* 79, no. 314 (April): 188–99.

Thomas Aquinas, St. [1874] 1951. *Super evangelium S. Matthaei lectura*. Ed. P. Raphaelis Cai, O.P. Rome: Marietti.

———. [1267–1272] 1969. *Summa Theologiae*. 60 vols. Tr. R. J. Batten, O.P. Blackfriars. New York: McGraw-Hill.

Thomasius, Christian. [1718] 1979. *Fundamenta iuris naturae et gentium*. Darmstadt: Scientia Verlag Aalen.

Tolstoy, Leo. [1898] 1930. *What Is Art?* Tr. Aylmer Maude. London: Oxford University Press.

Tripp, Rhoda Thomas, ed. 1970. *The International Thesaurus of Quotations*. New York: Crowell.

Urantia Foundation. 1955. *The Urantia Book*. Chicago: Urantia Foundation.

Vega, Garcilaso de la. 1961. *The Incas*. Tr. Maria Jolas. New York: Orion Press.

Visser 't Hooft, W. A. 1982. *The Fatherhood of God in an Age of Emancipation*. Philadelphia: Westminster Press.

Walsh, Walter. 1920. *The Golden Rule*. London: C. W. Daniel.

Wang Yang-ming. 1963. *Instructions for Practical Living and Other Neo-Confucian Writings by Wang Yang-Ming*. Tr. Wing-tsit Chan. New York: Columbia University Press.

———. 1972. *The Philosophical Letters of Wang Yang-ming*. Tr. Julia Ching. Canberra: Australian National University Press.

Ward, Duren J. H. 1932. *A More Golden Rule*. Denver, Colorado: n.p.

Warren, Mary Anne. 1977. Do potential people have moral rights? *Canadian Journal of Philosophy* 7, no. 2 (June): 275–89.

Wattles, Jeffrey. 1987. Levels of meaning in the golden rule. *Journal of Religious Ethics* 15, no. 1 (Spring): 106–29.

———. 1993. Plato's brush with the golden rule. *Journal of Religious Ethics* 21, no. 1 (Spring): 69–85.

Weill, Julien. 1929. Nephtali et la "règle d'or." *Revue des Études Juives* 82: 127–31.

Weiss, Paul. 1941. The golden rule. *Journal of Philosophy* 38, no. 16 (July 31): 421–30.

———. 1950. The golden rule. In *Man's Freedom*. New Haven: Yale University Press.

Welch, Claude. 1972–85. *Protestant Thought in the Nineteenth Century*. 2 vols. New Haven: Yale University Press.

Westermarck, Edward. 1906. *The Origin and Development of the Moral Ideas*. London: Macmillan.

Whately, Richard. 1857. *Introductory Lessons of Morals and Christian Evidences*. Cambridge, Mass.: John Bartlett.

Wilder, Amos N. 1951. The Sermon on the Mount. In *The Interpreter's Bible*, vol. 7. New York: Abingdon.

William, Bishop of St. Davids. 1679. *The Comprehensive Rule of Righteousness: Do As You Would Be Done By*. Cornhill, England: William Leach.

Williams, James G. 1990. Paranenesis, excess, and ethics. *Semeia* 50: 163–87.

Wilson, Bryan. 1988. On a Kantian argument against abortion. *Philosophical Studies* 53: 119–30.

Wiseman, Mary Bittner. 1978. Empathetic identification. *American Philosophical Quarterly* 15, no. 2 (April): 107–13.

Wispé, Lauren. 1986. The distinction between sympathy and empathy: To call forth a concept a word is needed. *Journal of Personality and Social Psychology* 50: 315–21.

Wolbert, Werner. 1986. Die goldene Regel und das ius talionis. *Trierer Theologische Zeitschrift* 95: 169–81.

Woods, Ralph Louis, ed. 1966. *The World Treasury of Religious Quotations*. New York: Hawthorn Books.

Wu, Yi. 1986. *Chinese Philosophical Terms*. Lanham, Md.: University Press of America.

Wyschogrod, Edith. 1990. *Saints and Postmodernism*. Chicago: University of Chicago Press.

Zahorsky, John. 1913. *Golden Rules of Pediatrics*. Golden Rule Series. St. Louis, Mo.: C. V. Mosby.

Index

Printed in the United States
21544LVS00001B/178